The New Radicalism

tThe New Radicalism

BRYAN MAGEE

'Men fight and lose the battle, and the thing that they fought for comes about in spite of their defeat, and when it comes turns out to be not what they meant, and other men have to fight for what they meant under another name.'
WILLIAM MORRIS: *Dream of John Ball*

LONDON

Secker & Warburg

First published in England 1962 by
Martin Secker & Warburg Limited,
14 Carlisle Street, Soho Square, W.1.

Printed in England by
The Windmill Press Ltd
Kingswood, Surrey

To
Tyrrell, Joan
Russell and Marc

Contents

Acknowledgements

THE passages quoted in this book from Aneurin Bevan's *In Place of Fear* are reproduced by kind permission of Messrs MacGibbon & Kee Ltd; from Universities Quarterly by kind permission of the Editor, and of the Turnstile Press; from John Strachey's *The Great Awakening* by kind permission of Encounter; from Bertrand Russell's *The Conquest of Happiness*, *History of Western Philosophy*, and *Portraits from Memory* by kind permission of Messrs George Allen & Unwin Ltd; from Boris Pasternak's *Dr Zhivago* by kind permission of Messrs Wm. Collins Sons & Co Ltd; from C. A. R. Crosland's *The Future of Socialism* by kind permission of Messrs Jonathan Cape Ltd; from G. D. H. Cole's *A Short History of the Working Class Movement* by kind permission of Messrs George Allen & Unwin Ltd; and from Evelyn Waugh's *Black Mischief* by kind permission of the author and Messrs Chapman & Hall Ltd.

Preface

I WANT to write about what is wrong with the Left in Britain, and I think the root of the trouble lies in fundamentally mistaken ways of looking at things – approaches to politics that have been left behind by both intellectual and social developments.

So inappropriate have some Socialist attitudes become that they are now the direct opposite of what they should be. For instance one of the most odious regimes in the world is that of East Germany. After fifteen years of power, during which three million people have fled the country, it can stop more millions leaving only by building a wall to keep them in. Yet Labour M.P.s pay friendly visits to East Germany and are on amiable terms with the politicians who run it. Three of the best-known British business men doing trade with it (which means doing trade with its Government) are also Labour politicians – Ian Mikardo, Arthur Lewis and Sir Leslie Plummer. At the same time Socialists hate Fascist Spain and no Labour M.P. would either want or dare to have friendly relations with Franco – his career would be ruined if he did. Yet by any standards the East German régime is the worse of the two. This is just a simple example – there will be more later in the book – of how Socialist attitudes and behaviour can be in flat opposition to reality. The reasons are illuminating. They are partly that the attitudes in question relate to the past and not to the quite different actuality into which that past has changed; and partly that most Socialists are the prisoners of words – the East German régime is 'left-wing' and therefore bound to be acceptable to some extent, whereas the Spanish is not merely 'right-wing' but Fascist, which is the worst possible thing to be.

If we could free ourselves from preconceptions and look at the world as it now is and build a political outlook on the basis of today's reality the results would be very different from today's left-wing attitudes. Similarly if we could set up our left-wing organizations from scratch in response to present-day realities they would have a quite different structure from the Labour Party, the Trade Unions and

11

the Co-operative Movement. We live in a revolutionary world, a world of global conflicts – not only the Cold War but the clash of White and non-White everywhere; the majority of mankind that has always lived in destitution is suddenly starting to develop at an explosive rate; colonies are being liberated – three-quarters of Africa is already independent. We live in a world of nuclear energy, hydrogen bombs, rockets and space travel. At home in Britain we have full-employment and a welfare state, prosperity for most, inflation always with us, automation on the way. The historic isolation of Britain from Europe is about to end. It is to all this that a contemporary political outlook has to relate. And such an outlook cannot possibly be cast in the nineteenth-century categories of 'Capitalism', 'Socialism', and all the rest of those terms that no one nowadays can even agree on the meaning of. In both logic of language and structure of theory it has to meet the unprecedentedly high standards set by contemporary philosophy. It has to take full account of modern psychology's revelations about human behaviour. It has to take full account of Einstein's revelation of the conjectural nature of all theories and all knowledge. No political outlook that does not do at least this is now tenable.

So this book is an attempt to re-examine the very foundations of left-wing thinking. Nothing less will meet the need that now exists. There is a great deal of intelligent discussion going on about the lost elections, the internecine struggles, the ramshackle organization, the feeble Opposition, the outmoded policies – all the obvious inadequacies of the Labour Party in day-to-day and year-to-year politics – but none of it so far has got down to the bedrock of assumptions and emotions on which these more ephemeral manifestations rest.

A serious difficulty is knowing where to start. For what I have to say about any one aspect of the subject can be understood only in the light of what I have to say about others. Rousseau, chafing under a similar realization while writing *The Social Contract*, suddenly cried out before he was a quarter of the way through: 'All my ideas fit together but I cannot articulate them all at once.' I have cudgelled my brain about this problem in my own case and found, as Rousseau did, that there is no satisfactory solution. What I have finally done is to begin with an exposition of what I believe to be the only tenable political philosophy for Socialists, then tried to show how it has become mixed up with other, untenable views, and finally looked at the contemporary political situation, especially the Labour Party's, in the light of this analysis. So the book moves from philosophical argument to topical polemics. It would have been more arresting to plunge straight into the current argument; but my views in this are ultimately intelligible only in the light of the basic philosophy contained in the early chapters. It is these that say what I believe most needs saying on the Left today.

There is already a widespread but repressed suspicion that the old categories of thought will not do. The realization began to grow in secret from about 1947 onwards. Before that time British Socialists of every kind took it for granted that if the basic industries of the country were taken into public ownership and there was a Socialist Government the Good Society would more or less automatically come into being. And if they had been guaranteed in addition full employment, the Welfare State, a free health service and the liberation of India they would almost have expected to find Utopia round the corner. But all these things were done and Utopia was not round the corner – in fact it seemed as far off as ever. The appalling idea began to creep into some people's minds that what they had always believed was wrong.

I am not saying that Socialists in general faced the fact that some of their basic traditional assumptions were false. On the contrary, as one would expect, most of them tried to evade it. From some there was a cry of 'We have been betrayed!' and a search for scapegoats that lighted on all kinds of quarry from the leadership of the party to the United States. Others began to argue that public ownership did have the magic properties Socialists had always claimed for it, only in forms other than the one the Socialist Government happened to have used, namely the Morrisonian public corporation. Yet others said that the Socialist Government had carried out not the full programme of Socialism but only a fraction of it. This assertion, which in some way underlies all the others, is the opposite of the truth. The Socialist Government of 1945–50 did more than any pre-war Socialists had thought would be possible in the lifetime of a single government. This is shown in detail in Chapter Three of *The Future of Socialism* by C. A. R. Crosland, where he compares the actual pre-war programmes drawn up by individuals and groups, as well as by the party itself, with what was subsequently accomplished. The plain fact is that the Socialist Government did carry out the traditional Socialist programme and this did not produce the Good Society. Socialists had always been wrong.

What was wrong, though, was not what they did but what they expected. What they did was magnificent. They gave independence to India, Pakistan, Ceylon and Burma, which is to say about a fifth or a sixth of the human race; they maintained full employment in Britain for the first time ever in peace-time; created the National Health Service; passed the 1947 Agriculture Act; built the Welfare State; nationalized Electricity, Gas, Atomic Energy, Civil Aviation, Cable and Wireless and The Bank of England, all of which run with outstanding efficiency, together with Steel and Road Haulage (which have been denationalized by the Conservatives) and Railways and Coal Mines – and did all this in six years, in the teeth of hysterical opposition, at a time when Britain was exhausted by six years of war. In my view that post-war Socialist Government was beyond all question the greatest government Britain has ever had, and by its controversial measures it improved the lot of hundreds of millions of people. But those measures, wonderful in themselves, did not have all the results that Socialists had confidently expected of them – they did not, for example, promote a classless society. In fact the Socialist Government, because of its mistaken beliefs about public ownership, left the British class structure intact.

This failure of ideals to materialize caused disillusionment, dissension, recrimination. It is at the bottom of the present troubles in the Labour Party. But it is vital to be clear about what exactly it was that was missing. The measures carried out by the Labour Government were not bad – on the contrary, most of them were splendid. Nor were the ideals bad ideals – they were splendid too. What was missing was a causal link between the two. Socialists had always believed that the measures would actualize the ideals, and it is this belief that was wrong. But this means that something fundamental to the whole Socialist philosophy was wrong.

Another, quite different, illustration of this lies in the fact that it is common now for Socialists to complain that politics is not exciting any more. As someone said in a letter to the *New Statesman* on 29 December 1961: 'Many of my friends were "fanatical Socialists" until about six years ago. Now they are not. They still bring up some of the idealistic concepts of Shaw and are occasionally roused by a speech of a reminiscing party member. But the stomach is not in them any more for fighting for important "socialistic" causes . . .' Yet the issues facing mankind today are the biggest in human history. Even the things that Socialists got so inflamed about in the nineteen thirties –

unemployment and Fascism – were less important than the issues that face us now, from the imminence of universal death downwards. Do Socialists need yet bigger issues to get their teeth into than the preservation of peace, the development of backward peoples, the liberation of colonies, the ending of the Cold War, the use of nuclear energy and automation, the abolition of Britain's class structure? Or do there need to be more such problems crying out for alternative solutions? Or does the Conservative Government need to be *more* incompetent in dealing with them? No, these Socialists are listless not because of a lack of urgent issues but because almost nothing that happens seems to evoke a strong response from their political attitudes – and this shows that there is something fundamentally inappropriate about their political attitudes.

For years, both as a parliamentary candidate and as a television reporter, I have been immersed in day-to-day politics and current affairs. It is my job to follow them in some detail, and I am constantly having to investigate cases and argue practical proposals. However, in this book I am not concerned to put forward a specific policy or programme. My object here is quite different. It is to look afresh at political fundamentals (a job that, like painting the Forth Bridge, should never stop; as soon as it has been done it is time to do it again). This involves discussing some of the basic elements in our civilization. Anyone who takes on such a task is bound to be indebted to many others. Goethe remarked once that if all the ideas he had got from other people were removed from his writings there would be virtually nothing left. I say the same. In fact not only have I used other people's arguments without inhibition, I have even on one or two occasions used their illustrations where these struck me as unusually apt. My debts are too numerous to specify. Most of them are to the dead – to those rare men of genius from Socrates to Einstein who have made fundamental changes in man's understanding of himself and his environment. But the biggest direct influence on my thinking has come from someone who is very much alive, Karl Popper, and it is an influence that is deep and all-pervading – him I must thank. I make no claims to originality in anything I have written. The most I have done is to absorb ideas of others into a single political philosophy. This is of such urgency, however, that I feel no shame in being the one to put it forward.

CHAPTER ONE

The Importance of Theories

POLITICAL theory is one of the most important things in life. Nearly half the human race now lives in societies whose every aspect has been influenced by the political theories of Karl Marx. The American Constitution made a conscious and successful attempt to found a society on the principles of John Locke. Every school history-book lists Rousseau and Voltaire among the 'causes' of the French Revolution. It is therefore astounding that the importance of political theory, so vast and obvious, is constantly denied.

This denial comes from two main sources. First from naïve realists, a category that includes most people. Most people accept their environment as they find it, adapt themselves to it, live in its terms. They regard as 'airy-fairy' any attempt to appraise its institutions or investigate its past; these activities, they suppose, have nothing to do with real life. They regard as important what is directly present to their experience: all else is abstraction – and abstractions are not real, not important. The second group of people, overlapping with the first, assert that human behaviour is not rational. Theories, they say, are chiefly rationalizations – they come after behaviour, not before it. People are motivated by emotional considerations: to take a political example, they do not become Communists through an intellectual conviction of the correctness of Marxist theory, or cease to be Communists because they have spotted the mistakes in Marxist arguments; most Communists have never studied Marx at all, and of the few who have, only a small proportion achieve anything like a comprehensive understanding of his theoretical system. No, the objection runs, if you want to understand politics it is not necessary to understand political theory, it is necessary to understand human nature, personal relationships and practical situations.

Both these forms of anti-intellectualism are mistaken. But the former, naïve realism, is a major factor in political affairs because it embodies the attitude of most people. And the latter, which I will call

17

'irrationalism', contains an important element of truth which needs to be unravelled from the general confusion of its argument. Let us take irrationalism first.

I

The important truth which irrationalists have grasped is that the objects of human activity are not determined by reason but by our physical and emotional needs. We need first to satisfy our appetites for food, drink and sex, then to be clothed and housed and kept warm; we want companionship, love, comfort, recreation, excitement, adventure; we need outlets for our destructive instincts such as aggression, jealousy and the will to power; and we are subject to fears and uncertainties. These and other irrational forces determine our wants and needs. And in accordance with our wants and needs, so we act.

All this is true. But the irrationalist errs in supposing that this conflicts with the principle of rationality. For rationality is not about the purposes of action, it is about the relationship of means to those purposes. Of course we do not eat because we have reasoned things out and decided to eat: we eat because of a basic physical and instinctual need. But miracles of reasoning and planning go into *meeting* that need. Even primitive peoples sow in the spring so that they shall harvest six months later, so that in turn they and their animals shall eat during the following winter. This behaviour is rational in a high degree: it means repressing the natural desire to take it easy now, and working instead, yet not for any immediate gain but so as to eat next year. It is based entirely on reasoning from past experience. And when we come to consider the feeding of a modern community, say a city like London, our imagination is baffled by the complexity and sophistication of the reasoning involved.

This example illustrates what happens in every aspect of life, great or small. If I want to know the date I do not look at my watch; equally, if I want to know the time I do not look in my diary. If I want to eat I do not put food in my ears; if I want to wash my ears I do not put soap in my mouth. People who do behave like this are either babies or, as we sometimes put it, have 'lost their reason'. They are unable to look after themselves, and if they are not cared for by someone else they quickly die. Rationality – the appropriate relation of means to ends – is successful living. This is something which irrationalists either ignore or do not understand. On the contrary, many of them talk as if rationality were anti-life, and irrationality the down-to-earth, practical thing. 'There is in many people a dislike of rationality, and where this exists the kind of thing that I have been saying will seem irrelevant and unimportant. There is an idea that rationality, if allowed free play, will kill all the deeper emotions. This belief appears to me to be due to an entirely erroneous conception of the function of reason in human life. . . . In passionate love, in parental affection, in friendship, in benevolence, in devotion to science or art, there is nothing that reason should wish to diminish. The rational man, when he feels any or all of these emotions, will be glad that he feels them and will do nothing to lessen their strength, for all these emotions are parts of the good life, the life, that is, that makes for happiness both in oneself and in others. There is nothing irrational in the passions as such, and many irrational people feel only the most trivial passions. No man need fear that by making himself rational he will make his life dull.'[1]

It is irrationality that is anti-life. In fact if it were not for rationality there would be no human life. Man would have died – the human race would never have survived the evolutionary struggle – had it not been for reason. It is a platitude that 'man is a rational animal' and that he owes his survival and supremacy to his rationality. But survival is the end and rationality the means. It is never suggested that men wanted to survive because they hit on rational grounds for doing so. The wish to survive is instinctual. Where rationality has been indispensable is in choosing means which would accomplish that desired end. And the achievements of reason in this respect have been awe-inspiring – the development from nothing of language and of science, to name only two. Society itself can be looked on as one of the fruits of rationality. We live together because by doing so we can more successfully meet our most passionate desires – above all our passionate desire to survive. (A society can disintegrate with astonishing suddenness if it ceases to meet the needs of its members.) This is how the facts stated in the first paragraph of this chapter come to be facts. The creation of new societies, as in America in the eighteenth century – or the reconstruction of old ones, as in the French and Russian revolutions – is always partially the result of a conscious desire on the part of some people for a new kind of society. And concern with how to get

1. Russell: *The Conquest of Happiness*, Chapter 7.

the sort of society they want involves them in political theory; in other words the choice of means is, as always, a rational activity. If they choose the wrong means they cannot get the society they want.

In science the chief way of seeing whether a hypothesis is true or false is to try it out – this is what experiments are for. Governments too are continually experimenting – with this or that new kind of school, hospital, committee, coinage, form of local government finance or what have you. But mistakes above a certain level become too costly to be risked voluntarily, and then hypotheses are not put to the test. The Russian Government may doubt whether the United States Government will risk the death of the entire American population for the sake of defending West Berlin. They could easily test this by annexing West Berlin. But if the hypothesis is false the very making of the experiment might obliterate all life on the earth. So they do not make the experiment. However, even in science experiment is not the only way of testing theories. Scientists also examine the logic of theories, looking for self-contradictions or non sequiturs; they isolate and examine the assumptions on which a theory is based; they compare it with other, better-attested theories. It is even more important to do this in politics. When we have to act, and the results of acting wrongly will be tragic, rigorous examination of the theories and assumptions underlying our proposed actions is the only way we have of minimizing risk. Serious errors in our assumptions will cost us little if they come to light in this way. Otherwise they will come to light in practice, in the failure of our policies, and this may be catastrophic.

I have chosen political examples because this is a book about politics. I could as easily have chosen examples from other fields of activity. Everything we do is based on theories and theoretical assumptions, down to the most trivial activities of everyday life. In most cases familiarity with the activities makes us unconscious of the theories underlying them and we regard them as 'natural' when they are not. We *all*, as babies, put food in our ears and soap in our mouths – it is this, if anything, that is 'natural' – and it takes us months or even years to learn not to. Dressing ourselves, going to the lavatory – we are laboriously trained to all this by other people, at the cost of much time and patience, and for very good reasons. We eventually cease to think about the reasons, and our behaviour in these matters becomes unthinking and habitual, but it nevertheless rests on a deep foundation of learning and reason.

In all matters, if we do not examine the assumptions on which our behaviour rests, that behaviour will, with repetition, come to seem 'natural'. In such cases we become the victims of our assumptions: they limit what we do, and misguide us if they are wrong; and so long as we refuse to re-examine them we persist in our errors. On the other hand by keeping our assumptions under review we increase both our freedom and our success. For if they are faulty our analysis of them may show this and suggest alternative courses of behaviour which are more rational, i.e. more likely to achieve the ends we desire. Keynes pointed this out in connection with businessmen. Every big business decision is unavoidably based on an elaborate pattern of theoretical assumptions, and therefore those businessmen who most pride themselves on being hard-headed, pragmatic fellows who despise mere economic theory are the most abjectly governed by whatever happens to be the current business orthodoxy. In the very course of writing this book I have been told that I am wasting my time, since to suppose that the practical men who run the day-to-day affairs of the country in government, the civil service, the trade unions, the political parties and so on, might be influenced by a book was to be completely wrong about the simplest facts of life. In fact I can think of quite a few recent books that have influenced such people – *The Affluent Society* is an obvious example, though no doubt few of them have actually read it, and far more have been influenced by it than realize the fact. I do not assert for one moment that it is common for administrators and executives to be consciously influenced by abstract ideas: what I do assert is that they are so influenced, and the less conscious they are of the fact the stronger is the influence. 'Two opposite errors, both common, are to be guarded against. On the one hand, men who are more familiar with books than with affairs are apt to over-estimate the influence of philosophers. When they see some political party proclaiming itself inspired by So-and-So's teaching, they think its actions are attributable to So-and-So, whereas, not infrequently, the philosopher is only acclaimed because he recommends what the party would have done in any case. Writers of books, until recently, almost all exaggerated the effects of their predecessors in the same trade. But conversely, a new error has arisen by reaction against the old one, and this new error consists in regarding theorists as almost passive products of their circumstances, and as having hardly any influence at all upon the course of events. . . . For my part, I believe that the truth lies between these two extremes. Between ideas and practical life, as everywhere else, there is reciprocal interaction; to ask which is cause and which effect is as futile as the problem of the hen and the egg.'[1]

At this point the irrationalist will perhaps object that although all behaviour may be based on assumptions that can be analysed in rational terms, the *causes* of those assumptions are invariably irrational. This could be true – in fact I think it is – but so what? To invent an example: Keynes may have been led by a deep, unconscious sense of personal insecurity to create a technique for abolishing the worst form of social insecurity, namely mass unemployment, and this might even have come to light had he been psychoanalysed. But why he did it is irrelevant to the technique itself. The important question there is, does it work? And in fact it does. So it has become an indispensable instrument in our social affairs. If it had not worked it would have been abandoned. The truth of a theory is ascertained not by tracing it to its origins but by testing it. *The origins of a theory are irrelevant to its truth.* Thus a scientist, say, may propound a theory because he dreamed it, guessed it or stole it; because he wants to make himself famous, or hopes to get rich; because the theory articulates his unconscious desires; or for any other reason. These considerations are interesting solely from a psychological or biographical standpoint. They have nothing to do with the value of the man's work or the truth of his theory. The scientific world will ascertain its truth not by investigating his reasons for putting it forward but by testing it in controlled experiments. It is tests, not sources, that determine knowledge. The assumption that the truth of a statement depends on its source is almost the hallmark of pre-scientific thinking, and furthermore is intimately connected with authoritarianism. But this is to anticipate my argument.

Now getting back to politics. Lenin may have been driven by a love of mankind or by a hatred of mankind. It would not be difficult to interpret his career on either assumption. But in either case the facts are the same: he did what he did. And it is that that matters. It may be that I am a Socialist because of my early relationship with my mother, or with my sister, or because I want to love everybody, or because criticism of society is an effective outlet for my aggressive impulses; or it may be because I was born into the working class; or because my father was a Socialist. Or it may be none of these. I don't know, and the point is it doesn't matter – it is quite irrelevant to how my political

1. Russell: *History of Western Philosophy*, p. 620.

proposals, and the arguments with which I support them, should be considered. They should be considered on their merits. They should be looked at for inconsistencies and non sequiturs, their assumptions should be exposed and tested, they should be set against observed facts and experience, and if tried out they should be tried out critically. If they work they should be adopted.

Many irrationalists are irrationalists out of self-defence – some because they do not want to accept the burden of rationality, others because they do not want to face the fact that numerous theories which they do not understand play a fundamental part in shaping the world they live in, and hence their lives. In my observation intelligent people are just as prone to this latter vice as unintelligent ones. They have a strong urge to understand their lives, and this leads many of them to exclude from their estimation the theories they do not know about.[1] Too many scientists pooh-pooh the arts, too many artists pooh-pooh academics, too many academics pooh-pooh the world of business, too many businessmen pooh-pooh politicians. All are protecting themselves in the same way, assuring themselves that they do not really need to know about these things because it is *they* who are doing what really matters and therefore *their* experience that really illuminates life. It would impose an intolerable strain on them if they felt they could not attain intellectual mastery of their environment without informing themselves about a mass of things which do not spontaneously interest them, so they limit their conception of what is important to their own interests.

II

What Keynes said about some businessmen applies to all naïve realists: the less interested they are in the reasons for what they do and what happens to them, the more they are the victims of theories they know nothing about. If the Government tries to meet a balance-of-payments crisis by raising the bank rate, this will lead to cuts in investment in many parts of industry, and this in turn may create unemployment. As a parliamentary candidate I have discussed this with people who have been thrown out of work in precisely this

---

1. 'Shaw's contempt for science was indefensible. Like Tolstoy, he couldn't believe in the importance of anything he didn't know.' Russell: *Portraits from Memory*.

way, only to discover that many of them (not all, but many) are not interested. However lucidly one explains what has happened – that it results from a choice made by the Government; that there are alternative choices; that one of these is preferable and worth agitating for – the whole subject has no significance for them. It is outside their world. Unemployment is being out of work and is 'real life'. Economics and political theory have nothing to do with real life, and therefore nothing to do with being out of work. Because many people have this sort of attitude they live in a world controlled by forces beyond their ken. (*See also* Chapter Six.)

A good antidote to naïve realism is education. And by this I mean not only school education, though that is most important, but also books, television, radio, newspapers, political meetings, everything that stimulates interest and provides information about how our society works. But the best antidote of all is responsibility. Most people suppose theory to be unimportant not because they are engaged in important practical matters but because they are not engaged in important practical matters. The doctor knows that medical theory is a matter of life and death to thousands of individual men and women every day, and that the most rarified researches in pure bio-chemistry may result in the relief of pain. The engineer knows he cannot build railway bridges without higher mathematics. The members of the Cabinet know they owe their ability to control unemployment to the economic theories of Keynes. It is above all when people have to participate in major practical decisions that they are likely to realize the importance of theories.

CHAPTER TWO

The Unimportance of Words

WORDS are signs which we use for communication. They are not the only signs we use for this purpose: there are thousands of others, ranging from musical notation to traffic lights. The meanings of all of them are settled by some sort of social agreement or convention. For example, on traffic lights the red light means '*Stop!*', because that is what we use it to mean. It could equally well have been used to mean '*Go!*', and for all I know there may be countries in which it is so used. Parliament could pass a bill changing its use in Britain to '*Go!*', and we should grow accustomed to the new usage. The point I am making is that it has no intrinsic meaning, no meaning independent of the way we use it. Its meaning is its use; and this may differ in different places, or in the same place at different times; and we can change it deliberately. Even on British roads a red light does not always mean '*Stop!*' On the back of a vehicle, or beside a hole, it means '*Beware of this*'. In a Soho doorway it means '*You can get a prostitute here*'. The situation in which the sign is used contributes to its meaning, is part of its meaning, and therefore we seldom confuse different meanings of the same sign. Of course the possibility of misunderstanding exists, for every sign is capable of ambiguous use, but in virtually all cases we are clear what is meant. So it makes no sense to ask: 'Ah yes, but what does a red light *really* mean? What is its *essential* meaning?' For it has no essential meaning. It does not really mean anything. It means only what we agree to use it to mean in a given kind of situation.

All this is true of words too. When I am talking to people in Scotland the word 'Loch' immediately means a lake. But when I am talking to people in Germany it means a hole, and then we do not think of lakes at all. The question: 'Ah yes, but what does "Loch" *really* mean?' is gibberish. (Is it 'really' Scots or German?) Language is a human artefact, albeit the most important one. We made it and we determine its use.

In case any of my readers think this is obvious I must tell them that

it is a recent and revolutionary discovery. It is the central discovery
of what is often called 'the revolution in philosophy' that has taken
place in this century.[1] Before that an entirely different theory of
meaning was assumed by the whole of mankind. Socrates asked 'What
is justice?', and this set the pattern of intellectual enquiry for two
thousand years. What is truth? What is beauty? What is motion?
What is life? It was assumed that these words were the names of
things that had some independent existence, and therefore that their
meanings were fixed, regardless of us or the way we chose to use the
words. These are mystical assumptions. They presuppose that words,
all by themselves, encapsulate the essence of different aspects of
reality, and of course from this it follows that enquiry into the meanings of the words will give us knowledge of the reality. Such language-
mysticism is as old as language itself. Many primitive peoples have
believed that your enemies would gain power over you if they could
discover your name. The God of Moses deliberately withheld his name
from Abraham, Isaac and Jacob (Exodus VI.3) and when he revealed
it to Moses he did so with strict instructions (the third commandment)
that it should not be used except in a religious context. Rome had a
second, secret name, and any attempt to discover it was punishable
by death. The proof of Elsa's absolute trust in Lohengrin was that she
should not ask him his name; the moment she did so and he replied
he had to abandon the world of ordinary mortals. To this day there
is a widespread feeling that knowing who somebody is means knowing
his name; that knowing and loving birds, say, or flowers, trees, anything, involves above all else knowing their names. This notion that
knowledge of words gives us access to a reality behind the words, a
reality with which those words have a unique and privileged relationship, has existed throughout human history and at all levels of
sophistication from the bronze-age superstitions of the Old Testament

---

1. The charge commonly made against modern philosophy by people who
know little about it – that it is concerned merely with words, whereas the great
philosophy of the past was about important issues – is grotesque. The importance of language in thinking is enormous, and for this reason considerations of
language are commonly involved in intellectual problems. The main purpose of
linguistic analysis is to isolate this verbal element, for one of the chief technical
concerns of modern philosophy is to avoid problems which are merely linguistic. Unless such analysis is carried out the problems one is facing are almost
bound to contain an unrecognized verbal element. So it is if one *neglects*
linguistic analysis that one is likely to become enmeshed in verbal problems.
However, it is true that one particular group of philosophers has become
absorbed in linguistic analysis for its own sake.

to the passionate insights of Wittgenstein. It is, I believe, supposed by most people. I took it for granted myself until my student days, and I still remember the slow and disturbing process by which I ceased to do so.

It is hard to learn that words do not have essences – do not 'contain' meanings or emotions. Yet such realization is a major awakening. It is not all gain, because it lessens the vivid emotional impact that words have on the child and the primitive person, something of which is felt by everyone who assumes an 'essentialist' theory of meaning. A great deal of poetry, ritual and rhetoric ceases to move one, or moves one less. The sort of discussions that gave one such deep pleasure as an undergraduate, keeping one up far into the night talking about Love, Death, Art and the rest, cease to be interesting, because one no longer supposes that by manipulating words one is in contact with reality – or, to put it another way, one no longer supposes that there are 'things' that the words 'stand for'; whereupon that whole universe of discourse seems, as indeed it is, empty. But the gains outweigh the losses. For in direct proportion as the emotional importance of words decreases, the emotional importance of actual feeling and observation increases. The quality of living is enriched.

I

There is a widespread illusion that you cannot have a profitable discussion without first defining your terms. This view embodies two mistakes. First, if acted upon it leads to an infinite regress of definitions. For instance if I were to insist that before we could discuss the problems of democratic government you must first define 'democracy' you might reply: 'By "democracy" I mean "government by the people".' And you might then think you had settled the matter, for you would have given what is the standard definition of the word, the definition given by the Concise Oxford Dictionary, a definition in accord with the Greek from which the word is derived. But I could then say: 'What do you mean by "the people"? After all, children are people. Does this mean that no society can be called democratic unless children participate in its government?' If you then redefined 'the people' so that the term excluded children I could go on to say: 'Well, what about Switzerland? In Switzerland women don't have the vote, and even on your new definition, women are still included in "the people". Does this mean Switzerland is not a democracy?' And so we could go on. We would have embarked on a discussion of words which need have no ending, for every time you defined a term you would have to introduce new terms – otherwise your definition would be circular – and we should then have to define the new terms. So if it were really the case that we could not discuss anything without first defining our terms we could never discuss anything at all, for we could never complete the necessary preliminaries. This is made even worse by the fact that definitions introduce not only new terms but also more terms. In my example the single term 'democracy' is defined by the three terms 'government', 'by' and 'the people'. I have developed my illustration with the simplest of the three: but you would also have to answer the vaster question 'What do you mean by "government"?' and the subtler question 'What do you mean by government "*by*" the people?' And again every definition would spawn an increasing number of terms requiring definition.

The second mistake embodied in the view that you cannot have a profitable discussion without first defining your terms is the assumption that knowledge is partially derived from language, so that precise knowledge depends at least partially on precise definition. I have already suggested what is wrong with this assumption, but let me give an illustration. The most precise knowledge we have in any field is that derived from the physical sciences, yet in the physical sciences there is little discussion about terms and their meaning. Terms are introduced as a convenient shorthand for descriptions. As far as a scientist is concerned the statement: 'A proton is the unit charge of positive electricity in an atom' is an answer to the question 'What shall we call the unit charge of positive electricity in an atom?', not an answer to the question 'What is a proton?' 'Proton' is just a handy substitute for a long description, and that is its reason for existence. It does not tell us anything. And if all definitions were eliminated science could carry on just the same, except that communication would be absurdly laborious. Scientists know that facts remain unaltered by the language in which they are described. Therefore neither observations nor conclusions should depend on words. Hence the rarity of argument about definitions in science. What this illustrates is that a preoccupation with definitions, far from being necessary to clear thinking and precise knowledge, tends to obscure both, and leads, as in my example about 'democracy', to endless argument about words instead of about matters of substance. (In fact it almost seems as if the various fields of human enquiry have developed in inverse proportion to the extent to which they have concerned themselves with words.) Because of this I shall try to avoid terms that have a variety of conflicting uses, or else to make it quite clear what use I am giving them. I shall try to write in such a way that no part of my argument depends on securing my reader's agreement to use terms in my way. I am not writing this book merely to recommend new ways of using words. For people to understand my arguments it is not necessary that they should use words in the same way as I use them but merely that they should understand the way I use them.

In a book about left-wing politics in Britain it is impossible to emphasize too strongly the unimportance of words. Even Aneurin Bevan, that master of bewitching language, thought it necessary near the beginning of his book *In Place of Fear*: 'The student of politics must,' he says, 'be on his guard against the old words.'

> 'We talk of free enterprise, of capitalist society, of the rights of free association, of parliamentary government, as though all these words stand for the same things they formerly did. Social institutions are what they do, not necessarily what we say they do. . . .'

> 'The words persist when the reality which lay behind them has changed. It is inherent in our intellectual activity that we seek to imprison reality in our description of it. Soon, long before we realize it, it is we who become the prisoners of the description. From that point on, our ideas degenerate into a kind of folk-lore which we pass to each other, fondly thinking we are still talking of the reality around us.'[1]

This point has long been reached in Labour politics. At any gathering, from Annual Conference downwards – but most of all in the private meetings and committees of local parties – one hears folk-lore being passed round by people with the fantastic delusion that they are talking about the real world. Proposals will be applauded or condemned not according to their substance but according to the language they are couched in. An acquaintance of mine boasts that he can get anything through a Socialist committee by manipulating the language and the folk-lore – either by couching his proposals in the compulsive jargon that most active Socialists are emotionally incapable of resisting, or, more sinisterly, putting them in a form which

---

1. These three quotations from *In Place of Fear* occur on the same page (13 of the first edition) but in reverse sequence. It is typical of Bevan's writing that they should contain good thoughts, well expressed, but in the wrong order.

the members will be frightened of seeming to oppose. This is done over and over again, not always consciously, by Labour politicians and speakers, and exponents of 'committeemanship'. (Not only Labour ones, of course, but it is those I am chiefly concerned with here.) Almost the first thing to be learned by anyone active in politics is that what one should really concern oneself with is the substance, not the words. Politics is what happens, not what people say about it.

II

In this book I am not to any significant extent writing about words. For instance I am not concerned with questions like 'What is Socialism?', which is merely a request for a definition. It would be quite possible to compile a volume-size anthology of definitions of the word 'Socialism' – quite possible and quite pointless. Stalin, Trotsky, Hitler and George Lansbury meant different things by the term 'Socialism', though they were contemporaries. Within England, at the same time as them, Ernest Bevin, James Maxton, Bertrand Russell, Harry Pollitt, G. D. H. Cole, John Strachey and George Orwell all believed in 'Socialism' and all meant different things by it. Today Hugh Gaitskell, Frank Cousins, R. H. S. Crossman, William Carron, Ian Mikardo, Anthony Crosland and Palme Dutt all regard themselves as 'Socialists', but again mean quite different things by 'Socialism'. My readers will find that I rarely use the word, because since there is little agreement as to its use it has little meaning. Some may criticize me for this – I have often heard speeches and pamphlets attacked on the ground that they 'did not even mention the word "Socialism"', or mentioned it 'only once', twice, etc. I despise such word-magic. 'I believe that nothing depends upon words, and everything upon our practical demands or upon the proposals for framing our policy which we decide to adopt.[1]

When I first heard the definition 'philosophy is what philosophers do' I wrote it off as an evasive wisecrack, not even particularly funny, but my respect for it has increased since then. In fact I would now be inclined to say that Socialism is what Socialists advocate. I use the word 'Socialist' frequently in this book, and by it I mean someone who habitually votes for, or would if he voted, the Socialist Party of the country he lives in. Thus I could say with perfect clarity: 'Nearly all America's Liberal Democrats would be Socialists if they lived in

1. Karl Popper: *The Open Society and Its Enemies*, Vol. I, p. 91.

Britain.' This use of the term is genuinely descriptive and at the same time free from emotive content. It takes account of the fact that an enormous variety of conflicting views are held by different people all commonly called Socialists – from near-Conservatives like Patrick Gordon Walker to near-Communists like Konni Zilliacus. And it leaves me free to get on with the question of what I think the approach of Socialists to politics should be.

I seldom use the word 'Capitalism', for the reason that it has many conflicting uses and hence little in the way of clear meaning. Many people use it to denote a society in which the means of production, distribution and exchange are almost all privately owned. On this definition Britain, in which a third of the industry and half the capital investment are in the hands of the state, is not a Capitalist country. Many other people, however, object to this usage – for example, the delegate at the 1959 Labour Party Conference who said: 'Now we have Mr Gaitskell who talks about a mixed economy. What the heck is a mixed economy? We have a Capitalist economy, and where is this tripe getting us about a mixed economy?' Such people tend to regard all societies in which the economy is not *entirely* state-owned[1] as 'Capitalist'. This splits the world neatly into Communist and Capitalist countries. On this definition Spain and Sweden are both Capitalist countries, as are the sheikdoms of the Middle East. There are yet other people who confine their use of the word 'Capitalism' to *industrialized* economies which are chiefly in private hands. On this definition the England of 1860 and the England of 1960 are both 'Capitalist' despite the fact that the two societies were different in almost every major respect. Yet again, Trotskyites and quite a few Socialists describe the system in the Communist countries as 'State Capitalism'. So altogether the word is not much use for clear communication. When it does occur in this book its use is almost always attributed, if obliquely, to others, for instance in statements like: 'Before the war nearly all Socialists believed that unemployment was inevitable under Capitalism.'

1. And they mean state-*owned*. Thus they regard Fascism as a form of Capitalism despite the fact that thoroughgoing state *control* of the economy has been a major feature of the chief Fascist societies, such as Hitler's Germany and Mussolini's Italy.

CHAPTER THREE

The Rational Basis of My Case

SINCE the beginning men have found the fact of their existence and the facts of their experience amazing. And since the beginning this wonder at what is has led them to seek explanations – interpretations of the world that would enable them to understand it and to predict (and hence plan and control) its workings. The great myths were in part attempts at this. So were the great religions. The great philosophers were trying to do it. Science is doing it. But there is a crucial difference between scientific and other concepts of explanation.

The scientist – like the mythmaker, the theologian and the traditional philosopher – confronts a problem and constructs a hypothesis which, if true, will solve it. But unlike these others he does not stop there. He goes on to test his hypothesis, to see whether it does in fact explain what it is supposed to explain. And this is the crucial difference. He considers what sort of evidence would prove his theory to be false, and then checks it in actual situations.

The way to test theories is to subject their assumptions and structure to critical examination, to view them carefully in the light of other theories, and to test their factual content. This sums up the essence of scientific method. It may seem obvious, but it is revolutionary. The human race, for most of its history, has assumed quite different things – has assumed that the way to check a theory is to discover its source, and that the way to find out facts is to derive them from first principles. Indeed, theories about both the natural world and the human condition are still most commonly accepted on the ground that 'X says so'. X may be God, tribal custom, the Bible, Muhammad, the Pope, the dictator, Karl Marx, the Government, a political party, this or that wise man or oracle or written text, 'they', convention, tradition, the head of the family, Mummy, or a number of other sources. Critical examination of the theories is taboo on the grounds that it is blasphemous, subversive, disrespectful or shocking. Similarly, facts have usually been asserted and believed on the ground that there were good reasons for them. Aristotle proved to his own satisfaction that men have more teeth than women. They do not, and he could have ascertained this by having a look (he was married twice). The point I am making is that *this did not occur to him* – he took it for granted that reasoning is the way to find things out. Hegel used very profound arguments to prove that the number and position of the planets known to him were the only ones there could possibly be, and therefore that no planet could exist between the orbits of Mars and Jupiter. Just such a planet, Ceres, had been discovered only a few months before he wrote, and over two thousand have been discovered since. When Darwin's theory of evolution first appeared most people opposed it not because it had been tested and found to be false but because it flouted the authority of the Bible. In attacking it they took for granted that it could be disproved by argument – whereas of course it could only be either confirmed or disconfirmed by scientific observation of animals (which is what Darwin had already carried out). The plain fact is that knowledge cannot be attained by argument alone. The whole method is misconceived. Reasoning is never enough: there must always be tests. But the realization that this is so is still recent. It is the basis of scientific method.

The last of the great 'pre-scientific' thinkers was – for all his scientific pretensions – Karl Marx. That is to say he was the last man of genius to try to explain *everything* – cosmology, biology, history, economics, politics, religion, ethics, art, personal and family relationships, the whole of human experience – and to explain it without reference to tests. For instance he said that the causes of all wars were economic. This was not because he had investigated the causes of all wars, or even of a few wars, and found them to be economic. It was because the causes of all wars had to be economic to fit in with his theory of history. Similarly with his crucial prediction that the proletariat was doomed to ever-increasing poverty: he made this not because he had investigated workers' living conditions everywhere over a period of years and discovered (*a*) that they were worsening, and (*b*) that the causes of this deterioration were permanent and unavoidable. He just deduced it from his economic theory. If he had checked it against all the available facts he would have discovered that it was false (and this would have led him to the realization that his economic theory was also false). The principle of dialectical materialism itself is wholly pre-scientific. In the first place it is derived not from the world it purports to describe but from – as Marx himself tells us – the basic principle of Hegel's system of logic. And in the second place it is untestable.

There is something apparently 'natural' about these ways of trying to interpret the world, the ways of speculation and argument unchecked by observation. The whole human race, with very few exceptions, did it until about three hundred years ago. Children do it still, and most uneducated adults. On the other hand scientific method requires discipline, and though it looks simple it is new and highly sophisticated, only developed in individuals after much thought and training.

I

The way of building up knowledge by testing theories instead of arguing from first principles is called 'scientific method' only because it originated in the physical sciences. It applies to all attempts at knowledge. Any statement of the form 'it is the case that p' must be testable before it can be asserted. If it cannot be tested, that means we have no way of discovering whether it is true or not, and therefore we cannot assert it. This is why, in about the last hundred years, so-called 'scientific method' has spread to other forms of human enquiry: biology, history, economics, jurisprudence, sociology, psychology and the rest; even to literary criticism. The name 'scientific method' has become an embarrassment, for it gives pre-scientific prejudice a seeming loophole: 'Ah, yes, but history (or literary criticism, etc.) is not a science, so scientific method is inappropriate with respect to it.' This purely verbal argument would collapse if we merely used some term other than 'scientific method' – say, 'empirical method'.

Scientific method demands not merely that a theory be tested against the facts but that it fit *all* the known facts. From this it follows that a theory can be permanently disproved but not permanently proved. A theory which has been 'proved', i.e. which fits all the known facts, may be disproved in the future by new facts which have yet to come to light. However many observations have supported a hypothesis it is always possible that the next one will contradict it. And if one single observation is established that conflicts with a hypothesis then the hypothesis must be changed. So theories have to be tested at their weak points, not their strong ones – by seeking evidence that will refute them, not evidence that will confirm them. A theory that no conceivable evidence would refute is untestable. It is therefore uninformative, since it is unconnected with what the truth is. But if no theory can be definitively proved – if indeed a theory is only worth anything so long as it may still be disproved – why do we accept some theories and reject others? We accept a theory on two main conditions: first, that it fit all known facts, and second, that it be useful – i.e. explain the hitherto mysterious and, above all, yield accurate predictions. We say that a theory has been 'proved' when it meets these conditions and 'disproved' when it does not.

Let us take an example from the history of physics. Classical physics was given its final shape by Newton, whose work can also be said to be the chief foundation of Western engineering, if not of Western technology. For two hundred years Newton's laws held sway, explaining all physical phenomena from planetary motion to the workings of machinery. They were 'proved' literally millions of times. Understandably they were regarded as objective and unaltering Laws of Nature, and they were taught as such in schools and universities all over the Western world. Yet towards the end of the nineteenth century certain problems arose in mathematical physics which could not be solved if Newton's laws were universally valid. All sorts of ingenious *ad hoc* theories were evolved to explain the discrepancies. But in the end a man of courage and genius, Einstein, took the alternative course of rejecting Newton's laws. The result was that the whole science of physics had to be reconstructed on different foundations. And now relativistic physics explains everything that Newtonian physics could explain, plus a great deal more – and its heuristic power is greater.

Here, then, is a perfect illustration of my point – the point that there is no question of a scientific theory, such as one of Newton's laws, being 'true' in any permanent sense, since however often it is confirmed it can never be definitively established. There is, on the other hand, a question of its being false, because it might be definitively confuted. So a scientific theory is used for as long as it works. When it ceases to work it is replaced. Thus it may be that problems will arise in a hundred, or two hundred, or five hundred years time that are not soluble on relativistic assumptions – and when this occurs a successor to Newton and Einstein will sweep relativistic physics into the same limbo as that now occupied by classical physics. But meanwhile we shall continue to use our relativist assumptions, and to get results.

I could have used examples from other fields. For instance Aristotle was thought to have done for logic what Newton was thought to have done for physics – discovered its immutable laws. More than 2,000 years after Aristotle had laid down these 'laws of thought' Kant wrote[1]: 'It is remarkable that to the present day this logic has not been able to advance a single step, and is thus to all appearance a closed and completed body of doctrine.' Yet since Kant it has come to be realized that Aristotelian logic no more contains 'laws' that 'govern' valid reasoning than Newton's laws govern planetary motion. They are rather a system of rules (based on certain assumptions) for deductive arguments. On different assumptions we can build different systems, systems more comprehensive and useful. As a result Aristotelian logic has shrunk from being the whole of its subject to being a corner of it.

One final example. Euclid's geometry was thought for 2,000 years to be an established body of facts – of provenly accurate descriptions of the objective properties of space. Yet now it is realized that it does not consist of facts at all but rather of the logical consequences of certain definitions. It is useful as a calculus, but from other definitions we can derive other geometries with other uses – for example Riemann's geometry, which is used in Einsteinian astronomy. So Euclidean geometry, like Aristotelian logic, is now seen as one of an infinite number of possible systems. Indeed, mathematics itself has suffered an analogous change of status. Long regarded as the archetype of unassailable knowledge about the world, it is now realized to be a man-made calculus (albeit a prodigiously useful one).

All these changes are in the same direction. Natural laws, physics, logic, geometry, mathematics – all these which, until Kant, had been accepted by everyone as inherent in the world are now seen as products of the human mind. *Their principles characterize not things but ways of looking at things.* They are subject to alteration. They are theories, hypotheses, which even if relied on successfully for 2,000 years may still prove faulty and have to be revised or replaced. The popular notion that the sciences are bodies of established fact is wholly mistaken. Nothing in science is established, nothing certain. What distinguishes science from non-science is not its certainty but its method. Science *is* scientific method. Not that all sciences share a single methodology. Each field of inquiry develops its own appropriate techniques. But all the techniques have something funda-

1. in the Preface to the Second Edition of *Critique of Pure Reason*, 1787.

mentally in common – the free propounding of theories which are then critically examined and tested – and it is this that is the distinguishing characteristic of science.

II

From this certain things of the greatest importance follow. First, it is always possible that we are in error about even our deepest beliefs. Indeed, it is not merely possible, it is likely: I doubt whether anything that is taken for granted now will still be taken for granted three thousand years from now. Therefore we should not hold our beliefs and assumptions with unalterable certitude. The best reason we can have for holding them – the only good reason for holding them – is that they have stood up to critical examination *so far*, and stood up better than any known alternative. It does not follow from this that they are incorrigible. The only general statements about matters of experience that can be made with complete confidence are certain kinds of negative statement. We can show that an opinion involves self-contradiction, or that it is incompatible with observation, and in such cases we can assert that it is false. But we cannot assert an alternative, positive view with the same certitude. (That is why the common counter-argument: 'Then what are you going to put in its place?' is a foolish one, used chiefly by people who are determined to cling to what has been refuted.)

So the first demand that the pursuit of truth makes on us is that we hold our beliefs rationally. In other words we should be honest with ourselves and with others about the *status* of each of them, for this is what it is, independent of our wishes. If something is dubitable it is dubitable. If the evidence for it is weak it is improbable. If the evidence for it is strong it is likely. If it is incompatible with the facts it is false. We should never pretend to anyone, least of all ourselves, that uncertainties are certainties, or wishful thoughts probabilities, or unlikelihoods likelihoods, or matters of speculation matters of fact.

The second requirement is tolerance. For since all our beliefs are corrigible, all must be open to criticism. Indeed it is chiefly by the critical examination of theories that knowledge advances. So the pursuit of truth requires freedom of discussion and publication. Nothing should be exempt from questioning – the more fundamental the assumptions that are successfully revised, the greater the advance. So in addition to holding our own beliefs rationally we should demand freedom for others to attack them.

The scientific outlook, then, commits us to a certain form of society. It commits us to what we may call the 'free' society. The pursuit of truth is a radical activity and can be carried out only in freedom. It involves a permanently critical attitude to authority and to traditional assumptions. It involves a refusal to regard anything as final and unquestionable, much less infallible. It is incompatible with closed and completed systems of thought, and also with the fixed political goals that such systems characteristically produce. It involves free enquiry, rational discussion, open debate, freedom of speech and publication – and in consequence of these a willingness to revise beliefs. These are revolutionary requirements. Most social, political and religious systems are based on authority, and to them criticism of traditional assumptions is the worst of crimes, because it 'undermines the foundations of society'. They give it names like 'blasphemy', 'treason', 'heresy' and 'revisionism', and commonly punish it with torture or death.

It is vital to grasp that there is an organic connection between pre-scientific attitudes and authoritarianism, just as there is an organic connection between scientific attitudes and freedom. The pre-scientific approach in politics, as in knowledge, aims at certainty, at finality, at establishing something which, once established, will be permanent. Nazism aimed at setting up a 'thousand-year Reich' – an unending, unchanging New Order. Communism aims at creating a classless society which will put an end to the dialectical development of human affairs: the state will wither away, and henceforth there will be the administration not of people but only of things – in other words the historical process as we know it will come to an end. Some such static Utopia has been the aim of nearly all philosophies, however seemingly dynamic. Even those proposing the most violent immediate change aim ultimately at the arrest of all change. Movements based on such philosophies are totalitarian. Once they get into power they try to halt all political development. They destroy the institutions through which governments can be replaced. They forbid the forma-tion of any groups or parties other than their own. They limit the schools and universities to teaching their own historical dogmas. They compel the press to publish the party line and nothing that conflicts with it. They even try, usually, to seal off their countries from the rest of the world by banning foreign publications, jamming foreign broadcasts and controlling travel.

So the pursuit of truth creates conflict with authoritarian government. From Socrates to Pasternak men have found it so. And as for originality in fundamentals, this has been readily possible in very few times and places – and then only in free societies, or at least where authority was on the defensive. It is no coincidence that the richest harvests of individual creativity have been reaped in ancient Greece, the Renaissance, Protestant Europe, or the rest of Europe since the dawn of liberal thought; while authoritarian cultures – ancient Rome, classical China and India, medieval Christendom, contemporary Communism – have been comparatively barren. In authoritarian societies individuals are *not allowed* to call fundamental assumptions into question. Galileo was tried by the Inquisition and forced to renounce his theories in public. Descartes, who probably knew of this, went into voluntary exile in Holland for twenty years to do his work – yet failed even so to keep out of trouble. Hobbes had to flee England and live as an exile in France during the Protectorate. Spinoza was excommunicated by the Jewish Church, and only avoided persecution by the state authorities through publishing all his books (except one) anonymously – in fact not only anonymously but under false imprints and with false title-pages. Leibniz left most of his serious work unpublished during his lifetime. Marx had to flee Germany for France, where he wrote *The Communist Manifesto* – and then had to flee France for England, where he lived the rest of his life and produced almost all his work. Einstein had to leave Germany too – first for Switzerland, then the United States. Freud had to leave Austria for England.

In Russia Einstein's Special and General Theories of Relativity are still not allowed free circulation, even after half a century, because they are incompatible with dialectical materialism. The work of Freud – in fact psychoanalysis as such – can be neither published nor practised, for the same reason. In short, in every sphere of life – not merely in politics but in all the arts and all the sciences – nothing is permitted that cannot be reconciled with a closed system of metaphysics that was laid down in the first half of the nineteenth century. No fundamental assumptions can be revised. So no Communist society can ever harbour a Galileo, a Newton, a Darwin, an Einstein or a Freud – not to mention a Socrates or a Spinoza. This means that it has only the choice of abandoning Marxism (not necessarily in word but in deed) or falling farther and farther behind the front line of human advance.

Some people may be surprised by these remarks, in view of the fact that Russia now leads the world in rocket technology. If so their surprise is misplaced, for two reasons. First, they are failing to distinguish between science and technology. Russia's great success is in the application of scientific discovery to technical problems, and she is facilitated in this by her government's ability to mobilize and direct resources, skill and manpower in a way that democracies cannot do except in time of war. There is nothing in this remotely comparable with scientific discovery itself – with the work of people like Newton and Einstein. Second, even this technological virtuosity has been achieved only in the Khrushchev era, under a regime whose most striking feature is its greater liberalism than its predecessors. As Russian scientists and technologists press ever harder against the limits of our present conceptual framework, so they will be working on assumptions ever farther removed from Marxism. The strain this produces in individuals is already evident. For instance when the scientist Oleg Lenchevsky was sent on a mission to England in 1961 by the Russian Government and decided not to return, he wrote to Khrushchev: 'I have for you very great respect, as a person who sincerely loves our people and strives in such an energetic manner to achieve a better life for them, as well as for the populations of the rest of the world, but, alas, by the use of completely non-contemporary conceptions and methods, as it seems to me.' (*The Observer*, 25 June 1961. An earlier passage in the letter runs as follows: 'I am possessed by the conviction that every kind of intolerance towards any kind of person, be it even for the sake of the loftiest ideals, is nothing but a tremendous anachronism in our atomic and space age, which has come upon us so suddenly – an anachronism which can only be explained by the existence of a certain time-gap between human thinking and reality. I am profoundly convinced, Nikita Sergeyevich, that only the greatest tolerance towards all heterodox individuals, including even those whose thought is hostile, is the only means of salvation for humanity from mass fratricide and degeneration both physical and moral – and that no alternative exists in our age. As a member of the Communist Party of the Soviet Union I must follow the Party statute which calls for unanimous support for the moral-political course of the Central Committee without hesitation and without criticism. On the other hand, the same statute demands that every Party member should be absolutely honest and sincere before the Party. Being unable to combine both these requirements, and desirous of remaining really honest and sincere before my Party colleagues, as well as before you, I find myself compelled to leave the ranks of the Party. Because the Communist Party and the Soviet Government are inseparable, my leaving the Party stipulates the necessity for me of abandoning my Motherland and asking the Government of the United Kingdom for political asylum, regardless of the gravity of this step for me.')

This is why I think Communism is doomed – not because it is morally wrong but because it cannot withstand conceptual change. And I am optimistic about the future of political freedom not because I have a sentimental belief that 'right must triumph in the end', nor because I assume that 'my side will win', or think that what I desire for the future is bound to happen, but because in the long run (if there is a long run) authoritarian societies will get left behind by free societies in intellectual development, and therefore in wealth and power, unless they evade this by themselves becoming more liberal. All this is independent of moral considerations. The moral arguments for social tolerance and political liberty are well-known, and by themselves would be compulsive. They are also the most important arguments. But it is generally believed that they are the only arguments. Erroneously, it is supposed that no rational justification can be given for belief in freedom, but rather, on the contrary, that logic is on the side of the centrally-planned society. Nothing could be farther from the truth. The fact is that the free society is the only society compatible with logic, the only society that rests on rational foundations. The major argument of this chapter is that the case for the free society and against authoritarianism is overwhelming even when all moral considerations are left aside.

III

The heart of freedom is political freedom: free choice of government by the governed. This involves the right to criticize and oppose the *status quo*, and therefore to say, write and teach what is unacceptable to the authorities. Above all it entails the right to organize in opposition to the government – indeed it means keeping alternative governments permanently in being. So political freedom is the root from which all other freedoms grow – freedom of speech, freedom of the press, academic freedom, freedom of organization and so on. A society that has it must have them. Without it they have no defence.

This means freedom must be thought of in terms of *institutions*. The preservation of freedom means the preservation of ways of changing rulers at reasonable intervals without violence. This is, I believe, the only way of defining a free society without contradiction. To think of it as a society in which there is rule by the will of the majority is self-contradictory. For what if the majority chooses a government that repudiates rule by the will of the majority – a Communist or Fascist government? The supporter of freedom would then have to support the destruction of freedom. His dilemma would be insoluble. But to think of freedom in terms of institutions involves no such paradox. One can defend free institutions against all attacks on them with equal consistency whether these come from minorities or majorities.

So for a society to be free, two basic conditions are necessary and not just one. First, governments must be chosen by a majority of the governed. Second, they must leave intact the means whereby this process can be regularly repeated – which means leaving intact the means whereby they themselves can be removed from office. In other words, when a group advocating a particular policy has gained power it must not persecute its defeated opponents, but on the contrary allow them to go on campaigning against its policy with the prospect of replacing it as the government if the governed change their minds. Thus the government of today may be the opposition of tomorrow, and vice versa. This is a framework within which differences of interest and policy can be reconciled; but, more important, it is a framework within which, when such reconciliation proves impossible, it can be decided *without violence* which interest to serve or policy to pursue, and how to proceed thereafter.

A society whose government's only concern is to enforce the will of the majority cannot remain a free society. This fact incorporates the fundamental difference between the so-called liberal tradition on the Continent of Europe and in the Anglo-Saxon countries. Continental liberalism, from Rousseau onwards, has always been concerned with the general will, and this has led straight to intolerance of minorities and the sacrifice of the individual to the collective. It has created a new form of tyranny: authoritarianism based on mass-movements. The French Revolution for liberty, equality and fraternity was the first, culminating in the dictatorship of Napoleon (which is why he is rightly considered the first modern dictator). In our own day we have had Mussolini's *corporate state*, Hitler's movement calling itself both *national* and *Socialist*, and now Communism with its *dictatorship of the proletariat* and *people's democracy*. All applaud the same basic concept (derived, incidentally, from the same source), the concept of an intolerant majority. By contrast Anglo-Saxon liberalism has always been chiefly concerned with the individual – with protecting his life, liberty, property and pursuit of happiness *against* the majority, or the government, or anyone else who might want to interfere – and powerful institutions have been developed to accomplish this. So the tendencies of Continental liberalism and of Anglo-Saxon liberalism are not merely different, they are diametrically opposed. A firm grasp of this fact is essential to an understanding of modern politics, because today's legatees of collectivist authoritarianism, that is to say Communism and Fascism, use the same key terms as liberal democracy – 'democracy', 'freedom' and the rest – but in opposite senses.

Almost all science and freedom are pluralist: when theories and facts are incompatible science demands that the former, not the latter, be rejected; and when the members of a society are free to shape their own lives they will pursue a million different ends. By contrast almost all pre-science and authoritarianism are monistic – that is to say they are single, unified systems that embrace the whole of human experience in a single theory: when the theory is then contradicted by facts it is the facts that are rejected; and a society can only be organized in the light of such a theory if its members are forcibly prevented from shaping their own lives. A free society cannot have a unitary purpose. In a free society power is widely diffused, and there is a great multiplicity of purposes among the individuals and organizations contained in it. The chief function of its institutions is to defend this licence, especially against the imposition of uniform purposes by the government. And the consistent pursuit of long-term goals is made virtually impossible by the fact that the government itself can be changed, and its policies dropped or reversed, every few years. By contrast, the steadfast pursuit of an ideal state of society means adopting an unchanging policy, preventing effective opposition to it, and bringing individuals and organizations into line. It therefore involves a great deal of suffering and intolerance. And it does not compensate for this by reaching its object. No society has ever achieved its kingdom of heaven on earth, its classless, peaceful anarchy, or its thousand-year Reich. These are superstitions, the result of pre-scientific attitudes, of closed and completed systems of thought. They rest on such silly assumptions as that some or all societies have a 'destiny'; that we can know what this destiny is by simple deduction from the right political theory; that we can reach it in practice by successful long-term social planning; and that once the destiny is fulfilled there will be no further change. Most of these assumptions are demonstrably false – for example the assumption that successful long-term planning is possible in social affairs, which is merely another way of asserting that the future is predictable and, what is more, predictable in detail. Others, such as the belief in destiny, are untestable. The truth is, as we all know perfectly well from personal experience (as well as from the whole history of mankind) in human affairs we can see only a short way ahead, and even then our predictions are highly fallible and often wrong.

We cannot sit down now and work out a theory that will tell us what to do in all future situations. We cannot foresee all future situations, and furthermore each situation is unique. We shall always need to assess the facts of each *actual* situation, and decide what to do in the light of them – and therefore only partially in the light of general rules (which are necessary but must be permanently open to revision). Over and over again people fail to understand this. Intellectuals in particular (but not only they) are continually demanding a political attitude that will settle difficulties *in general*. In argument they often pose universal questions, such as 'Should a democracy allow free operation to anti-democratic parties?' (the implication being that if it does it may allow itself to be destroyed and if it does not it is not a democracy). The assumption, almost always unconscious, is that painful decisions can be obviated and dilemmas avoided if only we hit on the right theoretical approach – as if *actual* judgement and *actual* responsibility in *actual* situations could be done without. This approach represents a flight, again usually unconscious, from responsibility – or from the harsh, imperfect world of reality with its unavoidable conflicts, burdens and anxieties to a harmonious world of theory where knowledge and judgement are not required in actual situations because there are general rules for all situations. But – to take up the same illustration as before – there *is no* general rule that free societies ought *or ought not* to tolerate political movements whose aim is the destruction of free institutions. The effective banning of the

Nazi Party in Germany before it came to power in 1933 would have been justified, but the banning of the Communist Party of Great Britain in the 1960s would be foolish. These things are matters for political judgement. And the decision to be taken is a highly practical and dangerous one. To suppress a party which constitutes no real threat to free institutions is to open the door to McCarthyism, yet to fail to suppress one that does may be to let it succeed in its aims. And worse still, there will always be genuine differences between people, however intelligent and benevolent, in their assessment of such situations. In short the need to make decisions is permanent and inescapable, yet all decisions will be fallible and some will be wrong.

This is frightening. It is so frightening that resistance to it is a major factor in the formation of political attitudes. We all wish at some level to escape the risk of taking decisions, by discovering an authority (whether a person or a system) that will take them for us. This desire for security, in politics as in knowledge, is the strongest of all temptations to a pre-scientific attitude. Its roots lie deep in our psychology – in a fear of insecurity which is fundamental to our make-up. In fact these attitudes meet basic emotional needs. But this is not a reason for embracing them, or even an excuse. After all, we all have aggressive impulses, and these are 'natural' in a similar sense, but we do not allow this as a justification for aggressive behaviour. On the contrary, precisely because the impulse to aggression is in all of us we erect defences against it, both internally in the form of self-discipline and externally in the form of social institutions. And in the same way the fact that we are all powerfully impelled to adopt irrational attitudes is a reason for making every effort we can to be rational, both in our personal lives and in our social organization.

There is, of course, a strain here, a tension. Rationality is a burden. But rationality and freedom are, as I have shown, two sides of the same coin. And given the desire to be rational or free there is no escape – long for it though we may, and deeply – from responsibility.

IV

Choice between different policies or conflicting interests can only be made without violence in societies that have free institutions. That is why free institutions are the most important attribute a society can have. But most societies do not have them. Therefore to people living under tyrannical governments the most important question is how to get them.

This is also the most difficult practical problem anyone can have to face. One possible solution is revolution. A revolution may be justified if its aim is to overthrow a tyrannical regime and replace it with free institutions. It is certainly never justified otherwise – a revolutionary movement that aims to replace one tyranny with another is merely playing at Ins and Outs, and still leaves a need for revolution after it has succeeded, while a revolutionary movement that aims to overthrow free institutions is the most evil phenomenon in politics.

There is much to be said against even the most justified revolution. A lot of people get killed, most of them probably innocent, and widespread suffering of all kinds is inflicted. Hatred, bitterness and distrust are created which are bound to continue for decades afterwards and will poison the whole lives of many people. A great deal of material damage is done, too, taking years of subsequent privation to make good. The use of unrestrained violence to gain political ends is corrupting to almost everyone concerned. And not the least important consideration is that revolutions are not controllable: once the structure of a society disintegrates and successful violence becomes the only law it is not wholly within the power of any individual or group to direct events. They all become to some extent the victims of events, and are driven to all kinds of unforeseeable extremes by the sheer need for survival. Then, when the fighting stops, it is never possible to set up free institutions at once, because in such a situation the second of the two conditions for a free society set out on page 42 cannot be observed. If you have just reached power by being more successful in slaughtering your opponents than they have been in slaughtering you, you know that if you allow them to replace you, however peacefully, they will almost certainly take their revenge. Revolutionary leaders like Colonel Nasser or Fidel Castro, who promise to hold free elections within a year or two of the revolution, are almost never able to carry the promise out, however sincere they may have been in making it (and Castro for one was not sincere). They find themselves committed to authoritarian rule, while holding out freedom as no more than an indeterminate goal. And men in power are not given to abnegation. It is not only Communist dictatorships that obstinately refuse to wither away. Dictators of whatever kind are more likely to fortify their position over the passing years than to deliberately weaken it. There have been exceptions, like Kemal Ataturk, but not many.

So revolution is a chancy business. The only certainty is that it will bring death or misery to many. Whether good will come of it is very uncertain. So a revolutionary carries an appalling load of moral responsibility. Is the current tyranny really so bad as to justify all the tragedy inseparable from revolution? (And now, in the modern world, he must consider whether revolution in his country might not involve the Great Powers and precipitate nuclear war.) In any case, what would be its chances of success? And is there really no alternative? (This question of alternative must be most seriously considered, because most of the countries that have free instituions have evolved them without bloodshed from authoritarian forms of government.) The political revolutionary is the extreme case of someone confronted with the need for what I have just referred to as '*actual* judgement and *actual* responsibility in *actual* situations.' He shares this position with the nationalist leader in a colonial territory, who has to choose between co-operation with the imperialist power, revolt, and passive resistance as alternative roads to freedom. There are no general rules except *Choose the lesser evil*. And deciding what that is is often inhumanly difficult, though such decisions cannot be avoided.

V

You cannot be a lover of freedom without also being an egalitarian. For freedom promotes equality – in the sense of both equal opportunity and egalitarian feeling. I have shown already some of the ways in which it does this: by encouraging a critical attitude to authority, and hence a disbelief in the right of any person or persons to command others; by making us aware of our own permanent fallibility, and hence of the indispensability to us of the criticism and opposition of others, however much less able than us they might be.[1] I have also shown how the chief function of government in a free society is to prevent unnecessary restrictions, including material ones, on the individual liberty of its subjects.

Where the main purpose of institutions is to protect the individual,

1. This last has been superbly put by Burke in his *Reflections on the Revolution in France*: 'In my course I have known and, according to my measure, have co-operated with great men; and I have never yet seen any plan which has not been mended by the observations of those who were much inferior in understanding to the person who took the lead in the business.'

and where each individual has a vote, each must be taken notice of. The history of every country that has developed free institutions illustrates this. A government that rests on consent is sensitive to pressures and cannot afford to let any large number of its citizens harbour a sense of common injustice. So, even if in spite of itself, it is driven to prevent avoidable poverty; to open the doors of education to all; to ensure that the victims of illness or accident are cared for; that the old are not abandoned. And these things, besides being good in themselves, promote equality of opportunity, because they mitigate handicaps that are suffered by some and not by others. They also involve redistribution of wealth from richer to poorer, and hence promote equality of real income. Yet another point: to free the members of a society from avoidable handicaps and restrictions increases not only their happiness but also their working efficiency. So the argument for social equality, as for freedom, is overwhelming even when all moral considerations are left aside.

CHAPTER FOUR

The Moral Basis of My Case

THE moral basis of the case for free institutions is simple. In any society there will always be differences of opinion and conflicts of interest, and broadly speaking these can be solved in one of only two ways: either by force or by agreement. If it is to be by agreement there must be ways in which differences can be discussed and compromises reached. And when decisions are finally arrived at those who wanted something else must acquiesce in them for the time being and not be tempted to try to nullify them by force. In practice they are likely to do this only if three conditions are observed: first, if in the process by which the decision was reached their views and interests were fairly represented; second, if there are still means open to them of getting the decision reversed without force; and third, if they are confident that their opponents have obeyed the rules and will continue to do so. If any of these conditions is consistently broken there will sooner or later be demands for reform from whoever is discriminated against, and if these continue to be pressed and refused there will eventually be violence or the threat of violence, either by them or against them. If, on the other hand, the conditions are consistently observed, this means there are institutions permanently in being for the representation of everyone's opinions and interests; that policies are arrived at by discussion and compromise and not by dictation; that people who continue to disapprove either of the policies or of the people executing them are free to go on criticizing and campaigning against both with some genuine hope of getting them changed; and that everyone, whether they have power or not, is subject to the rule of law. This is what is meant by free institutions.

The moral basis of the case for free institutions, then, is that they are the only alternative to government by violence. It is on violence, or the threat of it, or the fear of it, that all authoritarianism rests. It is this that makes authoritarianism of any kind repulsive, no matter how benevolent some of its intentions may be. Of course some people *like* violence, and enjoy the use of it for its own sake as well as for its help in solving political problems. Describing a private conversation with Lenin, Bertrand Russell writes[1]: 'When I put a question to him about socialism in agriculture, he explained with glee how he had incited the poorer peasants against the richer ones, "and they soon hanged them from the nearest tree – ha! ha! ha!" His guffaw at the thought of those massacred made my blood run cold.' To people who enjoy murder I have no arguments to offer in this book. But to people who abhor violence the case for free institutions is overwhelming.

Although the fact that they are the only alternative to violence is the chief moral argument for free institutions it is not the only one. Belief in veracity is also a moral belief. I showed in the last chapter how the pursuit of truth required free institutions, and how this led to success in science and an increase in power, but I also made it clear that I believed in veracity as a value and not only because it brought material results. So anyone who believes in the pursuit of truth is committed to free institutions. Conversely anyone who believes in authoritarianism is committed to contempt for truth. As Saint Ignatius Loyola, founder of the Jesuit Order, wrote in his *Spiritual Exercises*: 'If the Church defines anything that seems to us white to be black, we must at once assert that it is black.' Of course Loyola is not here *professing* a contempt for truth, he is exhibiting it. ('Jesuitical' has entered our language as a word meaning 'intellectually dishonest'.) His point is not that one should assert what one knows to be false if the Church requires it: it is that if the Church requires it, one knows it is not false, even if all experience, all evidence and all reason go against it. This total submission to authority in matters of truth is indescribably immoral in its consequences. It also leads to the perpetuation of error.

This is one of the most devastating indictments of all authoritarian systems. Governments in free societies make mistakes too, of course, but these can be publicized and criticized and discussed, so that more often than not they have to be corrected in the end. But infallible authorities, like the Catholic Church and Communist Governments, are almost incapable of admitting error and therefore can scarcely ever permit discussion and criticism of their errors. Their mistakes go uncorrected, and the consequences of these snowball until they become, quite often, nightmarish. An example is given by one of the characters in Pasternak's *Doctor Zhivago* (page 453): 'Collectivization was both a mistake and a failure, and because that couldn't be

1. in *Eminent Men I Have Known*, to be found in *Unpopular Essays*.

admitted, every means of intimidation had to be used to make people forget how to think and judge for themselves, to force them to see what wasn't there, and to maintain the contrary of what their eyes told them. Hence the unexampled harshness of the Yezhov terror, and the promulgation of a constitution which was never intended to be applied, and the holding of elections not based on the principle of a free vote.' Once more, the only alternative to this kind of thing is free institutions.

The extraordinary difficulty that authoritarian governments have in acknowledging and correcting mistakes, and their inability to do so without the most far-reaching upheavals (like those accompanying 'de-Stalinization') expose the myth about their being more efficient than democracies. This has always been one of the chief defences of tyranny – that it is 'more efficient'. Mussolini, it was said, 'made the trains run on time'. Hitler cured unemployment and built the best road system in Europe. But this represents a partial view of efficiency, to say the least. Mussolini also led his country into a war in which it was bankrupted and beaten and stripped of all its overseas possessions. Hitler brought his people down in unimaginable ruin and reduced their cities to burning rubble. I should have thought that this was inefficient of them. In other words, even if one ignores questions of morality and judges governments only by their material results authoritarian governments can be regarded as efficient only if one overlooks half the balance-sheet. Some people have a weird gift for seeing only the good in tyrannies. But if one is going to give credit to the Soviet régime for, say, making the Russian people literate, industrializing the country, leading the world in rocketry, and so on, one must also debit it for the huge famines caused by forced collectivization and the millions of deaths, the purges, the terrors, the liquidation of whole populations, the revolt and destruction in the satellites, the poisoning of the earth's atmosphere, and also so on. On balance it comes out as a markedly inefficient form of government. Literacy, industrialization and technological development can be achieved without all that. The most the systematic use of terror can do is bring them a little quicker – and is it worth it? The difference in pace is marginal. Is it *economically*, let alone morally, worth it? If Russia and China bring, on balance, catastrophe to the human race, as Hitler did, in what sense can their régimes be said to have been efficient?

In estimating the efficiency of governments one really must look at the whole balance sheet and not just the credit side, the long run and not just the short run. Failure to do this results in exaggerated respect for tyrannies even among people who do not like them. The illusion that Communism is efficient and produces the goods is as widespread in free countries now as the same illusion about Fascism was in the thirties. Russia would have developed into a major industrial power by the middle of the twentieth century under any form of government; and in any case the country with the world's highest rate of industrial growth is not Russia but, by a long way, Japan. If the *whole* material performance of Russia is compared with that of any of the free societies of the West it is immeasurably inferior. Or take a different example:[1] 'It is a mistake to think that in spite of all her spectacular achievements – some of them are very spectacular – China has actually raised the standard of life of her people more than India has done. The economists try to make comparative estimates, and the last one I have seen was made by Professor J. K. Galbraith. It wasn't his personal work but the work of many statisticians; and in this view per capita income in India is running at about $77 per annum and per capita in China is running at about $60 per annum. I don't want to stress the difference between those figures: I don't think that anybody can estimate the per capita income of hundreds of millions of people in an undeveloped country as accurately as that. All I would say is that those estimates indicate that if people suppose that the Chinese, so far at any rate, have raised their standard of living well above the Indians, they are quite wrong.'

In addition the Chinese Government has made exactly the same mistake as the Russian Government made in the thirties – and with exactly the same results: by forcing through the collectivization of agriculture it has created widespread famine. (Agriculture is where Communism breaks down completely. Nearly half a century after the Russian Revolution Khrushchev publicly admits that Russian agriculture is in a ramshackle state. Poland, the only Eastern European country to have abandoned collectivization, is the only one to have made any real progress in agriculture. Meanwhile America, for comparison, has uncontrollable abundance – for many years now she has been giving away billions of tons of food, storing billions more at public expense, and subsidizing farmers *not* to produce, on the ground that such subsidies are cheaper than the problems created by increasing the already-fantastic surplus.) China has mobilized workers into

---

1. From the fourth of John Strachey's five lectures delivered in Singapore in the spring of 1961 and published under the title *The Great Awakening*.

communes with a ruthlessness that appals even sympathetic observers. And she has committed aggression against most of her neighbours – started wars in Korea and Laos, annexed Tibet, infringed the frontiers of Burma and India. Meanwhile the Indian Government keeps out of the Cold War, is developing free institutions, and does not regiment its people. In what sense is China's government more efficient than India's?

Newly independent countries should take the direst warning from this. To say that Communism is better suited to their situation than free institutions is a lie – expertly fostered and widely believed, but still a lie. Not only that: *any* form of authoritarian government contains for them the most frightful dangers, because of this almost irresistible tendency to persist in mistakes. Criticism is essential to efficiency. Both the Russian and the Chinese governments have brought avoidable death to millions of their people by persisting in policies which no democratic government could pursue, and for results which could have been achieved without them. When backward countries are going through the process of industrialization it is only too easy for them to make colossal mistakes, and most of them have. Free institutions are no guarantee against such mistakes but they do make them less likely, and they do make it easier to back out of them after they have been made.

Because free societies are more efficient *in their overall performance* than tyrannies, and because tyrannies persist in cataclysmic mistakes of a kind that free societies are protected from by their institutions, it is not easy to see why the myth of the greater efficiency of tyranny retains such a hold. Perhaps it is partly because rulers and ruling classes, including the most benevolent, are always likely to feel that they could do so much more if only they had more power. Such impatience is a danger to be guarded against, not a temptation to be yielded to. However, I suspect that the roots of the myth are in individual psychology. We are brought up from babyhood to think that 'Mummy knows best', to do as Father says, to obey teacher and so on, and we do in fact learn from experience that if we go our own way things come painfully unstuck whereas if we submit to authority everything turns out right. This is our first training, and it goes on for many years. Secondly, there is an element in nearly all of us of the feeling that it is 'realistic' to be tough. There is a widespread feeling that it is somehow naïve to put one's confidence in free institutions, whereas to put confidence in the solution of political problems by violence is grown-up. Democracies are felt to be 'soft', and slightly contemptible even when preferred, whereas monolithic government is awe-inspiring and to be respected even if feared and disliked. All this is contradicted by evident fact. For the reasons given so far in this chapter I take the view that there is nothing especially 'realistic' about force: on the contrary, to base a political method on it, as authoritarianism of every kind is based on it, is unrealistic in the sense of being unfitted to reality and therefore productive of mistakes and inefficiency on an unnecessarily large scale. Nor is there anything starry-eyed about believing in free institutions: they happen to work better than unfree institutions. When people persist in believing something which is evidently untrue it is usually because, consciously or unconsciously, they want to believe it – because it satisfies a need. The systematic overestimation of the accomplishments of authority meets, I think, infantile needs: it reflects our sense of insecurity, our impatience and our aggression.

I

Moral codes fall into two main categories: those which are couched in positive terms and tell you what to do, and those which are couched in negative terms and tell you what not to do. The difference is enormous. The former, leaving you no choice, are authoritarian and characterize tribal forms of social organization. Only the latter are compatible with freedom, and the moral codes which are honoured in civilized communities are all of this second, negative kind. Like the Ten Commandments, the most important words they contain are 'Thou shalt *not* . . .' The things forbidden are those that would make social life impossible if they were universal practice – killing, lying, stealing and so on. Civilized people are generally agreed that within some such limits individuals should be free to live as they wish.[1] We go further and agree that when the general rules clash with the extreme needs of individuals it is the general rules that should be sacrificed. Circumstances alter cases. We almost all assent to the general rule that it is wrong to kill, but we also think that in some circumstances killing may be justified – for instance in self-defence against a homicidal attack. And although we are agreed that it is wrong to lie we are

1. The law in civilized communities takes a similar form. By creating crimes, and thus laying down what one cannot do, it defines the limits within which one can do as one likes.

also agreed that it is sometimes right to lie – to avoid, say, betraying an innocent man to his death. In other words we are well aware that moral principles are not principles in the same sense as logical principles. The latter, being necessarily true, are compulsive and binding regardless of circumstances – if all A's are B's and X is an A, then X is a B, and this is true no matter what we substitute for A, B and X. Authoritarian moral principles claim this same status of necessary truth regardless of empirical fact, but their claim can be disproved; for whereas logical principles have no empirical content, moral principles contain both inductive generalizations and value judgements. They are practical guides to behaviour, and can be applied only in the light of actual circumstances. Values, after all, relate to individuals, and it is in the light of its effect on individuals that any course of action must be judged. The sacrifice of human beings to principles is a great evil, and comes from regarding moral principles as unqualified, as if they were logical principles.

Or, to put it another way, it comes of confusing practical problems with theoretical problems. Theoretical problems may be clear-cut and have definitive solutions – for instance an arithmetical problem has a correct answer, and all other answers are incorrect. To make do with or propagate any answer other than the one 'correct' one would be intellectually dishonest. If there is an argument between two people it must end with one of them giving in completely – unless both are wrong. The question of compromise does not arise: in this context compromise is lack of personal integrity. But practical problems are not like this at all – they rarely have 'solutions' in anything like this sense. They are normally full of imponderables and unpredictables, their limits cannot be defined, the full consequences of alternative courses of action cannot be calculated. They involve conflicts of will and interest. They are a matter not of correct and incorrect but of pros and cons, a balance of advantage that is seldom easy to assess. You can usually get part of the outcome you want only by sacrificing something else of what you would like.

We all accept this in the day-to-day problems of our personal lives. We may daydream about 'ideal solutions' but we know that to try to put them into practice would be to ride roughshod over other people in all those respects in which their feelings and interests differ from our own; in short, what would be ideal in theory would be thoroughly immoral in practice. So no one expects to get all his own way in his family, or among his friends or his colleagues at work, nor even thinks it desirable that he should, for that would be to trample over everyone else. We look on give-and-take as not just the best of a bad job but as positively the right way to live. In practical matters it is the *refusal* to compromise that we regard as immoral – we despise, not admire, the man who insists on getting his way in everything and sacrifices family and friends all the time to his own unqualified demands. We regard such a person as monstrously selfish and cruel. But alas, there are such people. And there are even more who regard it as the right way to behave in matters of politics. There is an extraordinarily large number of people who think it is wrong and corrupt for a politician, but right and necessary for everyone else, to compromise in practical affairs. And of course totalitarian organizations, for reasons that have already been made plain, systematically confuse theoretical matters with practical matters (note for instance the Communist use of the term 'correct' in relation to policies and attitudes) and denounce all compromise in practical affairs as either immoral or impossible. The natural results of this attitude are the stake, the concentration camp and the salt mine. It involves treating people as means instead of as ends in themselves. But in free societies so overriding is our conception of human beings as ends in themselves that even when they most need our help we subordinate this to their wishes. For instance our laws are such that a man cannot be kept in hospital against his will no matter how ill he is (unless he is certified as insane); and if his life can be saved only by an operation which he refuses to have he is allowed to die. Similarly with those who plainly need our help in everyday life, such as invalids or the blind: we often leave them alone rather than risk imposing on them. The man who continually thrusts his help on others unasked-for is looked on as an interfering nuisance, and resented. We help others only if they do not mind. We do not force our help on them, and we regard it as an intrusion if they force their help on us.

We expect these 'ordinary' rules of behaviour to be obeyed not only by individuals but by social groups – for example those of the family, or our friends, or our workmates. As Jefferson said, 'I know but one code of morality for men whether acting singly or collectively.' The Roman Catholic Church is at one with humanists on this: 'The Gospel has not one law for individuals and another for States and nations' (Pope Benedict XV in the encyclical *Pacem Dei Munus*, 1920). No one has ever produced a valid argument for limiting the application of moral behaviour to groups of less than a certain size. All the moral arguments and all the logical arguments demand that they apply to every group. So no society however big, and no government, has a right to kill its members, or lie to them, or steal from them. It should alleviate misery and remove injustice but it should not try to make its members happy or force them to live in a certain way. Unfortunately, however, when groups get bigger than a certain size there are *psychological* barriers. We do not *feel* the same sense of obligation to people we have not met as we do to people we have, despite the fact that all moral teaching, whether religious or otherwise, and all logical argument, tell us we should. As a result we have things done to people we do not know which we would never dream of doing ourselves, or of having done to people we know. For instance we pay the public hangman to break the necks of strangers, whereas if called upon to do it ourselves most of us would break down and demand the renunciation of the whole business; or if it were a friend who was being hanged and we had the power of reprieve we would use it. Many British men and women who would be appalled at the idea of beating up a difficult customer to make him do what they wanted nevertheless approved of Britain's invasion of Egypt in 1956. Czechoslovakia, said Neville Chamberlain in 1938, was 'a faraway country' of whose people 'we know nothing' – and gave this as his excuse for betraying it to the Nazis.

The point of these examples is threefold. First, the farther removed a piece of immoral behaviour is from our own experience the less we feel it as such. Second, this remains true even when we ourselves are responsible for it. And third, in the huge societies and complex international relationships of the modern world we are responsible for innumerable things that happen at a great distance from ourselves. In a completely closed tribal society the limits of personal acquaintance are also the limits of responsibility, so that little harm is done by a failure to project moral principles beyond the immediate experience of private life. But we of the British electorate, by contrast, are responsible for, say, the present and future well-being of millions of Africans; if we are indifferent to this the results can be, as they have sometimes been in the past, utterly damnable. At one of the darkest times in the history of British colonialism I opposed the Colonial Secretary in a General Election;[1] and I was appalled at the indifference

1. I stood against Alan Lennox-Boyd in Mid-Bedfordshire in the General Election of 1959 after nursing the constituency for eighteen months. During most of that period the British Army was trying to hold down the people of

of ordinary men and women to what was being done by their elected representative. They thought it airy-fairy to care about such things – nothing to do with 'real life'. The opposite, of course, was the truth, and it was they who were being unrealistic, both in failing to envisage what was actually happening and in failing to face up to their responsibility for it. Such psychological limitations in our sense of moral responsibility are in no sense whatever good, and considerations of personal and social maturity, self-interest, moral considerations, rational considerations, and the brute facts of life in the modern world all alike demand that we make every possible effort to overcome them – and this means not only trying to think and feel more realistically but also building positive safeguards against our own indifference into our institutions.

Cyprus by brute force. Shortly before the election the Devlin Report described Nyasaland as 'a police state' – and shortly before that eleven people had been beaten to death by Government officers in Hola Camp, Kenya, in circumstances that cast responsibility on the Colonial Secretary. . . . Perhaps I had better not leave that last remark unexplained. I can best amplify it by reproducing a letter of mine published in one of the local newspapers in the constituency, the *Biggleswade Chronicle*, on 19 June 1959: 'Britain maintains four concentration camps in Kenya. In one of them, Hola, eleven Africans were beaten to death on 3 March of this year. The following day the Kenya Government issued a statement that they had died 'after drinking water from a water cart'. That this story of water poisoning was a pack of lies was revealed by the inquest. One man had a fractured skull, another had laceration of the mid-brain. 'In each case,' said the medical report on all eleven men, 'death was found to have been caused by shock and haemorrhage due to multiple bruising caused by violence.'

As the truth came out it was discovered that the murdered men had been victims of the so-called Cowan Plan. This was a plan to make political prisoners work by using violence on them – in other words a plan for forced labour in the detention camps. It had been approved by the Kenya Government, despite the fact that forced labour is against the law.

In recent months many quite terrible stories have leaked out about the use of violence in Kenyan camps, and the Labour Party has asked again and again for an independent inquiry to be held, but again and again Mr Lennox-Boyd refused. He said an independent inquiry was unnecessary because the Government had itself carried out the closest inquiries and was satisfied with the conduct of the camps. On 24 February Colonial Under-Secretary, Mr Julian Amery, speaking on the Colonial Secretary's behalf, said: 'Our contention is that the organization of the prison service is right and is what it should be.' Exactly a week later the eleven Hola prisoners were battered to death.

If Mr Lennox-Boyd had agreed to an inquiry these men would probably still be alive.

Only two alternatives are possible. Either the Colonial Secretary and his deputy knew all about the Cowan Plan *and approved of it*, or they had not carried out the closest inquiries into the conduct of the camps. In either case the only honourable course left open to them now is to resign.'

II

Christianity asserts that all men are of equal importance to God. Whatever the church, it constantly uses phrases like 'all men are equal in the sight of God', or, as the last Archbishop of Canterbury preferred to put it, 'all men are equal in the love of God'. Other major religions employ the same concept. Aside from religion, we look on the principle of 'equality before the law' as a necessary foundation for any ordered society. In short, the principle of equality is already central to all civilized law and civilized ethics. This principle consists not in the assertion that people are all the same – that would be not a principle but a description, and a false one. It consists in the demand that all people should be treated as of equal importance.

Nearly every religion known to us has formulated this in the so-called Golden Rule: treat every other human being as you would wish yourself to be treated. Jesus put it much more strongly, starting with 'Love thy neighbour as thyself' and rising to 'Love your enemies'. However it is formulated, this acceptance of other people as being as important as oneself leads naturally to caring about them. And as I have already shown, logic and morals alike demand, as do religious injunctions, that this feeling extend to everyone. Man as a moral entity is not just the people we approve of. He is not just Christian man, or Western man, or White man, or literate man. He is all men. What all human beings have in common by virtue of their common humanity is such that by comparison the differences are negligible. However bestial some people may be, the fact that they are people is more important than the fact that they are bestial. And as for distinctions such as male and female, able and incompetent, rich and poor, educated and illiterate, Black and White, Communist and democrat – these pale into insignificance beside the fact that we are all people.

Caring about other people is the emotional basis of radicalism. 'The capacity for emotional concern for individual life is the most significant quality of a civilized human being. It is not achieved when limited to people of a certain colour, race, religion, nation or class. Indeed, just to the extent that this or that group commands our exclusive sympathy, we are capable of the most monstrous cruelty, or at best indifference, to others who do not belong to the group. Describing a hanging scene at Tyburn gaol not so much more than a hundred years ago, the learned and observant diarist, Charles Greville, "was astonished by the incomprehensible attitude of some of the boys sentenced to be hanged. Never", he is reported as saying, "did I see boys cry so". These children belonged to a different social class from Greville's. Their terror apparently made no claim on his emotions or understanding.'[1]

Even today it is common, and in England more than in other Western countries, to treat children as if they were not people. It is common to look on women as grade two people, and many women accept this valuation of themselves. I frequently hear the old, or the mentally ill, or the poor and overcrowded described as 'living just like animals'. Those who believe in killing murderers or political opponents commonly categorize them as 'mad dogs'. 'In much the same way the Nazis put the Jews outside the walls of their personalities, except as objects of sadistic pleasure. So, too, races of a different colour from their own, or groups that stand in the way of their ambitions, are regarded by some of our contemporaries.'[2]

This denial of full humanity to other human beings is the root of most evil. Often it is due to lack of imagination – in which case it can be cured by direct experience. Only recently a likeable young man who had just been through public school and Cambridge was telling me about the transformation his period of National Service had brought about in his attitude to 'the lower orders'. With eyes wide and great emphasis he said: 'I discovered they were *people*!' Perhaps it is natural, in the sense in which selfishness is natural, for our personal experience to set the limits of our human sympathies in such a way that we withhold these from men and women outside the narrow range of our own lives. But the most important thing education can do is to break down this barrier between experience on the one hand and understanding, imagination and sympathy on the other.

I would go so far as to say that this is the measure of maturity. Does a man really *feel* women to be his equals as human beings? Does he really *feel* children to be his equals? And old people? And beggars? And illiterates? And lunatics? And Communists? And Jews? And foreigners? And Negroes? And prostitutes? And homosexuals? And murderers? If he excludes any of these from his human sympathies his humanity is to that extent incomplete. The wonderful words of Donne apply here. 'No man is an island, entire of itself. Every man

1. Aneurin Bevan: *In Place of Fear*, Chapter 10.
2. *Ibid.*

is a piece of the continent, a part of the main. If a clod be washed away by the sea, Europe is the less; as well as if a promontory were; as well as if a manor of thy friend's or of thine own were. Any man's death diminishes me, because I am involved in mankind.'

III

From this it follows that 'equality of opportunity' is not enough. In fact in the modern world 'equality of opportunity' is becoming a Conservative slogan, a formula for retaining injustice. For it is compatible with extreme inequality. To take an instance, one can easily imagine a system of education in which *all* children went to primary schools (a suggestion which was in fact made by the Minister of Education at the 1961 Conservative Party Conference) and after that went through a process of grading, strictly on the basis of ability, as a result of which most of them, as now, were sent to overcrowded classrooms at the age of eleven and out into the world at the age of fifteen; a few of the remainder were sent to technical schools; even fewer to grammar schools; a handful to public schools; and the élite of the latter two groups, the *crème de la crème*, made their way, still strictly on the basis of merit, to universities. Such a system would embody perfect equality of opportunity and extreme inequality. It would be totally unacceptable to anyone who agrees with what I said in the previous section of this chapter.

'It implies that very unequal rewards and privileges are distributed solely on the basis of, if not one, at any rate a particular group of traits of human personality, for any selection must in practice be based on a limited number of more or less known and measurable aspects of character. Let us suppose that intelligence is made the main criterion. . . . Why should this one trait, or even a group of traits, alone determine success or failure, riches or poverty, a high or low prestige? Why should no marks be given for saintliness, generosity, compassion, humour, beauty, assiduity, continence, or artistic ability? These questions denote no anti-intellectual bias – matters would be in no way improved if we chose some other trait to be the sole criterion for exceptional rewards. It is the injustice of isolating, as a basis for extreme inequality, certain selected ones out of the multiple strands that go to make up the human personality, which constitutes the fundamental ethical case against any élite or aristocracy.

Of course the practical reasons for rewarding outstanding ability generously are obvious enough; and any society would be foolish not to offer such rewards as will attract the ability into the service of the community. But if this requires such large differential privileges as to create a distinct élite, differently educated and socially select, it must be regarded as an unpleasant concession to economic efficiency, and not as being intrinsically just. In practice, however, I do not believe, after studying the experience of the U.S. and Scandinavia where the selection is highly efficient yet social equality much greater, that the inequality and class segregation, which would characterize an élite of ability in Britain under our present educational system, could possibly be justified by any considerations of efficiency.'[1]

Conservatives like inequality, believe in it and want to preserve it. The intelligent ones realize that the most dangerous opponents of inequality are able people who have been victimized by it. They are therefore coming more and more to favour opening the doors of opportunity to all able people as a way of helping to preserve inequality. I happen to think that this willingness should be seized on and exploited to the full, but it is no substitute for equality. 'The doctrine which throws all its emphasis on the importance of opening avenues to individual advancement is partial and one-sided. It is right in insisting on the necessity of opening a free career to aspiring talent; it is wrong in suggesting that opportunities to rise, which can, of their nature, be seized only by the few, are a substitute for a general diffusion of the means of civilization, which are needed by all men, whether they rise or not, and which those who cannot climb the economic ladder, and who sometimes, indeed, do not desire to climb, may turn to as good account as those who can.'[2] In Britain most of our children do in fact leave school and start work at the age of fifteen. A million old age pensioners are so poor they have to go to the National Assistance Board to keep alive. Altogether about seven million people are living in poverty – while nearly half the privately-owned wealth in the country belongs to one per cent of the population. When one looks beyond our local society the dark picture becomes a nightmare. Half the human beings in this world live in such poverty that they do not even have enough to eat. Getting on for half are illiterate. Well over

1. C. A. R. Crosland: *The Future of Socialism*, pp. 235–6, Mr Crosland appends to this passage a footnote saying: 'My views on this point owe much to discussions with Mr Michael Young.'
2. R. H. Tawney: *Equality*, Chapter 3 (ii).

half live under tyrannical governments. To be conservative in such a world is a sign of some major defect of imagination or sympathy. To advocate equality merely of opportunity is grotesque. What is clearly needed is a massive and 'general diffusion of the means of civilization'. If you really care about people and regard them as the only ends you will want a huge increase in, quite simply, *equality*. You will want a large part of the resources of our world to be devoted to improving people's lot regardless of their IQ or their level of literacy or their skill in passing examinations, or for that matter their strength of character or any other personal advantage they may happen to have or lack – in fact the fewer they have of these things the more help they need. Equality of opportunity alone means that the prizes go to the strong, that the lion's share of the good things of life goes to those who can win them by their own efforts – whereas what is wanted is almost the opposite: institutions that give preferential treatment to the weak, the poor, the ill, the old, the exploited, to all who are not in a position to fend successfully for themselves. And in present circumstances that includes most of the human race.

I want the giant aggregates of wealth and power that characterize the modern world to be put at the service of individual men and women as the sole justification for their existence. This means, when tackling any problem – whether starvation in India or education in Britain – starting with *people*: what their situation is, what their needs and wants are. One should not, to take the example nearest home, try to work out how one can fit children into the schools, but on the contrary, how one can adapt the schools to the needs of the children. This approach automatically involves a radical attitude to institutions and a willingness to keep changing them in response to human needs. It is also, I am convinced, the only approach that can reconcile personal freedom with the huge concentrations of power and organization that are inevitable in contemporary life. Furthermore the institutions themselves should be so constructed as to ensure that their purpose is always the service of individuals. Where a service has to be organized in a monolithic way, as with a national transport system or a basic industry, it should be controlled by a democratically elected government. Where it does not need to be monolithic the maximum devolution of power should be encouraged and a multiplicity of independent ventures – not only business enterprises but co-operatives, trade-union undertakings, professional associations, non-profit-making organizations and the rest. In every kind of organization, no matter what it is, the people actively engaged should share in the making of policy *on the level at which they are engaged*. And finally, when all these safeguards have been built into institutions, the fact must be faced that the rights and freedoms of people are still not wholly secured. From then on the price of freedom is eternal vigilance.

In the world as it is today there are two great challenges to this way of doing things. First from Conservatives, who from the most backward countries to the most advanced promote a form of society whose major aspects – industry, commerce, social life, communications, and even government itself if they can get away with it – are controlled by small groups of privileged individuals. Conservatives fear collective action, believe in the inferiority of the unfortunate, and defend each inequality to the last ditch (by contrast with Communists, who love collective action but fear freedom with the same hysteria as Conservatives fear equality). Fortunately we do not live in a Conservative world. We live in a world of unprecedentedly fast change, of revolutionary change. Conservative governments in backward countries have the same future as rotting dykes before a flood. But there is a long-term danger from Conservatism in advanced countries. When primary poverty has been abolished the appeal of radical change dwindles and societies can begin to stagnate, as Britain today is stagnating. The only effective answer to this is for radical parties to keep up to date in both their outlook and their methods, to stir the imagination of electorates, convincing them that radical policies are more relevant than Conservative policies. I suspect also, though this remains to be seen, that material complacency is a stage through which populations pass: certainly John Kennedy's 1960 election campaign showed that it could be challenged successfully even in the world's most affluent society.

Just as Conservatism is only really to be feared in advanced countries, so Communism is only to be feared in backward countries. For there it has something to offer. It promises to mobilize the whole resources of a nation, including its population, to the task of modernizing its economy. It hastens the process by holding down personal consumption to a level which the members of a free society would never accept, and is thus able to devote a higher proportion of production to capital investment and economic growth than a free society could. And it ensures the continuity of this process by outlawing opposition and having no changes of government. There is no baulking the fact that this programme has enormous appeal to the potential leaders of backward countries – an appeal that can be softened only by convincing them of two things: first, that a free society need not lag too far behind the same rate of economic development; and second, that the difference is worth nothing like the price that has to be paid for it. It is worth pointing out, too, that this programme, which in fact constitutes both the appeal and the function of Communism in the modern world, is almost the opposite of Marxism. According to Marx the historical function of Capitalism is to industrialize society, and Communism will come only after that: but in the real world the appeal and function of Communism *are to industrialize society*. The working class in every single one of the advanced industrial countries, which according to Marx were the only ones which could effect the transition to Communism, have rejected it decisively, and the only way in which Communism might come to them now is under the bayonet-points of foreign armies after defeat in war – which they would certainly resist. Or to take another point: according to Marx nearly all the human evils that spring from Capitalism are due to the fact that it holds wages down to subsistence-level and robs the workers of 'surplus value'. But in fact it is Communism that bases its economic programme on this, while the only countries in which the workers live in affluence are Capitalist countries. Thus, quite apart from the fact that Marxist theory is wrong and Communist practice evil, the two flatly contradict each other. There are four separate lines of criticism here, all of them valid.

1. Marxist theory is indefensible.
2. Communist practice is evil.
3. The realities of Communism flatly contradict what Marxist theories say they must be.
4. The development of non-Communist societies flatly contradicts what Marxist theories say it must be.

IV

Because politics is for people the ultimate aims of politics are non-political. Peace and better standards of living, health, education, housing and the rest are to be promoted not for society's sake but for the individual's sake. In so far as they are means at all it is to the end of maximizing the freedom of each man and woman to live his own life as he wishes. I repudiate the Communists' belief that politics is co-extensive with life, and I deny their right to subordinate the individual to the collective, or to sacrifice present to future generations. Similarly, I despise the Conservatives' worship of institutions and the way they make individuals subservient to these even in thought. People, and only people, are ends. All else is means.

In an absolutely vital sense politics is only about means. Political action can free people from socially avoidable limitations and give them that security which is a necessary basis for civilized life. How they live beyond that is for them to decide. If you advocate a free society and assert the right of each individual to decide for himself what aims, within the limits of a free society's laws, he is going to pursue in life, you thereby also assert that it is not for anyone else to say what those aims shall be. They lie outside legislation, outside the sphere of government, outside politics, in the world of private life and personal choice. Your political convictions do not relate to ultimate aims, nor should they. You are insisting on the right of other people to pursue aims of which you disapprove.

In affluent societies the precept of 'choice' needs to be propagated in a purely political context just as Aneurin Bevan successfully propagated the precept of 'priorities' in post-war Britain. At that time it represented a great leap forward to have a job for every worker and medical attention for everyone who was ill. Such things had never been known in Britain before. But in the changed conditions of today they represent a conservative standard. It is now possible, and essential, for every worker to have a *choice* of jobs. Every patient should have a *choice* of doctors and hospitals. Every parent should have a choice of *different kinds* of school for his children. Every family should have a choice of *different kinds* of housing. Such provision of choice in fundamentals like work, health, housing and education is far and away the best use to which abundance can be put – more useful than making consumer goods, desirable and enjoyable though those are. It means more freedom, and a richer diversity of social possibilities, than have ever been known before, with correspondingly greater opportunities for individual development and fulfilment.

V

Chapter Three and this one taken together outline a whole political approach or 'philosophy'. It is not a programme but *a way of looking at things*, from which follows a way of doing things. In politics the way things are done matters more than what is done. The most obvious example of this in the world today concerns disputes between nations: the way these disputes are settled – is it to be by violence or compromise? – is infinitely more important than what the disputes are. The same is true within nations: whether disagreement about policies is resolved by counting heads or breaking them matters more than what is resolved, and does more to shape the structure and character of the society. So although what I am advocating is a method I do not regard it as subsidiary but as fundamental. Just as science is scientific method, so politics is political method. The heart and soul of a political attitude is contained not in its conception of final goals, if indeed it has any, but in its view of how change should occur. Final political goals are figments of the imagination. They are based on the fiction that one day time will stop. People who are trying to bring about a particular state of society forget that, even if they were to achieve it, it would presumably be as transient as any other. The world will, I take it, change as much if not more between the years 2040 and 2060 as it did between 1940 and 1960. The human race will always be travelling, never arriving – unless there is a catastrophe in which it is totally destroyed. So political attitudes – whether conservative, utopian or totalitarian – that are concerned with establishing states of society are incompatible with the real world. Only political attitudes that are concerned with change are realistic. Whether we realize it or not, it is our attitudes to social *change* that constitute our political outlook. And if it is said that most people need a stable vision of the good society to give them their bearings through the complexities of political action I reply, first, that this is a religious and not a political need, and second, that it is patently not true of most people – every parliamentary candidate knows that it is a herculean task to interest most people in anything beyond the here and now.

What the approach I am advocating is *called* does not matter: that is a purely verbal question. It so happens that in Britain it has for some time been called 'democratic socialism'. For instance it is clearly the sort of approach Aneurin Bevan was describing when he wrote in *In Place of Fear* (Chapter 10):

'The philosophy of democratic socialism is essentially cool in temper. It sees society in its context with nature and is conscious of the limitations imposed by physical conditions. It sees the individual in his context with society and is therefore compassionate and tolerant. Because it knows that all political action must be a choice between a number of possible alternatives it eschews all absolute proscriptions and final decisions. Consequently it is not able to offer the thrill of the complete abandonment of private judgement, which is the allure of modern Soviet Communism and of Fascism, its running mate. Nor can it escape the burden of social choice so attractively suggested by those who believe in *laissez-faire* principles and in the automatism of the price system. It accepts the obligation to choose among different kinds of social action and in so doing to bear the pains of rejecting what is not practicable or less desirable.

'Democratic socialism is a child of modern society and so of relativist philosophy. It seeks the truth in any given situation, knowing all the time that if this be pushed too far it falls into error. It struggles against the evils that flow from private property, yet realizes that all forms of private property are not necessarily evil. Its chief enemy is vacillation, for it must achieve passion in action in the pursuit of qualified judgements.'

It is the sort of approach recommended by Evan Durbin in *The Politics of Democratic Socialism*, and by Bertrand Russell in the quotation on page 78, in which he also uses the term. On this definition Socialism is not a system of society but a method of changing society; not a state of affairs but a way of doing things. However, there are other people who use the term 'Socialism' in a sense incompatible with this, and for the reasons given in Chapter Two I do not propose to get into a wrangle about words, so for the sake of clarity alone I will avoid the term 'Socialism' and use 'radicalism' as a label for what I am advancing. I hasten to add, though, that no one would be more pleased than I if the term 'Socialism' came to be universally understood in this sense.

I am not under the illusion that everyone can be got to agree on the radical approach. People will always disagree about political problems

– even radicals will always differ in their degree of radicalism. This is partly a matter of temperament and partly a matter of standpoint. Also, what can be done in the way of tackling political problems depends not only on what people want but on the resources available, so even people who agree both about what the problems are and about how they should be solved will give different priorities to their claims on available resources. Therefore, anyone offering a single set of opinions to everybody is wasting his time: the worthwhile thing to offer is a framework within which different opinions can be reconciled, and even more important, within which it can be agreed what to do when such reconciliation proves impossible. That is what I think I have done. If people can agree on the way of going about things set out in these two chapters they will have agreed terms of discussion in which they *can* discuss, instead of resorting to violence, and in which they can agree on how to proceed after discussion has failed to resolve differences. And I think this approach can be successfully recommended to enough people in most societies to enable it to work. The fact that it embodies both the morality and the self-interest of everyday life, that it appeals to common sense as well as common decency, makes it acceptable, I believe, to most ordinary men and women. And an overwhelming argument is that unless the human race as a whole accepts ways of settling major differences without violence it will eventually destroy itself.

The radical approach is down-to-earth, not only in the theoretical sense of being justifiable to most people, and in the pragmatic sense of being demanded by the actual problems confronting us, but also in the practical sense of being already represented by powerful political forces in the world. There would not be much point in recommending a political attitude that was not. The first country to try something like it was the United States, under Franklin Roosevelt and the New Deal. Then came New Zealand. In the Scandinavian countries it has been brought to an advanced state of accomplishment under long-established Socialist governments. It is already accepted by the great majority of British Socialists, and was the basis of the Labour Government's approach during the period 1945–51. Most Western European countries, and in particular their Socialist parties, are moving in this direction, while underdeveloped countries as diverse as Yugoslavia and India are taking the first fumbling, seemingly-hopeless steps, from entirely different starting-points, in an attempt to get on to the same path.

In Britain most radicals are Socialists. Nevertheless quite a lot of radicals are not Socialists, and quite a lot of Socialists are not radicals. This is because although the Labour Party is mainly a radical party it contains a number of incompatible elements: it contains conservative elements, class-war elements, authoritarian elements, Marxist elements, and just plain cranks – to name only five. This attracts into it a lot of people who are not radicals, and keeps out of it a lot of people who are. These are matters I shall return to later.

I am a Socialist. But my really deep loyalty in politics is to the beliefs set out in this book, and my loyalty to the Labour Party is subordinate to this. If the Labour Party were to be irredeemably captured by any of the five elements listed in the previous paragraph I should leave it. The crying need would then be the creation of a radical party, and I should without hesitation help to form such a party, or join it if it already existed. However, as things are in Britain at the moment, the only political party with any hope of forming a radical government in the foreseeable future is the Labour Party. In the 1959 General Election Socialist candidates received 12,216,166 votes as compared with Conservative candidates' 13,750,965. The fact that the Conservatives got a parliamentary majority of a hundred seats seems to have misled people into thinking as if the difference between their vote and the Socialists' is much bigger than in fact it is. The Conservatives got less than half the votes cast – 49.4%, compared with the Socialists' 43.8%. And not only does the Labour Party retain, like the Conservatives, the support of forty-something per cent of the electorate: it has a nation-wide organization, the support of the entire trade-union movement, and big financial backing. A huge section of the nation regards the Labour Party as representing its interests. None of this can be said for, say, the Liberal Party, which got 1,640,761 votes (5.9% of those cast, despite the fact that it attracts a lot of temporary support from middle-class voters between General Elections. (Analysis of recent by-election figures shows that it is deriving most of this increased support from disillusioned Conservatives.) To talk as if the Liberal Party were about to replace the Labour Party is to disregard all the realities. The most it can hope for is to merge its radical elements with those of the Labour Party.

Britain's greatest political need is for a party which whole-heartedly pursues a radical approach *and is generally accepted as doing so*. The Labour Party is capable of becoming this, but whether it will or not still hangs in the balance. Quite apart from the country's need the matter is one of life and death for the party itself. If it does not present itself as a thoroughgoing radical party it has, in my opinion, no future as an effective instrument of social change: it will never again become the government, and will suffer only the same decades-long decline as the Liberals have gone through – not disappearing, but not accomplishing anything either. If this happens it will be a tragedy. Whether it does or not rests largely with the members of the Labour Party. That is why I, one of them, am writing this book. The need is threefold: first, for a fully-worked-out and coherent radical philosophy which is clearly understood; second, for the Labour Party to base itself and its policies firmly on this; and third, for these to be vividly projected to the electorate. At present confusion reigns in all three fields. Firstly, most people, even Socialists, are unacquainted with any systematic 'left-wing' philosophy other than Marxism, and the result is that Labour Party thinking consists of an unsystematic radicalism debilitated by major infections of Marxism and conservatism. Secondly, because of this the Labour Party contains Marxists and conservatives as well as radicals, and there is unending fighting amongst them; policies can be arrived at only by compromise among the different groups, and in consequence, although predominantly radical, they contain important Marxist and conservative elements. Thirdly, the resulting image projected to the electorate is extremely confused. The unending fighting is given maximum publicity by the party's opponents, as are all its Marxist and conservative characteristics, and it appears unsure of what it wants to do and unfit to govern.

My chief concern in this book is with the first of the three needs. I have already given a systematic outline of my radical approach to politics – and it so happens that this looks like an up-to-date version of the central traditions of the Labour Party. That is why I joined the Labour Party. And because my approach is an extension – perhaps not even that, perhaps only a fuller articulation – of its predominating attitudes I consider it realistic to hope for its general acceptance. One of the biggest weaknesses of the non-Marxist Left is an ideological inferiority-complex. There is a widespread sense of intellectual insecurity, of the unmet need for an approach to existing society which is more powerful and heuristic than Marxism, and at the same time productive of radical change. The realization that such an approach exists, followed by an understanding of it, could result in an immeasurable increase in self-confidence and boldness, a blood-transfusion of new political effectiveness. It could also give the Labour Party a new unity – the unity of a common outlook – and a clear identity. On this basis most of the radicals outside it would join it – and if most of the non-radicals in it were to leave, so much the better. We should then have what we need – a radical party with all the driving force of self-confidence and unity, routing the arguments of Conservatives and Communists alike.

CHAPTER FIVE

Conflicting Elements in Socialist Thought

THE position outlined in the last two chapters has behind it the greatest intellectual tradition of mankind, a tradition which seems to have begun with the pre-Socratic philosophers. Before them there was more or less no distinction between politics, religion and cosmology. There were just different sorts of tribalism, each community having its own conception of the universe, its own gods, its own priests, its own rulers and its own laws. The conception of the individual as a moral entity did not exist: he had significance only as a member of the tribe. Hence there was no distinction between morality and the law. And all these things – priests, rulers, gods, laws, the structure of the tribe and the structure of the universe – had magical significance. The worst crime of all, punishable by death, was to question them. Wisdom was handed down like orders – down through the social hierarchy, down through the generations.

The institutions thus created have been well described by Karl Popper:[1] 'Far from being places of critical discussion, they make it their task to impart a definite doctrine, and to preserve it, pure and unchanged. It is the task of the school [of thought] to hand on the tradition, the doctrine of its founder, its first master, to the next generation, and to this end the most important thing is to keep the doctrine inviolate. A school of this kind never admits a new idea. New ideas are heresies, and they lead to splits: should a member of the school try to change the doctrine, then he is expelled as a heretic. But the heretic claims, as a rule, that his is the true doctrine of the founder. Thus not even the inventor admits that he has introduced an invention; rather, he believes that he is returning to the true orthodoxy which has somehow been perverted.'

Such primitive schools of thought are still common – most churches, totalitarian parties and crank organizations are like this.[2] But the pre-

1. Presidential Address to the Aristotelian Society, 13 October 1958.
2. See also the words of the Candidate for Wimbledon at the Labour Party's 1957 Annual Conference: 'Harold Wilson has said that the document does not

Socratic philosophers introduced a new kind of tradition, which has run parallel with the other ever since – a tradition of critical discussion. 'It[1] was a momentous innovation. It meant a break with the dogmatic tradition which permits only *one* school doctrine, and the introduction in its place of a tradition that admits a *plurality* of doctrines which all try to approach the truth, by means of critical discussion.'

The pre-Socratics concerned themselves with the structure of the universe and the problem of change: they were not greatly concerned in their philosophy with mankind. The first person to make a rational approach to specifically human affairs was Socrates. The basic assumptions underlying personal morality, ethics, politics and all social matters were regarded by him as to be critically examined and openly discussed. His incredibly brave spirit of inquiry and his integrity (he suffered death rather than stop encouraging the pursuit of truth) went hand in hand with a deep concern for people. He was the first humanist, by which I mean he was the first to believe in the duality of fact and value, and thus to combine the two basic principles that have characterized humanism ever since: the principle that the truth is independent of what we may wish or authority say; and the principle that values relate only to human beings. The genuineness of his disbelief in authorities is shown by the fact that he did not attempt to set himself up as one, nor pretend to any special knowledge. As Aristotle said of him after his death: 'Socrates did not give answers, he raised questions; for he admitted he did not know.'[2] It is probable that mankind owes more to him than to any other single person.

A few hundred years after Socrates, in a nearby part of the Eastern Mediterranean, came another innovator, Jesus, whose contribution to the moral basis of civilization has been second only to that of Socrates. Jesus believed in the unique value and importance of every individual human being *as such*, regardless of all other considerations.

---

abandon our original concept of nationalization. He has said that the new suggestions for investment, and purchase of shares, are merely an addition to our old ideas. Even if we accept his contention, can we agree that we should add any new addition, however small, however slight, to the original Socialist concept unless we are sure that this idea is also a Socialist idea?'

1. Popper, *ibid.*

2. Asking a new kind of question is the hallmark of intellectual genius. Cf. 'Whatever criticisms may be made of Freud's theories the fact remains (and this is perhaps the supreme instance of his tremendous genius) that, whilst making no claim to know all the answers, he was well aware of the right questions psychology should ask.' J. A. C. Brown: *Freud and the Post-Freudians*, p. 187.

He dramatized this in the astounding maxim 'Love your enemies'. Because human beings and God were the only moral entities, relationships among human beings, and between them and God, were the only moral relationships. So being good meant not obeying the rules but loving God and other people. It is hard now to understand the almost inconceivable nature of this belief to a tribal society, or its revolutionary implications. For in a tribal society, as I said a little earlier, the notion of the individual as a moral entity does not exist: the tribe itself is the source of all morality. Jesus was saying the exact opposite of this: the tribe, he was saying, is not a moral entity; the only moral entities are God and human individuals. From this it follows that each individual should obey, in the last resort, the will of God and his own conscience rather than the law of the society in which he lives. This was a frontal onslaught on the very foundations of social morality as it had always been known. It was in the strict sense of the word anarchic, and would make all forms of social organization impossible except those actively assented to by each individual. So it invited persecution and death. But the Early Christians, though persecuted and killed in large numbers by the civil authorities, kept their basic beliefs alive. And these had so much in common with the tradition founded by the Greeks that the two streams quickly mingled and became the mainstream of what is good in Western civilization.

It would take me the rest of this book, indeed many books, to develop the history of these ideas to our own day. This is not necessary for my purpose. Tradition is a light, not an authority. The past, like language, is fascinating and prodigiously useful but should not be allowed to direct our thinking.[1] Conflict has never ceased between, on the one hand, the humanist values of freedom, love, tolerance, supreme regard for the individual, egalitarianism, the application of reason to human affairs, the scientific outlook and opposition to authority; and on the other hand authoritarianism, with its belief in the moral supremacy not of individual values but of group values – the institution, the church, the state or the past – from which follows the attribution to these of superhuman qualities, and thence pre-scientific outlook; also the authoritarian belief in the moral

---

1. This contention is fundamental to my whole position, and I want to make it absolutely clear that my purpose in mentioning the history of my ideas is not to drum up authority for them but merely to give the reader his (or rather my) bearings.

inequality of men, from which follows the subordination of individuals and the use of violence against the intractable – and thence intolerance in all its forms. The two most successful authoritarian ideologies of the last two thousand years, Catholicism and Communism, though belonging to the second of these two opposed traditions, both owe their founding inspiration to the first. Both began with a handful of revolutionaries inspired by humanitarian ideals. But both survived persecution and rose to become themselves the religion of governments. They have caused more human suffering and been used to justify more cruelty than any other set of beliefs, except possibly Nazism. But their adherents continue to pay lip-service to the ideals of their founders. Thus comes about the paradox even today that the Catholic Church, which preaches justice and mercy, is the chief pillar of military dictatorship in Spain, Portugal and elsewhere. (Similarly Protestant bishops in England used to say the Absolution in their cathedrals on Sunday – 'Almighty God, the Father of our Lord Jesus Christ, who desireth not the death of a sinner, but rather that he may turn from his wickedness and live . . .' – and then go into the House of Lords on Monday and vote for the retention of the death penalty.) In the same way Communists still talk about freedom, and the state withering away, while remaining responsible for the most ruthless and monolithic tyrannies in the modern world. It is important to acknowledge this opposition between the founding inspiration, to which lip-service continues to be paid, and the reality. Just as Marx insisted in later life that he was not a Marxist, so it is worth pointing out that Jesus was not a Catholic. Jesus was one of the greatest of mankind, and so in a quite different way was Marx; but my hostility to contemporary Catholicism and Communism is extreme, for they are the chief authoritarianisms of the world I live in.

The authoritarian tradition flourished almost unopposed from the fall of Athens to the Italian Renaissance, disturbed only by unsuccessful revolutionary movements such as Early Christianity. The rebirth of the libertarian tradition, which began in Italy at the end of the fifteenth century, was based on a conscious reversion to the values of Ancient Greece – humanism, scientific enquiry and the rational investigation of experience, including social experience.[1] In one

1. As in Greece it was accompanied by a momentous flowering of artistic genius and creation. Many people suppose that the spirit of science and the spirit of art are mutually antagonistic, but this is not so at all. A mere consideration of Golden Age Greece and Renaissance Italy should convince them of this. The fact is that art and science have triumphed at the same times and places. The

way and another the two attitudes have been in open conflict ever since.[1]

I

Of these two attitudes it is only the libertarian one that I regard as intellectually defensible, let alone moral. The chief recommendation of this book is that it become the fundamental attitude, the defining characteristic, of the Left in politics. Some people may think it is already. I wish that were so. Unfortunately the Socialist tradition is eclectic in these matters, and contains strong elements of authoritarianism as well as libertarianism.

Everyone who has seen or read Bertolt Brecht's *Life of Galileo* will remember that what it treats as centrally important is not Galileo's scientific achievement but the conflict between two criteria of truth – authority on the one hand, observation and experiment on the other. The social implications of this are presented, quite rightly, as explosively revolutionary. Liberalism rose directly out of physics. After Galileo came Newton, who built on both Galileo's method and his work. Newton dominated the development of empirical philosophy: he was the strongest intellectual influence on Locke, and furthermore 'the victory of Locke's philosophy in England and France was largely due to the prestige of Newton'[2] Voltaire devoted a lifetime to propagating the ideas of Newton and Locke, and through him they achieved most of their vast influence. 'Voltaire was not an original philosopher, but he did more to increase the prestige and the understanding of the new empiricism than any other human being. Locke seemed to him, as to so many of his most enlightened contemporaries, the genius who, in his tentative and modest fashion, had done for the human mind what Newton had done for nature.'[3] At the heart of these

---

reason is that both are based on the freedom of the individual to innovate, to present wholly new ways of looking at things – originality in fundamentals, as I called it on page 39 – and this has existed in comparatively few societies. Where it has existed there has usually been a flowering of both art and science; and conversely those authoritarian cultures that have produced almost no fundamental innovation in intellectual matters have also produced little great art – at least, little great individually-created art. (They may produce good social art, such as architecture.)

1. See Chapter 3 *passim*, but particularly pp. 39–41.
2. Russell: *History of Western Philosophy*, p. 666.
3. Isaiah Berlin: *The Age of Enlightenment*, p. 113.

ideas was the Socratic attitude. As Voltaire said of Locke in his *Philosophical Letters*: 'Aided everywhere by the torch of physics, he dares at times to affirm, but he also dares to doubt.' Locke was the most influential philosopher between Aristotle and Marx. He built virtually the whole edifice of modern Liberalism. His ideas dominated British politics for two hundred years, played an important role in bringing about the French Revolution, and were embodied in the Constitution of the United States. One of his disciples was the most famous of all English Radicals, Thomas Paine. And in the course of time his ideas were developed through Radicalism to Socialism. The outstanding British philosopher of the nineteenth century, John Stuart Mill, was an empirical philosopher in the central Lockean tradition and also an advanced radical Member of Parliament whose influence on the development of Socialism in Britain was enormous.[1] And the outstanding British philosopher of the twentieth century, Bertrand Russell, continues both traditions – he has been influenced more by Locke than by any other philosopher, and is a lifelong member of the Labour Party and hence a Socialist parliamentarian (he accepts the Labour Whip in the House of Lords). He once included in a famous lecture on 'Philosophy and Politics' (published separately, and also available in the volume *Unpopular Essays*) a forceful summary of this tradition, and then finished with these words:

'I conclude that, in our day as in the time of Locke, empiricist Liberalism (which is not incompatible with *democratic* socialism) is the only philosophy that can be adopted by a man who, on the one hand, demands some scientific evidence for his beliefs, and, on the other hand, desires human happiness more than the prevalence of this or that party or creed. Our confused and difficult world needs various things if it is to escape disaster, and among these one of the most necessary is that, in the nations which still uphold Liberal beliefs, these beliefs should be whole-hearted and profound, not apologetic towards dogmatisms of the right and of the left, but deeply persuaded of the value of liberty, scientific freedom, and

1. Thus G. D. H. Cole, talking of the 1880s and 1890s, writes in *A Short History of the British Working Class Movement* 1789–1947 (page 287):
'The movement among the masses, in as far as it was Socialist at all, created a Socialism almost without doctrines; and the new Socialism of the intellectuals began far more as an ethical and Utilitarian than as a class-war movement. It owed more to Mill than to Marx, and though it sought a radical reconstruction of the social system, was strongly disinclined to accept the class-struggle as the instrument of change.'

mutual forbearance. For without these beliefs life on our politically divided but technically unified planet will hardly continue to be possible.'

The majority of the Labour Party's active supporters have almost always been this kind of Socialist: believers in liberty, equality and the brotherhood of man; in short, heirs to the greatest traditions of Liberalism – undogmatic, humanitarian, peace-loving. The present leader of the party, for all his faults, comes in this category, as do most of the Labour M.P.s, and also the party's two most distinguished recent thinkers, Tawney and Russell. As for the electorate: just as nearly all Socialists voted Liberal before the rise of the Labour Party, so, thereafter, most Liberals came to vote Labour. In short the Labour Party inherited not only the best political traditions of Liberalism but also its electoral support. To this day the great majority of Labour voters are more in sympathy with those liberal attitudes that are the central tradition of the Labour Party than they are with the authoritarian attitudes of certain sects within it.

Historically the main cause of the aggressive element in Socialism is the fact that Socialism came into existence before universal suffrage. The Industrial Revolution in its early years reduced masses of people to life in such bestial conditions as had been known before only in time of plague, famine or defeat in war. Industrial slumdom was created: whole populations were herded into dark, satanic mills[1] and the hovel-cities that festered round them. These human beings were illiterate and starving. They were excluded from participation in government, which in each of the newly industrial countries consisted of the tyranny of a rich oligarchy. Socialists wanted, quite rightly, to change this whole order of society, but the means of doing that without violence did not exist. A few Socialists, the most patient or the most optimistic, thought their first task was to create such means. For instance the Chartists: 'The Chartist Movement was embryonic Socialism, based on the class struggle,'[2] yet all six points of their Charter were aimed simply at instituting parliamentary democracy. They failed – and the plain fact was that, in the absence of democratic institutions, all ways of changing the social order *at that time* involved the use of force.

It was from this situation that the greatest of all revolutionary

1. The word 'Socialist' was first used in the year of Blake's death, 1827.
2. G. D. H. Cole: op. cit., p. 109.

thinkers emerged. Marx's masterpiece, *Das Kapital*, is a history of the Industrial Revolution in England – or rather, to take a phrase from its own subtitle, it is a 'critical analysis' of that history. How the notion got about that it is unreadable I cannot imagine: it is one of the most excitingly written and deeply moving books I know. Even now, almost every time I open it to look up a reference I find myself reading on, swept forward by the compassion and intelligence that burn on every page, infected by the unique sense of outrage that informs the whole book. With huge, articulate passion Marx describes the life of the industrial proletariat up to his own time, not in generalizations but in terms of actual people. For instance, 'Mary Anne Walkley had worked without intermission for $26\frac{1}{2}$ hours, with 60 other girls, 30 in one room, that only afforded $\frac{1}{3}$ of the cubic feet of air required for them. At night, they slept in pairs in one of the stifling holes into which the bedroom was divided by partitions of board. And this was one of the best millinery establishments in London. Mary Anne Walkley fell ill on the Friday, died on Sunday, without, to the astonishment of Madame Elise, having previously completed the work in hand. The doctor, Mr Keys, called too late to the death-bed, duly bore witness before the coroner's jury that "Mary Anne Walkley had died from long hours of work in an overcrowded workroom, and a too small and badly ventilated bedroom". In order to give the doctor a lesson in good manners the coroner's jury thereupon brought in a verdict that "the deceased had died of apoplexy, but there was reason to fear that her death had been accelerated by overwork in an overcrowded workroom, etc." ' (*Das Kapital*, Chapter X, Section 3). Or, earlier in the same section, a quotation from a Children's Employment Commission report: 'When he was 7 years old I used to carry him on my back to and fro through the snow, and he used to have 16 hours a day . . . I have often knelt down to feed him as he stood by the machine, for he could not leave it or stop.' The book contains hundreds of such individual case histories, most of them taken from Parliamentary Reports and other official documents. The picture Marx paints is appalling, but no one seriously disputes its truth. Any understanding of Marx – indeed of the authoritarian element in Socialism, and therefore of Socialism itself – must include a grasp of these elementary facts: that the condition of the British industrial workers less than a hundred years ago (and therefore – astounding thought! – within the lifetime of some people now living) was as Marx described it; and that democratic means of altering it did not exist. To this day

Marx's theories have forceful appeal wherever a population is subject both to want and to tyranny. (I take it no one would deny that his influence has spread wider in a shorter time than that of any other individual ever.)

If Marx's theories had given expression only to his deep humanity and his refusal to accept social evils as permanent his influence would have been wholly good. Unfortunately there is much more to them than that. Starting from a critique of Capitalist production he went on to develop a view of society that led to a theory of historical development, which in turn became a philosophy of all human experience.

The commonest misunderstanding of Marxism – widespread among people calling themselves Marxists as well as among others – is the belief that Marx asserted the paramount importance of economic motives. Even people who realize that what he was doing above all was offering a scientific theory of historical change are commonly under the illusion that he showed 'the economic motive' as the driving force of the historical process. In fact he did the opposite – he asserted that motives of whatever kind, economic or otherwise, were irrelevant. The determinants of historical change are economic in his view, but they are autonomous, and human motives, far from being among the causes, are among the results. The economic forces that shape history do not arise from anything to do with human thoughts or feelings at all; on the contrary, our thoughts and feelings arise from them. 'It is not the consciousness of men that determines their existence, but, on the contrary, their social existence determines their consciousness.'[1]

He himself foresaw the misunderstanding and tried to forestall it. 'To prevent possible misunderstanding, a word[2] . . . My standpoint, from which the evolution of the economic formation of society is viewed as a process of natural history, can less than any other make the individual responsible for relations whose creature he socially remains.' His warning was in vain. A whole literature has grown up on the basis of the misunderstanding.[3] And the error is total and

1. Preface to *A Contribution to the Critique of Political Economy.*
2. Preface to the first edition of *Das Kapital.*
3. Most of the 'Marxist' and most of the 'anti-Marxist' writers I have read share this error, which renders worthless everything they have to say on the subject. Even some otherwise good books are marred by it – for instance Evan Durbin's *The Politics of Democratic Socialism,* whose section on Communist theory is nullified by this misunderstanding. As Karl Popper once wryly re-

devastating, for it concerns the very nature of the theory. *The whole point of Marxism, laboured by Marx throughout his life, is that it purports to be science.* Unfortunately Marx was an armchair scientist, and made the mistake, common to all armchair scientists between Newton and Einstein, of equating scientific method with determinism. He supposed that a subject became a science when its 'Natural Laws' were discovered, thereby making infallible predictions possible with respect to it.

The heart of Marxism is this: Marx believed that he had discovered the Natural Laws of historical change, and that these were scientific laws in precisely the same sense as that in which Newton's laws of motion were scientific laws. Their operation, like that of all other Natural Laws, was entirely independent of human wishes or motivations. The chain of reasoning goes something like this. 'The economic structure of society [is] the real foundation, on which rise legal and political superstructures and to which correspond definite forms of social consciousness. The mode of production in material life determines the general character of the social, political, and spiritual processes of life.'[1] From this it follows that all historical change is ultimately dependent on and caused by changes in the economic structure of society. 'With the change of the economic foundation the entire immense superstructure is more or less rapidly transformed.' But – and this is the point – 'the material transformation of the economic conditions of production . . . *can be determined with the precision of natural science*'. (My italics.) Marx, believing he had made a discovery analogous to Newton's (though of course many times more important, and far transcending it in implication – in fact the discovery of all discoveries) used Newton's terminology to describe his own work. In the Preface to the first edition of *Das Kapital* he says 'it is the ultimate aim of this work to lay bare the economic law of motion of modern society'. Just as, given any physical system at time *t*, with Newton's laws of motion we can accurately predict what the state of this system will be at any future time *t′*, so it is, says Marx, with 'the natural laws of Capitalist pro-

marked to me: 'Two things you discover when you read Marx – first, he has nothing to say about Communism or Socialism, and second, no one seems to have read Marx.'

1. This and the following two quotations are from the preface to Marx's *A Contribution to the Critique of Political Economy*. This preface is one of the key documents of Marxist literature, because in it Marx describes how he arrived at the theory of historical materialism.

duction. It is a question of these laws themselves, of these tendencies working with iron necessity towards inevitable results. The country that is more developed industrially only shows to the less developed the image of its own future'.[1] Having discovered the scientific laws of historical change he was able to predict all future states of the social system, up to and including Communism, as infallibly as we can predict all future states of the solar system. This is what he meant by saying he had put Socialism on a scientific basis. In a crucial sense he was no more 'advocating' Socialism or Communism than Newton was advocating the next eclipse of the sun. He had discovered the causal laws which would inevitably bring it about.

Khrushchev, I may say, understands this perfectly, and believes it. 'On the subject of revolutionary movements among small nations, Mr Khrushchev spoke specifically of three – Laos, Cuba and Iran. But for him these three are merely examples of what he regards as a world-wide and historic revolutionary movement – akin to the change from feudalism to capitalism – which is surely destined to bring the old colonial countries into the Communist orbit. I could detect no doubt or reservation in his mind that this will surely happen, that there is no alternative, that while he will help this manifest destiny and while we will oppose it, the destiny would be realized no matter what either of us did.... In his mind, Iran is the most immediate example of the inevitable movement of history in which he believes so completely. He would not admit that we can divert this historic movement by championing liberal democratic reforms. . . . His attitude to Cuba is based on this same dogma. Castro's revolution is inevitable and predetermined.'[2]

And of course not only Khrushchev but really intelligent Communists all over the world are quite clear about this. John Hendy, a member of the Communist Party of Great Britain who was described by Mr Justice Winn in the E.T.U. case as '. . . a man inspired, if not possessed, by the Communist creed, a man of intellectual honesty and power . . .' wrote to the *New Statesman* on 22 December 1961: 'Please don't go on repeating that Communists cheat because they

1. Preface to the first edition of *Das Kapital*.
2. From Walter Lippman's account of a whole day's conversation with Khrushchev on Monday, 10 April 1961 at Sochi, on the Black Sea. The account appeared in *The Observer* on 23 April 1961. Lippman's repeated use of the word 'destiny' shows the usual failure to understand that it is a *scientific* theory that is in question. (There is going to be an eclipse of the sun on 17 November 2161, but this is not because of destiny.)

are Communists. They have no need to, anyway, for their ultimate victory is inevitable, and there is now no power on earth that can long delay it.'

II

So Socialism is a hybrid, combining the best traditions of liberal science with some of the worst traditions of oracular pre-science; combining hostility to authority with elements of authoritarianism – crossing humanitarianism with collectivism, idealism with materialism, the belief in moral responsibility with a belief in determinism. The reasons for this are many. I have given two of them already – the fact that Socialism was born in an age when most people were poor and exploited past our imagining, yet had no means of improving their lot without violence;[1] and the fact that Socialist theory came into being before the rise of modern logic, philosophy and science. There are others – for example the accident that there has been no great Socialist political philosopher, so that the influence of the only great political philosopher there has been since the Industrial Revolution, Karl Marx, has seeped into Socialists and their organizations as into a vacuum. And the appeal of determinism to our sense of insecurity – and of authoritarianism to our aggressive instincts. And the sheer ignorance of most people about where the front line of intellectual advance has got to since the nineteenth century.

I am not going to launch into a full-scale critique of Marxism. For one thing, this has already been done by Karl Popper in the second volume of *The Open Society and its Enemies*.[2] I will content myself with one simple, devastating point that Popper does not make, and it is this. Because Marxism is a philosophy that claims to be both materialist and scientific, Marxists have no appeal from scientific arguments to other sorts of argument. I have compared Communists

1. In Europe, that is. In the oldest democracy, the United States, where free institutions preceded industrialization, philosophies of violent revolution have never had much appeal – except, significantly, among immigrant workers who were disfranchised because they were not American citizens. To this day the overriding aim of oppressed American minorities, e.g. the Negroes in the South, is not to destroy or even change the Constitution but, on the contrary, to secure its full operation.

2. '. . . the most scrupulous and formidable criticism of the philosophical and historical doctrines of Marxism by any living writer.' Isaiah Berlin, in the bibliography to the second edition of his biography of Karl Marx.

with Catholics in important respects, but there are also important difference, and this is one. Christians, possessing a theology which explains the whole of human experience, fiercely resisted the birth of science and its subsequent growth, but were driven out of position after position as science advanced. Eventually the cleverer theologians realized that if they were condemned to an endless succession of defeats in rational argument one possible solution was to repudiate rational argument. This position has in fact been put at its most powerful by non-Catholic theologians, such as Reinhold Niebuhr and Paul Tillich. The assertion is that it was always a mistake to try, as theology has tried for two thousand years, to establish the rationality of religion: religion is fundamentally irrational, as we now know man to be, and rational procedures, methods, arguments, criteria, have little relevance to religious experience. Religious theories are different *in kind* from scientific theories. Religious explanations are different *in kind* from other sorts of explanation. There is therefore no conflict between scientific procedures and religion, and religious assertions cannot be confuted by rational argument.

Christian theologians are not alone in having first claimed knowledge which was just like scientific knowledge – better, if anything – and then abandoned this for a position which they assert is immune from rational consideration. Psychoanalysts have done the same. But Marxists cannot do it. For the very heart of the Marxist claim, as I have pointed out, is that Marxism is science. If this claim is abandoned the whole edifice collapses. If Marxists are defeated in rational argument they have nothing else to turn to.

I am aware that in fact almost no Marxists hold their beliefs rationally: they hold them as a system of revealed truth, a religion fitted out complete with sacred books and prophets. My point is that this can be shown. The claims of Marxism to be science are *demonstrably* false, and the illusions can be and have been stripped away. In consequence a Communist is either a flat-earther who simply does not know that his primitive beliefs have been thrown on the scrap heap by intellectual developments, or else a mystic who holds them in a way which is incompatible with their own claim to be science.

Although one of my secondary purposes in this book is to combat the influence of Marxism on left-wing thinking today this does not require a detailed analysis of Marx's own writings but rather a consideration of the respects in which these have influenced left-wing thinking. And the first thing that needs emphasizing is that this influence has been transitory. The only generation to be dominated by it was that which came to political maturity between the two world wars. Previous and subsequent generations have not been Marxist. Of the foundation of the Labour Party G. D. H. Cole wrote:[1] 'In the successful formation of the Labour Representation Committee[2] Keir Hardie and his colleagues felt a not unnatural elation. What had they done? They had made a new Socialism, violent sometimes in its expression, because there were strong ethical impulses behind it, but essentially moderate and evolutionary in its conception of social change; British to the backbone in its policy and methods of expression, however internationalist and pacifist in its outlook; simple enough to be easily and widely understood, and so undefined in its doctrinal basis as to make recruits readily among persons of quite different types. There were weaknesses in these very sources of immediate strength. But it is certain that on no other basis could British Socialism have grown so rapidly or won so soon the alliance of the Trade Unions.'

In short, the Labour Party was the only Socialist Party of any consequence to come into existence outside the Marxist tradition. It remained non-Marxist in every important respect until the Russian Revolution. Then a profound change took place. 'Although[3] the Communist Party failed to attract more than a small following, the influence of the Russian Revolution was deep and widespread. . . . Indeed, it was scarcely possible, whatever view men might take of Communist doctrines and policy, for them not to feel differently about Socialism with a vast Socialist Republic actually in existence. In 1914, Socialism still seemed a distant ideal; after 1917, it presented itself to men's minds as a real and immediate possibility. The capitalist system had lost its inevitability; the sense of a possible alternative sank deeply into the minds of the active workers in the Labour Movement.'

Most of the people who occupied positions of power and influence in the Labour Movement between the wars were by that time, of course, in middle or late life and had formed their basic political outlook before the Russian Revolution. They remained, most of them, sternly anti-Communist. In fact in many cases their anti-Communism increased. The Communist Party of Great Britain, formed in 1920,

---

1. Op. cit., p. 290.
2. This name was changed to The Labour Party in 1906.
3. Op. cit., p. 383.

tried to affiliate to the Labour Movement, but was beaten at every attempt. Its members then tried to infiltrate local Labour Parties, and a highly organized underground movement went on throughout the early twenties with this object. The National Executive of the Labour Party countered by disaffiliating those local parties that were captured by Communists – by 1927 twenty-three of them had been thrown out. The struggle was bitter and dirty, for since Communists were ineligible for membership of the Labour Party their whole position was based on secretly-planned mass-lying, and they pursued their ends by their customary methods of ballot-rigging and character-assassination. (The unforgiving anti-Communism of many lifelong Labour activists dates from those battles.) So most of Labour's leaders at that time were not merely anti-Communist but militantly so – despite the fact that many of them had themselves been deeply influenced by Marxist ideas and nearly all of them were enthusiastic supporters of the Soviet Union. To understand the inter-war Labour Party it is essential to grasp this threefold distinction: being Marxist, being pro-Communist and being pro-Russian were three different things. They were not found together in any large number of Labour activists until the generation that grew up and formed its political outlook *after* the Russian Revolution. That generation, to which I now turn, was the only one in the history of the Labour Movement to be dominated by Marxism.

III

People who came to political maturity between the two world wars did so at a time when the economic system was visibly breaking down. The unemployment figure in England was never as low as a million; often it was over two million, and in 1932 it was nearly three million. 'Poverty in the midst of plenty' was a fact. The major attempts to alleviate the lot of large numbers of workers by direct industrial action were failures – for example the strike-threat in 1919 by the Triple Alliance of coalminers, railwaymen and transport workers; and above all the General Strike of 1926. Equally miserable were the failures of the Labour Movement's incursions into government: the first Labour Government of 1924 lasted less than a year, the second Labour Government of 1929–31 lasted two years and three months and ended in the expulsion of some of its leaders, including the Prime

Minister, from the Labour Party, and the reduction of Labour's 287 seats in the House of Commons to 52.

The economic break-down was world-wide, and in many countries free institutions were swept away. Fascism rose on the ruins. Most of the governments of Eastern Europe went Fascist in fact if not in name, the Japanese invaded Manchuria, Hitler took over Germany, Mussolini invaded Africa, a civil war broke out in Spain which the Fascists won, Hitler annexed Austria and invaded Czechoslovakia. In France democracy was seriously threatened, and even Britain saw Oswald Mosley and his Blackshirts marching through the East End of London beating up Jews and wrecking their shops. The only well-known social theory that seemed to offer a plausible explanation for all this otherwise-bewildering catastrophe was Marxism. The Russian Revolution had already opened the minds of British Socialists to Marxist influence, and most major political events from then on served to strengthen this influence. Marx's prophecies seemed to be coming true in front of people's very eyes, and the international Capitalist system was cracking up. It is in one way easy to see why young Socialists grew up to embrace Marxist political attitudes and why so many older Socialists, like Cole and the Webbs, shifted ground and inclined towards them. Socialists came to agree with Communists in their diagnosis of the sickness of the age. They agreed that the deadliest threat to world peace was Fascism. They agreed in their analysis of Capitalist society. They agreed in giving the name 'Socialism' to what each believed to be the only cure for the body politic, and they agreed in looking on the coming of Socialism as inevitable. If you scratched a Socialist in those days you were likely to find a Marxist.

Already by the thirties some of the most prominent figures in the Labour Party were Marxist in outlook. Even Attlee, whatever he may say now, was strongly influenced, as anyone can confirm by looking at his book *The Labour Party in Perspective*, published by The Left Book Club in 1937. I have heard Aneurin Bevan say, and say proudly: 'I grew up a Marxist.' John Strachey wrote what some still consider the best Marxist book in English, *The Coming Struggle for Power*. Laski at the London School of Economics was a thorough-going Marxist, Cole at Oxford was a reconstructed Marxist, and both were having an almost sensational impact on their pupils as well as writing many books – in fact both were world-famous. The Left Book Club, run by Laski, Strachey and Gollancz, was publishing mostly

Marxist literature, and this again was having great influence among left-wing intellectuals. So was the *New Statesman* under the editorship of Kingsley Martin. Meanwhile, the literature of the anti-Marxist Left included better work by better writers, but was without influence. Sometimes it was suppressed, as when Kingsley Martin refused to publish George Orwell's reports of what the Communists were doing in Spain.[1] But suppression was not necessary, since when Orwell's best book, *Homage to Catalonia*, appeared it was ignored. As the publishers say on the blurb of the Collected Edition, 1951: 'Originally published at the time of the Popular Front, *Homage to Catalonia* was deeply resented by the Left and long remained the least known of Orwell's books.' The book he wrote immediately before it was *The Road to Wigan Pier*, and when in 1937 this was published by the Left Book Club as one of its few non-Marxist books, Victor Gollancz thought it necessary to write a foreword consisting of a long apologia for publishing it at all. This foreword contains a good deal of detailed deprecation of the book: e.g. 'He even commits the curious indiscretion of referring to Russian commissars as "half-gramophones, half-gangsters".'

Nearly all intelligent Socialists who formed their ideas in this period took over the Marxist critique of capitalist production – in fact the whole Marxist analysis of social development in terms of economic class-conflict – and hence the Marxist philosophy of history and the Marxist prophecy. Many, for instance Sir Stafford Cripps and John Strachey, believed that even if the Labour Party were constitutionally elected to power it would have to establish a dictatorship of the proletariat in order to overcome first a Fascist counter-revolution and then a refusal of the Civil Service to serve the new government. And even this was a Marxist belief. Marx himself had constantly expressed it. For Engels writes, in his preface to the first English translation of *Das Kapital* (1887), of Marx as 'a man whose whole theory is the result of a life-long study of the economic history and condition of England, and whom that study led to the conclusion that, at least in Europe, England is the only country where the inevitable social revolution might be effected entirely by peaceful and legal means.

1. The *New Statesman* bears a heavy share of responsibility for the distortion recently acknowledged in its columns by R. H. S. Crossman (24 April 1961): 'In the 1930s the Spanish Civil War – not the war actually being fought in Spain, but the image of it projected into our minds – pervaded left-wing politics and conditioned the mental attitudes of many of those who lead the Labour Movement today.'

He certainly never forgot to add that he hardly expected the English ruling classes to submit without a "pro-slavery rebellion" to this peaceful and legal revolution.' (My italics.)

Socialists and Communists, then, seemed to have almost everything in common in the nineteen-thirties. Even their practical situation was the same – both were excluded even from political influence, let alone power. It seemed natural that they should become comrades-in-arms (a metaphor that took on literal truth in Spain). On the initiative of the Communist International of 1935 a United Front was formed, with the slogan *'No Enemies on the Left!'* The National Executive of the Labour Party regarded this as simply another Communist attempt to subvert the Labour Movement, and opposed it to the point of expelling Sir Stafford Cripps and Aneurin Bevan for supporting it. These expulsions themselves illustrate the strength of the United Front's appeal – an appeal that was strong to almost all Socialists who appreciated the threat of Nazism.

CHAPTER SIX

The Marxist Legacy

So almost everyone in the generation of Socialists that grew up in the 1930s was Marxist in outlook. The extent to which this is true can be illustrated by the fact that Anthony Crosland and Philip Williams were thoroughgoing Marxists, Roy Jenkins only somewhat less so, and Denis Healey a member of the Communist Party. It is that generation which is now stepping into most of the positions of power and influence in the Labour Movement, from constituency and shop-floor level upwards. Experience has shifted the opinions of nearly all of them, and some (including the four individuals named above) have long since adopted a rational approach to politics. But in many others the effects of their formative years remain powerful – not surprising, in one way, yet still surprising in another since almost all their main beliefs and expectations have been contradicted by experience.

Before 1945 most Socialists were in the habit of blaming social evils of whatever kind on 'the Capitalist system' – not only war and unemployment but also crime, prostitution, rubbishy popular entertainment, biased newspapers, every social phenomenon that merited criticism. Every one of these beliefs has been proved false. No one could say that the Korean war was due to Capitalism, nor the annexation of Tibet by the Chinese, nor the Russian invasion of Hungary. Different wars have different causes. By the use of Keynesian techniques Capitalist economies seem able to maintain full employment indefinitely. And in a full-employment economy neither crime nor prostitution can be said to be caused by poverty.[1] Popular entertainment is better in the Capitalist countries than in the non-Capitalist

1. In fact it is now being seriously suggested that a major cause of crime is prosperity. E.g. 'As more goods are produced and owned, the greater are the opportunities for fraud and the more property that must be protected. If the provision of public law enforcement services do not keep pace, the counterpart of increased well-being will, we may be certain, be increased crime.' J. K. Galbraith: *The Affluent Society*, p. 199. See also *The Causes of Crime* by Christopher Mayhew in *The Observer*, 18 June 1961.

countries. The only countries in the world where newspapers are free to print the truth are Capitalist countries.

So how wrong can you be? The pre-war Socialist analysis of society was utterly, totally, disastrously wrong. Socialists were even wrong about their own coming to power: the whole notion of armed resistance to their election was shown to be silly, as was the idea that the Civil Service would refuse to serve them. And since their diagnoses were so mistaken their cures, not surprisingly, have not cured. Pre-war Socialists, believing that all social problems were 'faults of the system' of private ownership of the means of production, asserted that all these problems would be solved by public ownership. Well, we brought into public ownership all but one or two of our basic industries, and over half the total investment of our economy goes into the public sector; yet crimes of violence have gone on increasing, and after the war prostitutes multiplied so rapidly on the pavements of London that they became an international scandal and were eventually 'cleared off the streets' by an act of Conservative legislation. Newspapers decrease in number without increasing in quality, and popular entertainment is, if anything, getting worse. We have had a dozen years of Conservative Government, and not only has there been no serious unemployment but the British working class is more prosperous than it has been at any time in its history.

You would expect people who have been so wrong about so much to re-examine their assumptions. And of course many have. But many have not. And I want now to list quite baldly some of the specifically Marxist theoretical assumptions which many active members of the Labour Movement, not themselves Communists, still incorporate in their thinking.

1. The belief that everything about a society is ultimately determined by the ownership of the means of production and distribution. Typical of hundreds of examples I could give are Barbara Castle's words in the *New Statesman*, 25 September 1960: 'We can't be a radical party unless we realize that the whole nature of a society is dictated by the methods by which it earns – and shares – its bread.'

2. From this it follows that the essence of any political theory is contained in what it has to say about ownership and distribution. So the essence of Socialism is public ownership and distribution.

3. It also follows that social life is co-extensive with political-economy, for all social phenomena, from philosophy to crime, are 'dictated by the methods by which society earns – and shares – its

bread'. Therefore religion, art, education, culture, entertainment and so on are all only seen in their proper light when regarded as politico-economic phenomena.

4. Again it follows – and this assumption has been of enormous importance and immeasurable harm to the Labour Movement throughout its history – that the only problems you have to concern yourself with are the economic problems. If you solve them the others will automatically come right.

5. Capitalism inevitably breeds war.

6. Capitalism inevitably breeds mass-unemployment.

In addition to these there is a deep reluctance to regard Communists as adversaries or to accept criticisms of Russia. There is a clinging to such customs as addressing people as 'Comrade'[1] and singing 'The Red Flag'; also a clinging to the Marxist use of such terms as 'contradiction', 'inevitable', 'Capitalist' and 'Socialist'.

The importance of the Marxist legacy is illustrated by the two main issues over which the Labour Party has recently been tearing itself to pieces – public ownership and defence. The first is a straightforward battle about Marxist assumptions. Underlying the second are two fundamentally different attitudes towards Communist societies – one sympathetic and trusting, the other hostile and suspicious. However, it is not only in crisis that the Marxist legacy makes itself felt. It permeates Socialist thinking all the time. Most of the trade union leaders are anti-Communist, many of them bitterly so, but that does not stop them accepting the Marxist thesis that economic questions are the only important questions. Some may plead that they are bound to give this impression because it is their job to concern themselves with industry and working conditions and rates of pay and the rest. My answer to this is threefold. First, their utterances commonly show that many of their *concepts* are Marxist. Second, they do not in fact need to confine their activities to the industrial field, and one of my criticisms of British trade unions is that they have much too narrow a view of their opportunities: they ought to be playing a leading role in

---

1. 'Even the single word "Comrade" has done its dirty little bit towards discrediting the Socialist movement. How many a waverer has halted on the brink, gone perhaps to some public meeting and watched self-conscious Socialists dutifully addressing one another as "Comrade", and then slid away, disillusioned, into the nearest four-ale bar! And his instinct is sound; for where is the sense of sticking on to yourself a ridiculous label which even after long practice can hardly be mentioned without a gulp of shame?' George Orwell in 1937, in *The Road to Wigan Pier* (Chapter 13).

housing, adult education, insurance, newspapers, television, the arts –
all aspects of our social life. And third, anti-Communist Labour
politicians commonly exhibit the same characteristics.

Aneurin Bevan, though anti-Communist to the end of his life
('Communism is the death-watch-beetle of democracy'. . . . 'The
Communist Party isn't a party, it's a conspiracy') was also a garbled
Marxist to the end of his life, and even after the 1959 General Election
was repeating the old, old mistakes. On 11 October 1959 he wrote
in his column on the front page of *The News of the World*: 'It is suggested, for example, that the defeat of the Labour Party implies a
decisive rejection of Socialism. This certainly would have been the
case if the Labour Party had held aloft the banner of Socialism in the
course of the Election and before it. But it did no such thing. On the
contrary, with the exception of steel and road haulage, Socialism had
been put firmly to one side. . . .' Socialism, in short, was public ownership, and public ownership was Socialism, and everything else was
not Socialism.

Or take a different example. Few Socialists are more anti-Communist than Herbert Morrison. Before the 1950 General Election
when the Labour Party, having exhausted its great 1945 programme
Let Us Face the Future, was looking round with some desperation for
a new election programme, a distinguished group of lawyers visited
him (he was Home Secretary at the time) to try to persuade him that
reform of the law on divorce, abortion, the penal system, etc., should
be put into Labour's manifesto. He listened to them and then, at the
end, told them that in his opinion the only important problems were
economic problems and he was not interested in law reform. This
assumption is still common – the assumption that if you deal with
economic problems you are tackling the very basis of society, whereas
if you deal with other problems you are wasting your time. (People
who accept it might ask themselves why a change in the ownership
of an industry is central to our social life while a change in family
relationships is not.) It is an entirely Marxist assumption: to be
specific it is the Marxist theory of the 'economic foundation' and the
'superstructure' (see page 82).

It is organically linked with the view that politics is co-extensive
with life – that all phenomena are ultimately reducible to politico-
economic phenomena. This is another Marxist dogma that is accepted
as true by a lot of non-Communists. It is the basis, for example, of
Raymond Williams's work (*Culture and Society*, *The Long Revolution*)

and of most of the articles in *New Left Review*; also of the work of a lot of writers outside politics who are sympathetic towards the New Left – e.g. both the Film Critic and the Theatre Critic of *The Observer*.[1] It entails, and is entailed by, the demand that art should be 'committed'. It is a wholly pre-scientific theory, at best mystical, at worst silly. It is also monistic, and can be given practical application only by a denial of personal freedom. Williams is open about this: he is strongly collectivist and anti-individualistic in his views. '"Totalitarian" describes a certain kind of repressive social control, but, also, any real society, any adequate community, is necessarily a totality. To belong to a community is to be a part of a whole, and, necessarily, to accept, while helping to define, its disciplines.' (*Culture and Society*, p. 291.)

I do not want to waste time here on the New Left, but they are interesting in that they exemplify a confusion – based in their case firmly on Marxist theory – that has bedevilled many Socialists. What do you do if the life you envisage for people is better[2] than what they want? To take a trivial example, what do you do if most people prefer trash on television to better programmes? Do you promote what you know to be inferior at the expense of the better things you care passionately about? Or do you impose those better things on people against their will on the ground that it is good for them even if they don't realize the fact? This apparent dilemma springs from a pre-scientific approach to politics. It springs from the failure to realize what I tried to establish in Chapters Three and Four, that the way things are done in a society matters more than what is done – e.g. the freedom of people to choose for themselves what television programmes they watch is of greater importance than what television programmes they watch. As I said in Chapter Four, if I insist on the right of individuals to shape their own lives it follows that I claim no right to shape them myself. I cannot both want others to do as they like and at the same time want them to do as *I* like. If you are a libertarian you regard the purpose of political action as the extension, not the making, of choice for individuals. I do not have opinions about

1. 'I became aware that art, ethics, politics, and economics were inseparable from each other; I realized that theatre was a branch of sociology as well as a means of self-expression. From men like Bertolt Brecht and Arthur Miller I learned that all drama was, in the widest sense of a wide word, political.' Kenneth Tynan: *Curtains*, p. 10.

2. There are no people who know what is 'better' for others, but I use the word here because even if there were I should deny their right to give effect to their judgements.

what television programmes other people 'ought to' watch – the very concept is silly, and its effects pernicious. I want the widest range of programmes available so that people can choose for themselves. Television in Britain is so bad at the moment because it abysmally fails – it does not even try, in fact – to provide this choice.

Many Socialists have benevolent impulses but mistake these for libertarian impulses. They do not realize that wanting other people to live as one thinks best is incompatible with wanting them to live as *they* think best, and can be given effect only by subjecting them to authority. Thus many Socialists, and in particular the New Left, do not want people to be free. The kind of society they want would be at best paternalistic: its members would be compelled to do what its legislators believed to be in their best interests. But paternalism and freedom are mutually exclusive, as any African will tell you. This kind of unconscious hostility to freedom is unfortunately shared by many non-Marxist Socialists. I have heard Dr Donald Soper, a Methodist minister, advocate the conscription of all young people into labour camps. And alas, these attitudes are not confined to advocacy. In 1947 the Labour Government passed the 'Control of Engagement' Order giving itself the power to direct labour – and was bewildered at the public outcry evoked. I later heard the man chiefly responsible, Herbert Morrison, defend this law on the ground that it had been used against only a dozen or so citizens. He did not understand that this made it worse, since it proved that this appalling legislation had been passed without the faintest shadow of need. Anti-libertarian Socialists do enormous harm to the Labour Party, for they give substance to the already common view that it is destructive of personal freedom.

I

One of Marxism's legacies to the whole Labour Movement is the accepted use of the terms 'Left' and 'Right'. First, they relate to public ownership of the means of production and distribution: the more public ownership a person or party wants, the more Left he or it is. In fact the definition is even narrower: the more *state*-ownership a person or party wants, the more Left he or it is. Other forms of public ownership, like municipalization or co-operatives, are less Left. Second, 'Left' is equated with 'progressive': the more state-ownership you want, the more progressive you are; the less you want, the more conservative you are. Third, 'Left' is a hooray-word, 'Right' a boo-word: it is good to be Left.

All this would make sense only if the first two of the assumptions listed in the previous section were true: that everything about a society was ultimately determined by the form of ownership of the means of production and distribution, and therefore that the essence of a political attitude was what it had to say about ownership. If these assumptions are not true then it is not of the first importance whether people are 'Left' or 'Right' in the accepted sense. And of course they are not true.

In Chapter Three I have given, at length, my reasons for believing that the most important thing about a political attitude is what it has to say about freedom. I can contrast the importance of freedom with the unimportance of ownership by drawing up a list of contrasts between Britain and Russia. For in Britain most of the means of production, distribution and exchange are still privately owned, whereas in Russia they are almost entirely state-owned. Yet Britain has free institutions and Russia does not.

1. In Russia political and economic power is more narrowly concentrated in the hands of a definable ruling class than it is in Britain. This is what Djilas, Tito's former right-hand man, has called 'The New Class'. Because of the absence of free institutions this class is not accountable to the people for the way it exercises power.

2. Personal incomes are more unequally distributed in Russia than in Britain – in plain language there is a bigger gulf between rich and poor. The social set-up in Russia is even more of a racket than in Britain, for not unexpectedly it is to itself that the ruling class directs the higher incomes.

3. The 'degree of exploitation' – in the strict Marxist sense of that phrase, namely the amount of 'surplus value' extracted from the workers – is higher in Russia than in Britain. Communists boast of this every time they point to the higher rate of capital accumulation in Russia.

4. The workers in Russia – in addition to being thus tyrannized over, underpaid even relatively, and over-exploited – cannot change jobs at will or even travel freely inside their own country. They are not allowed independent representation by Trade Unions or any other bodies, and do not have the right to strike.

5. There is rigid censorship, not only of news but of all the arts.

D

Foreign broadcasts are jammed. Newspapers are ordered by the government to lie, and are told what lies to tell.

To extend the list no further, it is clear that public ownership does not necessarily entail any political good. It does not necessarily entail any political evil either, but that is precisely the point: it is not a moral phenomenon at all. And it is certainly not the determining factor about a society. It is a way, morally neutral in itself, of running an economy, and whether the results are good or bad depends on a whole lot of other circumstances. 'Either collectivism or private ownership is consistent with widely varying degrees of liberty, democracy, equality, exploitation, class-feeling, planning, workers' control, and economic prosperity. And it is surely the degree to which these attributes are present or absent which makes people differentiate between societies.'[1] There are still a number of Socialists who regard public ownership as *morally good in itself*. Quite what this means I have no idea – considered as a theory it is a piece of muddled metaphysics, and as a statement about reality it is contradicted by the facts. But many Socialists still repudiate any attempt to designate public ownership as a means to other ends. 'What is this philosophical argument Hugh Gaitskell makes about ends and means? Many of the ends Hugh Gaitskell described at the end of his speech are in such general terms that the Tories could agree with them too. They do not carry them out, that is the difference. But so far as the words are concerned they say they believe in "social justice". They believe in "freedom". They use the same kind of words. And therefore it is a fallacy to try to separate the ends and the means – because Socialism, in my view, is a doctrine which reveals how only by mobilizing the resources of the community can you achieve the ends. That is what Socialism is.'[2]

1. C. A. R. Crosland: *The Future of Socialism*, pp. 74–5. In my own list I have not mentioned planning. The examples about planning given by Crosland earlier in his argument are (op. cit., p. 73): 'Post-war experience has shown that private industry can be subjected to a close degree of government control, while nationalized industries may behave in a rather independent fashion, and prove not altogether easy to plan. Generally, there is no practical or theoretical reason why a collectivist economy should not operate solely under the influence of the price mechanism, without interference by the government, nor why a privately-owned economy should not be subject, as the Nazi economy was, to state control of all major economic decisions.'

2. Michael Foot at the Labour Party Conference at Blackpool, 1959. It is characteristic of Foot and almost everyone who thinks like him that differences in the use of words are held to be of primary importance while differences of fact are considered merely incidental.

Not only is this Marxist analysis logically indefensible, as shown in Chapter Three: it is also totally at variance with the facts. It takes no account of political democracy and the power this confers on an elected government (e.g. the Labour Government of 1945) to dictate to the owners of the means of production. According to Marxist theory whatever the political set-up may be, ultimate power lies with the owners of the economy. The truth is the exact opposite: whatever the economic set-up may be, ultimate power lies with whoever has political power. A second and quite different objection to the Marxist analysis is that even the private economy itself is not controlled by its owners. The development of the joint-stock company and limited liability has led to a decisive divorce between the ownership of large-scale private industry and its control – a divorce which was already being emphasized by non-Marxist Socialists before the Second World War, for example by Evan Durbin.[1] Durbin's language and arguments were used nearly twenty years later by Harold Wilson, who proposed the policy document *Industry and Society* to the Labour Party Conference of 1957: 'It shows, in the modern world, the complete divorce of ownership through shareholding from control and management in these large firms: you have the largely functionless shareholders on the one hand sitting back raking in their profits, and above all, their tax-free capital gains, and you have on the other hand the management, an oligarchy responsible in effect to no one but themselves, appointing themselves and filling by co-option any vacancies which occur from time to time in the oligarchy. So there you have the divorce between ownership and control.'

Given the fact that our economy ceased decades ago to be controlled by its owners, and the more important fact that what is most valuable about a society is determined not by the form of ownership but by its political system, it is both an anachronism and a fallacy to characterize people or parties as 'Left' and 'Right' as if the most important thing about their political position were their attitude to ownership. Yet this view is still commonly held. For instance in a front page leader on 13 January 1961 the *New Statesman* wrote: 'The vital dividing line in British politics still lies between those who believe in a Socialist policy built around public ownership, and those who do not.'

1. See *The Politics of Democratic Socialism*. Part II, S.4, 'The Recent Institutional Changes in Capitalism'. See especially Part II, S.4 D., 'The Institutional Consequences of Limited Liability'; and Part II, S.4 D. (a) 'The Dispersion of Ownership and the Divorce of Ownership and Control'.

One of the side-effects of this view is to distort the relationship between parties. For instance anyone who plots political positions on the Left-Right axis sees Socialists as being next door to Communists, who are at the opposite end of the axis from Fascists and Liberals. I, on the other hand, who am inclined to plot political positions on the freedom-tyranny axis, see Socialists as next door to Liberals and at the opposite end of the axis from Communists, who are next door to Fascists. Or put it this way. Those Socialists who are to any serious degree Marxist in their thinking regard Conservatives as greater enemies than Communists. Yet this is fantastic. If we had had a Communist Government in power for a dozen years, as we have had a Conservative Government, we should by now be living in a fully-fledged police-state like Czechoslovakia.

In view of all this it only compounds the confusion to use the term 'Left' as if it also meant 'progressive'. This has the weird result of characterizing the victims of pre-scientific nineteenth-century dogmas as forward-looking, and people who revise their assumptions in the light of experience and renew their assessments of current and future problems as backward-looking. It leads to regarding say, Michael Foot, whose spiritual home is in not even the nineteenth but rather the eighteenth century, as more go-ahead than, say, Anthony Crosland, who is continuously making original proposals for dealing with problems that actually confront us.

If we continue to use the terms 'Left' and 'Right' we should purge them of their self-contradictions. That is to say if we use them to refer chiefly to people's attitudes to ownership we must recognize not only that they have a minor part to play in describing political attitudes but also that 'Left' has no laudatory connotations and no necessary connection with progress. Alternatively, if 'Left' is to have importance as a descriptive word and also laudatory connotations then it should refer to freedom, in which case, Communists are so far to the Right as to be outflanked only by Fascists. My own view is that the terms embody such long-standing confusions that it is better to dispense with them altogether. In this book I use the term 'Left' to distinguish Socialists and radicals *as a whole* from Conservatives, but not to distinguish *among* Socialists or radicals – except in one or two cases where this use is quite unambiguous.

II

It is not only the sharing of Marxist assumptions that makes so many Socialists reluctant to regard Communists as adversaries: it is also a matter of personal history and personal loyalties. The older ones went through the thirties shoulder to shoulder with Communists – the Spanish Civil War, the Left Book Club, the United Front and so on. All their lives they have had Communist friends and allies. They know them to be well-intentioned and cannot regard them as even malevolent, let alone dangerous. Many of the younger ones on the other hand, if not actually second-generation United Front Socialists (of whom there are a good number) were members of the Communist Party until Hungary.[1] These too have Communist friends or families, and may even have lived for years in more or less closed Communist circles, so that their attitude to Communists is based not on practical politics or theory or morals but on autobiography. In both cases Communism or Communists are deeply embedded in their personal development, sewn into the fabric of their private past and their present ways of feeling and assuming. It is a matter not merely of shared ideas but of shared lives.

Even after ceasing to be Communists they often retain a Communist pattern of thought. In particular they retain the Communists' conception of their opponents, even if they have rejected the Communists' conception of themselves. This struck me forcibly in the case of some of the young Hungarian refugees in 1956. No one knew better than they the fraudulence of Communism, and they were at almost pathetic pains to tell everyone that Communist states were not really the people's democracies they claimed to be but tyrannies of a ruling class based on a foreign army and the secret police. Yet at the same time many of them clung fiercely to the view of the West with which they had been indoctrinated: bogus-democracies ruled by big business-men bent on world-domination and nuclear war. It took some of them years of actually living in the West to modify this view. And a few of them, like many members of the British Labour Party, retain it. The Labour correspondent of *The Guardian* has written recently:[2]

1. The Oxford University Communist Club, for example, disappeared when the Russians invaded Hungary. Its leading members joined the Labour Party and founded *The Universities and Left Review*. The O.U. Communist Club was not re-formed until autumn 1961.

2. John Cole: *The Struggle for the Labour Party, The Guardian*, 4 January 1961.

'In discussions over the past few months with people on the Left of the Party and the unions I have discovered that more of them than has ever been realized have a perfectly honest but absolutely fundamental difference of outlook on the whole range of foreign affairs from what I still believe to be the majority view of Labour supporters. It is a difference which makes the defence split much more comprehensible. The argument begins at the Bomb and runs something like this: That, anyhow, as potential aggressors the Americans look more dangerous than the Russians; that there is no longer a military menace from the Communist block (the Chinese deviation is explained entirely by the failure to grant her United Nations membership); that the export of socialism by the Communist countries will principally be by economic means, and that on the whole this is to be welcomed.

'It is when one seeks to discover why this group stands apart from world communism and speaks earnestly of a 'third force' that difficulty arises. There are obvious dangers in generalizing, and I can only report an increasing tendency on the Left to argue that the differences in human freedom between East and West are by now matters of degree rather than principle; that economic freedom is at least as important, probably more important, than "so-called political freedom", and that the Communist economic system is demonstrably superior to "capitalism" (under which umbrella title is included the kind of mixed economy left to Britain by the Attlee Government).'[1]

Because they see Communists as having so much in common with themselves they have a natural tendency to partially identify themselves with Communists and to take Communists at something like their own valuation. In fact in some ways they take Communists at more than their own valuation. For example Communist theory proclaims the intention to dispense with the rule of law, e.g. 'Dictatorship is power, based directly upon force, and unrestricted by any laws. The revolutionary dictatorship of the proletariat is power won and maintained by the violence of the proletariat against the bourgeoisie, power that is unrestricted by any laws' (Lenin: *The Prole-*

1. R. H. S. Crosman seems to have embraced this last view wholeheartedly. For instance he said to a Public Meeting in Hornsey on 21 November 1961, and repeated in a letter to *The Guardian* on 1 December 1961: 'The last ten years have proved that the most backward totalitarian form of Socialism is superior to the decadent type of Capitalism we have in the Western World.'

tarian Revolution and the Renegade Kautsky). This theory, which they make no bones about, they put into practice – and they make no bones about that either. Mao Tse-Tung himself announced publicly that his regime had put to death 800,000 opponents of the Chinese Revolution *after the fighting had ceased*. Yet although both the theory and the reality are openly declared by Communists, enormous numbers of Socialists regard any reference to them as anti-Communist propaganda. And they say things like 'Communism is ideal in theory, in fact it would be the perfect form of government: the trouble is it's *too* perfect – it doesn't work in practice.' Similarly Communists do not believe in free elections in any circumstances, and they say so, and they never allow them. They would rather risk world war over Berlin than let the people of East Germany choose their own rulers. Even in countries that already have democratic institutions, such as Britain, Communists always put a stop to the freedom of any elections they are in a position to supervise, as they did until 1961 in the Electrical Trades Union. Yet many Socialists believe that Communist leaders represent their people and are supported by them. Or to take a general example, a great many Socialists accept the Communist claim to be forward-looking. They still think of Communism as in some vague way the politics of the future. This is so bizarre that I do not know how to explain it, for the most striking thing about Communism is that it is the politics of the past, a petrified faith from the early stages of the Industrial Revolution that is old-fashioned in every way. Many Socialists even accept the Communists' claim to be part of the 'working-class movement', yet this is even more bizarre. The Communist Party of Great Britain has tried ever since its inception to affiliate to the Labour Party or the T.U.C. and has been consistently rebuffed. The Labour Party has never allowed Communists in its ranks, and it proscribes all organizations and publications that follow the Communist Party line.[1] The biggest trade union in the country, the Transport and General Workers' Union, has a rule forbidding any Communist to hold office. And most important of all, the British working class, though voting in millions for Conservative candidates, does not elect a single Communist M.P. – in fact seventeen out of the eighteen Communist candidates who stood in the last General Election (1959) lost their deposits. *Saying* you are part of the working-

1. An ordinary Communist device is to give their organizations and publications names designed to confuse them in people's minds with Labour organizations and publications, e.g. Labour Research Department and *Labour Monthly*.

class movement does not make you so. If the Communist Party is to be looked on as part of the working-class movement then the Conservative Party is ten thousand times more so – and that, though nothing like so ridiculous, is still ridiculous.

When one considers the kind of society Communists advocate for Britain, and the existing societies they support, their claim to be part of the working-class movement appears less funny and becomes macabre. The most famous martyrs of the British working-class movement are the Tolpuddle martyrs, six labourers who in 1834 were sentenced to seven years' transportation to Australia. After a hundred and thirty years they are still famous, still used as a symbol of class oppression. Yet what actually happened? After two years and a public outcry they were pardoned and brought back home. Subscriptions collected by working men provided five of them with farms in Essex, while the sixth returned to Dorset. Likewise we still remember the killing by soldiers of eleven people in St Peter's Fields, Manchester, in 1819: we call it a 'massacre' and compare it with the Battle of Waterloo (the incident is universally known by its punning nickname 'the Peterloo Massacre'). Such are the bloodiest and most terrible incidents in the history of the repression of the British workers by the British ruling class. Beside the ruling classes' repression of the workers in Communist countries they vanish into virtual non-existence. How do you compare the transportation of the six Tolpuddle martyrs to Australia in the eighteen-thirties with that in the nineteen-thirties of millions of Russians – no one knows how many, but it must be an eight-figure number[1] – to Siberia to suffer the fate of Pasternak's heroine in *Doctor Zhivago*: 'One day Lara went out and did not come back. She must have been arrested in the street, as so often happened in those days, and she died or vanished somewhere, forgotten as a nameless number on a list which later was mislaid, in one of the innumerable mixed or women's concentration camps in the north'?[2]

How do you compare the killing of eleven people at Peterloo in 1819 with the liquidation of entire populations, like that of the half-

1. Gulag, the organization which ran the forced labour camps, had over forty major 'colonies', some of them so big and self-contained as to be almost autonomous republics. By 1941 they were administering nearly 20% of all new construction in Russia, together with over 10% of the national production of timber, 40% of chromium ore, 5,000,000 tons of coal annually, and innumerable other products.

2. These are the two closing sentences of the Conclusion (page 449 in the

million people of the Chechen-Ingush Autonomous Republic in February 1944?[1] To find crimes committed by Communist Governments against the workers which are small enough to compare with the crimes of Capitalist Governments against the workers you have to come down to such trifles as the revolt of the workers in East Germany in June 1953 or the Poznan riots in Poland in June 1956, though even these are considerably larger. But at least they were specifically workers' uprisings, on the traditional model, against class repression and exploitation. For instance the account given in Keesing's Contemporary Archives (14967) of the Poznan riots, in which 53 people were killed, begins: 'Widespread dissatisfaction with low wages, poor living conditions, and the extremely high cost of living led to serious rioting in Poznan on 28 June. . . . The demonstrating began at 8 a.m., when columns of workers – many of whom were from the Zispo engineering works – spontaneously left their factories and converged on the main square in front of the Municipal People's Council building (Town Hall), chanting slogans such as "We want bread". . . .'

The ordinary day-to-day workings of Communist societies represent the most cynical, savage and efficient mode of exploitation of the working class that has ever been devised. If facts mean anything at all,

---

first English edition). Three pages further on, in the Epilogue, comes another passage about concentration camps:

'We were told: "Here you are. This is your camp." An open snow-field with a post in the middle and a notice on it saying: "GULAG 92 Y.N. 90" – that's all there was. . . . First we broke saplings with our bare hands in the frost, to get wood to build our huts with. And in the end, believe it or not, we built our own camp. We put up our prison and our stockade and our punishment cells and our watch towers, all with our own hands. And then we began our job as lumberjacks. We felled trees. We harnessed ourselves, eight to a sledge, and we hauled timber and sank into the snow up to our necks. For a long time we didn't know there was a war. They kept it from us. And then suddenly there came the offer. You could volunteer for front-line service in a punitive battalion, and if you came out alive you were free. After that, attack after attack, mile after mile of electrified barbed wire, mines, mortars, month after month of artillery barrage. They called our company the death squad. It was practically wiped out. How and why I survived, I don't know. And yet – imagine – all that utter hell was nothing, it was bliss compared to the horrors of the concentration camp. . . .'

1. This was among the crimes for which Stalin was denounced by Khrushchev in his famous speech to the Twentieth Congress in February 1956. Other whole peoples whose destruction was subsequently admitted were the Crimean Tartars and the Volga Germans. The Karachays, the Balkars and the Kalmuks were also liquidated at various times.

Communist Parties, far from being working-class parties, are the most anti-working-class parties that have ever existed. That we must live at peace with Communist societies I uncompromisingly assert. But to be 'friendly' with their governments is a betrayal of their people. Thousands of those people *every day* are fleeing to the free societies of the West. In 1948–49 I had a year's personal experience of this on the Yugoslav frontier of Austria. Thirteen years later I picked up the *New Statesman* (issue of 21 July 1961) and read on its front page: 'The mere fact that Krushchev has announced he is determined to "solve" the Berlin problem has generated panic among the East Germans. They are now crossing the frontier at the rate of 2,000 a day.' This mass-defection of people from Communist societies has been going on month in month out, year after year, never stopping, a permanent feature of our modern world. At the time of writing the number of people who have fled from Communist countries since the end of the Second World War has passed twenty-five millions, and is of course shooting up all the time. I cannot help feeling that Socialists who praise these societies while at the same time hating the free societies to which their victims flee are in the wrong party.

Socialist apologetics for Communism is a fascinating subject. The obvious explanations for it, most of which I have referred to in previous pages, still fail quite to explain. For the truth about, say, Soviet Russia was never unobtainable. As early as 1920 Bertrand Russell visited Russia and wrote *The Practice and Theory of Bolshevism* – a book so accurate in its descriptions and predictions that when it was reprinted in 1949 without alteration it could still not be faulted on any major point. In a much later book, *Portraits from Memory*, published in 1956, he gives a moving account of the effect the earlier book had had on his life (pages 13–14):

'The end of the first war was not the end of my isolation, but, on the contrary, the prelude to an even more complete isolation (except from close personal friends) which was due to my failure to applaud the new revolutionary government of Russia. . . In this I differed from almost all the friends that I had acquired since 1914. Most people still hated me for having opposed the war, and the minority, who did not hate me on this ground, denounced me for not praising the Bolsheviks. . . . My visit to Russia in 1920 was a turning-point in my life. During the time that I was there I felt a gradually increasing horror which became an almost intolerable oppression. The country seemed to me one vast prison in which the jailers were cruel bigots.

When I found my friends applauding these men as liberators and regarding the régime that they were creating as a paradise, I wondered in a bewildered manner whether it was my friends or I that were mad.'

The Soviet regime, as Russell had predicted, lurched from holocaust to holocaust. In the forced collectivization, millions of kulaks were killed. Then came the treason trials. Then the purges. The number of slaves in the concentration camps passed the ten million mark. The crimes and cruelties committed were on such a scale as to numb the imagination – only two régimes in human history can bear any comparison with it at all, those of Adolf Hitler and Genghis Khan. Yet all this time most of the active Socialists in Britain were praising Russia and describing Stalin as 'building Socialism'. The truth about Russia was 'Capitalist propaganda', and anyone who criticized the régime – even if, as in the case of Russell, he was himself a Socialist and of conspicuous integrity – was a lackey of the bourgeoisie.

Yet what Khrushchev conceded in his Twentieth Congress speech showed that the truth had been a thousand times more bloody and horrific than the Capitalist press had ever dreamt of suggesting. Communists and their apologists throughout the world were confronted with the inescapable fact that it was *they* who had been pumping out lies, slander and propaganda all these years while the Capitalist press for once had been telling the truth. Yet I have never heard one of them admit this fact, let alone express grief for it. They merely appropriated 'Stalinism' as a derogatory name for the régime they had hitherto supported, asserted that Khrushchev was changing it, and continued to praise and defend Russia as before. Their actual behaviour remained unchanged.

And when the bloodletting began again almost immediately after the Twentieth Congress speech – in fact that very same year, 1956, in Hungary – there were the same old apologias. I was criticized by several different members of the Labour Party for taking in Hungarian refugees, on the ground that they were counter-revolutionaries. And some of the trade unions treated refugees with positive brutality. At about that time I took a young refugee with me to the Beaver Hall in London, to a Labour Party meeting called 'The Truth about Hungary'. The speakers were Peter Fryer, the *Daily Worker* correspondent in Budapest whose despatches had been suppressed and who was subsequently expelled from the Communist Party, and Paul Ignotus and George Paloczi-Horvath, two famous Hungarian writers who had been in prison in Hungary. The audience consisted of delegates from constituency parties and trade union organizations all over Southern England. They listened in silence while the speakers told of their experiences in Budapest. The only applause was for incidental criticisms of the United States, for instance of Voice of America. Then, when the meeting was thrown open to discussion, delegate after delegate rose to attack the speakers and defend the Russian action. Not all of them did so, but certainly more than half.

The British Labour Movement as a whole showed more indignation over Suez than over Hungary. I attended the mass-meeting in Trafalgar Square addressed by Aneurin Bevan, and there was another at the Albert Hall addressed by Hugh Gaitskell. There were no mass-meetings about Hungary. I know we thought we were in a position to bring pressure to bear on the British Government over Suez and not on the Russian Government over Hungary, but the fact remains that large numbers of the most active members of the Labour Movement *did not want* to attack the Russian action. I said at the time that these two events, Suez and Hungary, could be used as co-ordinates to plot a person's real political attitudes. If you disapproved of Hungary but condoned Suez you were a Conservative. If you disapproved of Suez but condoned Hungary you were a Communist. If you disapproved of both you were a Radical. I still think this is a fair approximation.

One of my bitterest criticisms of the British and French invasion of Egypt was that it was carried out just after the Russians had begun their invasion of Hungary. It diverted the wrath of the world. The uncommitted countries of Asia and Africa had much to learn and gain from this demonstration in Central Europe of Communism at work. But quite naturally they cared more about a demonstration in Asia and Africa of Imperialism at work. So Suez monopolized their attention to the exclusion of Hungary. In other words Eden and Mollet, by committing that particular crime at that particular time, enabled the Russians to get away with something far worse at nothing like the price they would otherwise have had to pay. In England it unleashed the sharpest political passions I can remember: not only were there the usual processions, petitions and mass meetings but also the rupture of life-long friendships, upheavals of political outlook, resignations. Suez filled the political consciousness of the nation, especially of Socialists, and only a corner was left for Hungary. Perhaps many pre-war Socialists were thus saved from disillusionment with Russia of the kind that befell so many Communists. As it was, the Russian invasion of Hungary had the paradoxical effect of giving the Labour

Party a fresh injection of Marxist influence. For many of the Communists who left the Communist Party because of it – and they tended to be those of greater integrity and intelligence, or else the younger ones who had not had time to strike deep roots – joined the Labour Party. Some of them were talented and energetic, and made an almost immediate impact on the Labour Party. They founded magazines, such as *The New Reasoner* and *Universities and Left Review*, and played a leading role in The Campaign for Nuclear Disarmament. They and their followers have come to be known as the New Left, a recognizable group within the Labour Movement, chiefly characterized by youth and Marxism.

Thus, incredible though it may seem, illusions about Communism and Communists are still common in the Labour Movement. Only a few days before writing these words I inflamed two people sitting in different parts of a Labour audience to uncontrollable anger by making incidental criticisms of Stalin's post-war foreign policy. Stalin's, mind you! One of them described my speech as 'anti-Russian propaganda'. Every active person in the Labour Movement is used to these attitudes, common in individual members and sometimes found as the prevailing mood of whole audiences. At the Labour Party's Annual Conference at Blackpool in 1961 the majority of delegates from the constituencies voted against the expulsion of the Electrical Trades Union from the Labour Party, regardless of the fact that the High Court had just found its leaders guilty of fraud and found also 'that the Electrical Trades Union was not only managed and controlled by the Communist Party but was so managed as to serve the ideals of that party'. *The Spectator* had some interesting comments to make (6 October 1961) contrasting the attitude of the Annual Conference of the Labour Party with that of the T.U.C. 'Compare the debate here on the disaffiliation of the E.T.U. with the debate on their expulsion from the T.U.C. at Portsmouth. There, the Communists were heard in a contempetuous silence, broken only by a roar of healthy laughter at such charming *mots* as Mr Goldberg's "I have always regarded ballot-rigging with loathing and contempt"; and Mr John Byrne, that lonely and courageous fighter for decency against corruption, was applauded all the way to the rostrum. When the Labour Party discussed the E.T.U. ,on the other hand, the same Mr Goldberg (whom Mr Justice Winn described as a "not very scrupulous henchman of Mr Haxell's") was repeatedly cheered and applauded for the same lies.'

Illusions about Marxism are even commoner. In fact my experience suggests that the majority of intellectuals in the Labour Party, taking the active membership as a whole, are predominantly Marxist in their social and economic assumptions. If anyone doubts this let him listen to the speeches at any Labour Party Annual Conference.

CHAPTER SEVEN

The Psychology of Politics

WHAT we can think and feel and experience is limited by the nature of the equipment we have for thinking, feeling and experiencing. To take an example from our sensory apparatus, we happen to be equipped not merely to respond to waves of certain frequencies – sound and light – but to organize our responses automatically and involuntarily into a picture of our surroundings. We happen not to be equipped to do the same with waves of other frequencies, though it is perfectly conceivable that we might have been – X-rays, or radar waves, or the frequencies on which radio and television are transmitted. If we had been, our experience would be different from what it is, and our conception of the world also different. It is conceivable that our apprehension of objects might then have nothing in common with what it now is – we might apprehend a chair without size, shape, mass, colour or texture, but in other terms which we cannot now conceptualize. We apprehend things not 'as they are', whatever that could mean, but as we are capable of apprehending them. And this must be true of all experience – as true of our intellectual and emotional activity as it is of our sensory activity. 'The problem of the nature of the world irrespective of our perceptive mental apparatus is an empty abstraction without practical interest.'[1]

The first person clearly to grasp this was Kant. His work is deep and demanding, and I shall not here summarize or criticize it. The conclusion of his that I want to draw attention to is that space, time and causality, which had always been regarded as objective categories relating things and events to each other in the real world, do not exist in the real world at all but are *categories of experience*. This notion is difficult to grasp. The traditional analogy for explaining it is something like this: if I had been born wearing a pair of rose-tinted contact lenses that I could not take off (and perhaps did not know I had) I would see everything as rose-tinted, and it would never be possible for me ever to see anything other than as rose-tinted. I would take it

1. Freud: *The Future of an Illusion*, p. 97.

as a self-evident fact that everything in the world *was* rose-tinted – the sky, the sea, the earth together with all objects on it, including other people and my own body. But in this I should be mistaken. The truth would be not that everything was rose-tinted: on the contrary, almost nothing is. The truth would be that everything *could only be seen by me* as being rose-tinted. The rose-tint would not be inseparable from objects but inseparable from experience: it would be built in to my perceiving apparatus, not built into the world. Now Kant says something of this sort about space, time and causality. They are, he says, not ways in which things and events are related to each other independently of us, but *ways in which our experience is structured.* They are modes of apprehension, without which we cannot apprehend. They are built in to our conceptual apparatus.

I mention this argument of Kant's not to commend it uncritically but to draw attention to the revolutionary insight it contains. It may recall to the reader my words on page 36 'Natural laws, physics, logic, geometry, mathematics – all these which, until Kant, had been accepted by everyone as inherent in the world, are now seen as products of the human mind. *Their principles characterize not things but ways of looking at things.*' Kant was the forerunner of this relativistic revolution. But like all pioneers he did not grasp the full consequences of his own discovery. He regarded the ways in which our experience is structured as necessary and unalterable, and it did not occur to him that they could change. This was because, like everyone else until Einstein, he took it for granted that the structure of the physical universe as revealed by Newton was fixed for all time. Yet even though he accepted Newtonian physics as definitive he destroyed the foundations of the empirical philosophy to which it had given rise,[1] and opened up the incredibly rich world of possibilities that has issued in modern science. He showed that knowledge of the world is inseparable from the observer – and once this had been shown the way to Einstein lay open.

---

1. It was what he remembered from reading the last and greatest of those philosophers, Hume, that set Kant off on his revolutionary road – or, in his own words, 'interrupted my dogmatic slumber and gave my investigations in the field of speculative philosophy a quite new direction'. (Introduction to *Prolegomena to any future Metaphysics.*)

Hume has acted as the vital catalyst to another of the world's greatest thinkers: Einstein told F. S. C. Northrop in Berlin in 1928 that he would never have dared to reject Newtonian science had he not read Hume.

I

When writing about the structure of experience Kant took his subject at the deepest level, the level at which we are all the same by virtue of our common humanity. But at more superficial levels, the levels on which we differ, something analogous applies. Each one of us structures his *social* experience largely in terms which he himself provides, while attributing this structure to the environment. It is not a question of 'seeing things as they are'. The very notion is meaningless. To everything we see and everything we hear we bring an elaborate mechanism of assumption, perception and interpretation. Because of this there is no such thing as unambiguous communication. Wittgenstein has shown this (it is related to the whole theory, summarized in Chapter Two, that words do not have independent meanings but that the meaning of a word is its use) and in doing so he employs a striking illustration:[1] 'I see a picture: it represents an old man walking up a steep path leaning on a stick. -- How? Might it not have looked just the same if he had been sliding downhill in that position? Perhaps a Martian would describe the picture so.'

In Chapter Five of *Black Mischief* Evelyn Waugh describes some of the sociological implications of this:

'Finally there resulted a large, highly coloured poster well calculated to convey to the illiterate the benefits of birth control. . . . Copies were placarded all over Debra Dowa; they were sent down the line to every station latrine, capital and coast; they were sent into the interior to vice-regal lodges and headmen's huts, hung up at prisons, barracks, gallows and juju trees, and wherever the poster was hung there assembled a cluster of inquisitive, entranced Azanians.

'It portrayed two contrasted scenes. On one side a native hut of hideous squalor, overrun with children of every age, suffering from every physical incapacity – crippled, deformed, blind, spotted and insane; the father prematurely aged with paternity squatted by an empty cook-pot; through the door could be seen his wife, withered and bowed with child-bearing, desperately hoeing at their inadequate crop. On the other side a bright parlour furnished with chairs and table; the mother, young and beautiful, sat at her ease eating a huge slice of raw meat; her husband smoked a long Arab hubble-bubble (still a caste mark of leisure throughout the land), while a single

1. *Philosophical Investigations*, p. 54.

healthy child sat between them reading a newspaper. Inset between the two pictures was a detailed drawing of some up-to-date contraceptive apparatus and the words in Sakuyu: WHICH HOME DO YOU CHOOSE?

'Interest in the pictures was unbounded; all over the island woolly heads were nodding, black hands pointing, tongues clicking against filed teeth in unsyntactical dialects. Nowhere was there any doubt about the meaning of the beautiful new pictures.

'See: on right hand: there is rich man: smoke pipe like big chief: but his wife she no good: sit eating meat: and rich man no good: he only one son.

'See: on left hand: poor man: not much to eat: but his wife she very good, work hard in field: man he good too: eleven children: one very mad, very holy. And in the middle: Emperor's juju. Make you like that good man with eleven children.

'And as a result, despite admonitions from squire and vicar, the peasantry began pouring into town for the gala, eagerly awaiting initiation to the fine new magic of virility and fecundity.'

I have elsewhere quoted[1] a non-fictional and less amusing example – the Russian students who visited Oxford and then on their return home published a report: 'The students eat together in gloomy stone halls hundreds of years old. They sit on backless wooden benches and eat off the bare table. And such is the overcrowding that these same halls, benches and tables have to be used for lectures as well as meals. . . .'

We all do this to some extent – we *can* only understand what we see in terms of our own patterns of assumption, and it is no good asking us to 'see' things outside those. That is why you can seldom convince people on important issues by simply 'showing them the facts'. The Russian students saw the facts. What you have to do is to *change their way of looking at things*. This is made doubly hard by the fact that scarcely anyone seems to realize how much of life as he knows it, how much of its very structure, is not *there* at all but is supplied by himself, from his view of the world and society right down to his most personal intimacies. (Lawrence Durrell has written a quartet of novels on this latter theme, showing how even the private relationships among a closed circle of friends have a fundamentally different reality for each one of them, for each a reality incomprehensible to the others.)

In this chapter I am concerned with differences among ways of

1. *Go West, Young Man*, p. 13.

looking at social and political matters. These differences are seldom
rational in origin. Their chief sources in Britain are, I think, class and
personality, and I shall discuss them in that order. The fact that in
England most people vote according to their social class is so simple
and obvious as to be often forgotten. (To be more precise, most people
vote in accordance with what they think is their self-interest, and the
result of this is that a clear majority of working-class people vote
Labour and a clear majority of middle and upper-class people vote
Conservative.) It is forgotten, for instance, by psychologists when they
try to explain voting behaviour as a manifestation of personality-
structure. And it is why the Liberal Party has no prospect of becoming
the Government: there is no solid body of electors who regard the
Liberal Party as promoting their interests. But from the fact that class
is the chief determinant of voting behaviour it follows that opinions
about controversial issues other than class issues (e.g. other than
education, housing, old-age pensions, taxation) are not. Such differences, as between most people who vote Labour and most people who
vote Conservative, are incidental. In view of that it is not surprising
that they are, as I shall now show, negligible.

II

'Society', I remember Aneurin Bevan once saying, 'looks very
different depending on whether you're seeing it from the top down or
the bottom up.' I still recall my incredulity on arriving at Oxford in
1949 to find it constantly being said by undergraduates that 'everyone had servants before the war'. Before the war (and indeed at any
time) more people *were* servants than had them. Well over a million
people in Britain were servants – it was the highest single category of
employment – and 'according to the British census returns of 1931,
personal service accounted for $12\frac{1}{2}\%$ of the total occupied population
– the highest percentage found anywhere in the world' (*Chambers's
Encyclopaedia*). Between them and their masters stretched that vast
majority of the population who neither were servants nor had them.
So the assertion, still often made, betrays two things about a person
who makes it: first, his conception of society is simply a generalized
picture of the experience he personally has had or would like to have
had; and second, his use of the term 'everyone' shows that as far as he
is concerned most people do not count as people.

I have since become used, perhaps too used, to the fact that few of those who share my educational background have much idea of what our society is like, or the sort of life most common to its members. But they are not the sole culprits. 'Our tendency to centre our conception of what is normal around our own experience contains an essential error'[1] from which none of us is free. Working-class people do it too.

This has inflicted serious disadvantages on the Labour Movement. Historically the Labour Movement is a working-class movement, and the limits of its outlook have in many ways been set by the limits of working-class experience. These are narrow. Most working-class people do repetitive jobs without much responsibility. They have had little education – they left school and started work by the age of fifteen – and that little has been bad. They have low incomes – in fact until the last twenty years most of them could fairly be called 'poor'. And because of all this the range of choice open to them in work, housing, travel, the use of leisure and many other things is small. All this has damaging effects on the personality. Indeed, that fact is almost the cornerstone of the traditional case for Socialism. And quite apart from anything else it is why idealization of the working class is silly. As Bertrand Russell puts it in the last paragraph of his essay on *The Superior Virtue of the Oppressed*:[2] 'If it were indeed the case that bad nourishment, little education, lack of air and sunshine, unhealthy housing conditions, and overwork produce better people than are produced by good nourishment, open air, adequate education and housing, and a reasonable amount of lesiure, the whole case for economic reconstruction would collapse, and we could rejoice that such a large percentage of the population enjoys the conditions that make for virtue. But obvious as this argument is, many Socialist and Communist intellectuals consider it *de rigueur* to pretend to find the proletariat more amiable than other people, while professing a desire to abolish the conditions which, according to them, alone produce good human beings.'

Working-class people are, on the whole, more rigid and intolerant than better-educated people, narrower in outlook, more conservative in their social attitudes. I make these assertions on the basis of not only personal experience but also impartial investigations carried out by others. Let us take as first examples religious prejudice, race-

1. David Stafford-Clark: *Psychiatry Today*, p. 60.
2. Russell: *Unpopular Essays*.

prejudice, colour-prejudice and sex-prejudice. In November 1958 Social Surveys (Gallup Poll) Ltd carried out a poll on the question: 'If the party of your choice nominated a generally well-qualified person as Parliamentary candidate and he happened to be a Roman Catholic/Jew/Coloured Person/Woman would you vote for him/her?' The percentage of people who said yes in each case, broken down simply on a two-class basis, was as follows:[1]

	Lower Class	*Upper Class*
Roman Catholic	82	85
Jew	69	79
Coloured Person	59	65
Woman	75	81

Taking the specific relationship between such attitudes and voting behaviour, the percentage of people who said yes to the above questions broken down on the basis of whether they intended to vote Conservative or Labour at the ensuing General Election was as follows:

	Labour	*Conservative*
Roman Catholic	85	84
Jew	70	77
Coloured Person	60	62
Woman	74	78

So it was only on the question of religion that Labour voters were less prejudiced than Conservatives, and then only by a margin of 1%. They were more prejudiced than Conservatives, and by bigger margins, against Jews, coloured people and women.

In July 1959 the Gallup Poll invited people to say yes or no to the assertion that Jews have more power than they should really have. Of people intending to vote Labour 38% said yes; of Conservatives only 30%. In the same month people were asked whether those parts of the country that forbid the sale of drink on Sundays should stop doing so: of intending Conservative voters 70% said yes, of Socialists 69%. When asked if they thought restricted laws for the sale of drink should be abolished altogether 51% of Conservatives said yes, but only 47% of Socialists. In December 1959 people were asked to state whether

1. All the figures in this and the next paragraph are reproduced by permission of Social Surveys (Gallup Poll) Ltd.

they considered the success of the United Nations 'very important', 'fairly important' or 'not so important'. Of people who had voted Conservative in the General Election two months previously, 70% said 'very important'; of people who had voted Labour, 62%. Even on hanging and flogging, support for which is especially associated with Conservatives, the difference is not particularly great. In April 1961, 81% of the people who had voted Conservative wanted corporal punishment re-introduced – but so did 73% of Labour voters. 13% of Conservatives wanted to abolish capital punishment, as against 21% of Labour voters. Indeed, on these issues the deciding factor is just as likely to be education as politics:

	% in favour of bringing back corporal punishment	% in favour of abolishing capital punishment
People who had left school by the age of 13	81	16
People who had left school by the age of 14	77	17
People who had left school by the age of 15–16	69	21
People who had left school by the age of 17 or later	65	23

For purposes of my present argument I do not need to assert that education is a bigger factor in these matters than political outlook, though I think it is. And I am not saying that Conservatives are more liberal-minded and tolerant than Socialists, though they may be – if they are it is probably not directly due to politics but simply because the better-off are better-educated. All I need to assert, and I do assert it, is that *Socialists are not strikingly more tolerant, more liberal-minded or more in favour of social reform than are Conservatives.*

How is it that the opposite is taken for granted by almost everybody? It is not because of the attitudes of the great majority who habitually vote Labour or Conservative in elections: it is because of the behaviour of Socialist and Conservative *activists*, that tiny minority on each side who stand for Parliament, write for newspapers, organize local parties, attend conferences, or simply talk a lot about politics. These are quite untypical people. They are even untypical of their own supporters. A high proportion of them are exceptions to the general rule that people's political behaviour is determined by class-interest and not by personality-structure. Among these I think it is generally true that Socialists are strikingly more humanitarian than Conservatives, more tolerant, more rational in their approach to problems (e.g. more averse to attempting solutions which involve physical violence, whether inside society – against, say, criminals – or by the society as a whole against other societies), more in favour of liberal reform, and less afflicted by prejudice on grounds of religion, race, colour or sex. And of course it is such people who form or influence governments – and in the last resort it is what governments do that really matters. This is the bedrock on which the supposed difference between Socialists and Conservatives rests. What Socialist Governments and Conservative Governments actually *do* is profoundly different,[1] that is the point. And it obscures the fact, or else is obscured by it, that political differences are not very great between the electors on whose votes they respectively depend.

On both sides of the political fence, then, the people who get into Parliament and form governments depend on the support of other people who do not share their attitudes. My experience of this as a parliamentary candidate must be typical: over and over again I was asked by individual supporters to soft-pedal my views on liberal reform (e.g. the death penalty) on the ground that these would turn away Labour votes. When in the General Election of 1959 I stood against the Colonial Secretary, Lennox-Boyd, I unremittingly attacked his record in office – Cyprus, Hola, the treatment of the Devlin Report – and here again some of my most active supporters asked me to stop, on the ground that most Labour voters were in favour of such policies. Of course I did not, and for that matter I am sure it made no appreciable difference to my vote (precisely because so very few votes are swayed by policy or ideology). But I must admit that the doubters were at least right in their preliminary judgement: all my personal canvassing revealed a predominance of illiberal attitudes among Labour voters, varying noticeably in proportion to education. On the

1. Some people seem inclined to deny this, but such denial flies in the face of fact. To take only one example, the last Labour Government gave independence to India, Pakistan, Ceylon, and Burma, nationalized nearly all Britain's basic industries and created the National Health Service: all these measures were of historic importance and to every one of them Conservative opposition was so passionate as to spill over into hysteria.

whole my 'middle-class' supporters were by far the more progressive, my 'working-class' supporters the more conservative.

So one of the major disadvantages of the fact that the Labour Party is a working-class party is that conservative attitudes to social affairs predominate among its supporters. It is this more than anything else that keeps it from being full-bloodedly radical. It ought, as a progressive reforming party, to be commanding the attention of the whole country in a public battle to abolish the death penalty, to reform our penal system, to civilize the divorce laws, to legalize homosexual relations between consenting adult males (as they have always been legal between consenting adult females), to allow people to drink when they wish and do what they like with their own Sundays – in short it ought at the very least to be fighting for those social reforms which are already agreed on by liberal opinion and which, taken together, would transform the life of the individual in Britain more than the nationalization of any particular industry. But it does not. And the reason it does not is that most of the people who vote for it are in favour of hanging murderers, putting homosexuals in prison, and all the rest of it, just as they were in favour of Suez.

III

The fact that the Labour Movement is historically a working-class movement carries with it an even bigger disadvantage than the one I have just mentioned. It is not easy to put into words because it is a set of assumptions at the back of the mind, a pattern of expectations that only indirectly influences behaviour. People who have not themselves lived in the working class rarely understand it, and certainly an imaginative effort is required of any such person if he is to get an inkling of it.

It all rests on the fact that the world of working-class people is run by outsiders. The factories and offices where they work, the shops where they buy everything, their schools and hospitals, their local government (which is remote) and their national government (which is even more remote) – all are firmly in the hands of non-working-class people. Connected with this is the fact that working-class people go through life without exercising significant choice in most of the crucial matters – what school they go to, what they do while they are there, when they leave, what sort of job they go into, where they live, how they educate their children, how much of the world they see. This means that they have almost no control over their environment. All they can do is adapt themselves to it. So the majority of working-class men and women accept society as *given*. They regard as 'natural' the roads and houses and factories and schools and hospitals, the industries, the systems of transport and distribution, the post office, the books and newspapers, the music, the television, radio, cinema. These things are *there* – taken for granted as being somehow 'laid on', without it being really grasped deep-down that they are all man-made and have to be conceived and designed and built and run by ordinary human beings – such activities being wholly outside their experience.

The human beings who do make and run (and perhaps own) them are for the most part unknown and unseen. Our caste-system sees to it that they live in other parts of town, shop in other shops, work other hours, wear other clothes and speak with other accents, are educated at other schools and even sit in other compartments on trains. Most working-class people live their whole lives without really getting to know a single person in authority or a single professional person – for all the world as if the two classes were, as a Conservative Prime Minister once said they were, two nations.[1] They see houses every day of their lives but they have never seen an architect. They have never met a don or a barrister or a diplomat (most of them would not be sure precisely what those words meant). They may like and respect their doctor but they do not know him as a person – do not visit his home and mix on friendly terms with his wife and children. The same goes for their dentist, whom in any case they see less of. They probably recognize a couple of schoolteachers by sight and meet an occasional clergyman and solicitor. In their jobs they meet few people above the rank of foreman, and these they normally address as 'Sir' or 'Mr So-and-so' while being addressed in return by their Christian name or bare surname.

This whole way of life creates a 'they-us' mentality. ' "They" are "the people at the top", "the higher-ups", the people who give you your dole, call you up, tell you to go to war, fire you, made you split the family in the thirties to avoid a reduction in the Means Test allowance,

1. Throughout the history of writing about class in the modern sense, from Disraeli to Nancy Mitford, it has been asserted that there is only one basic division – 'the two nations', 'the classes and the masses', 'U and non-U', 'either you are a gentleman or you aren't'. One can subdivide both of these groups indefinitely, but there remains this single chasm between the two. As a matter of observation about how our society works I agree with this.

"get yer in the end", "aren't really to be trusted", "talk posh", "are all twisters really", "never tell yer owt" (e.g. about a relative in hospital), "clap yer in clink", "will do y'down if they can", "summons yer", "are all in a click [clique] together", "treat yer like muck".[1] It is the psychology of the victim, the person to whom things are done. In the simple or sinister-minded it becomes a kind of animism: just as primitive man, surrounded by the workings of nature but having no understanding of them, attributed every event to the agency of unseen beings, so quite a number of people today are inclined to believe that social power is held by a conspiracy of people who are seldom observed yet in some mysterious way control everything from behind the scenes – 'the Jews' or 'the Freemasons' or 'the Capitalist class'. However, these are only the stupid or, more commonly, the emotionally disturbed.

As a result of this segregation the classes are almost unbelievably ignorant of each other. And because of 'our tendency to centre our conception of what is normal around our own experience', each tends to exclude the other from its conception of what is normal. Just as most upper-middle-class people will say things like 'Of course before the war everyone had servants . . .', even though they must know at some little-regarded level of their consciousness that in fact few people had servants, so working-class people tend for most of the time to envisage society as consisting of people like themselves. After all, their observable world *does* consist almost exclusively of people like themselves, and it is not surprising that things and people outside their experience have little reality for them. So working-class people rarely think of non-working-class people (a fact which non-working-class people do not believe). They have usually little idea how executives or professional people live or what doing their jobs is like. They themselves have never initiated, built up or run anything, and they have no conception of policy-making or administrative responsibility or the work these things involve. The very word 'responsibility' means something different to working-class people from what it means to others – to them it means not decision-making but the effective discharging of imposed tasks ('It's my responsibility to see there's always water in the fire-buckets'). When they say of someone 'He's got a very responsible job' they mean a lot is expected of him by his superiors.

1. Richard Hoggart: *The Uses of Literacy*, Chapter 3.

There is a general tendency for all of us, when we cannot imagine what other people do, to imagine they do nothing. Working-class people commonly suppose that the higher up people are – the farther away from the life they themselves know and understand – the less they do; some genuinely believe that business-men do nothing but eat expensive lunches and play golf, Civil Servants drink tea and members of the Government talk. They know what doctors and teachers do because these impinge on them directly, so they acknowledge that doctors and teachers work hard and do an important job (though they are resentful of teachers' long holidays). For the rest, they tend to assume that it is the working-class who do all the work.

This illusion has been incorporated in the economic theory espoused by most working-class movements. 'Workers by hand and brain' produced all the wealth: everyone else was a parasite. The role of the entrepreneur was overlooked because most Socialists did not know it existed: they supposed that 'the people at the top' could simply be dispensed with. In Britain after 1945 the discovery that this was not so came as a shock even to many responsible members of the Labour Party. By 1957 they had absorbed it, and set out to educate their supporters in it. And as if it were a discovery that would come to everyone as a blinding revelation it was stressed over and over again in policy documents put before Conference in that year. 'In the history of private enterprise, the owners of industry have played an indispensable role' (*Industry and Society*, p. 26). 'Too little attention used to be given to the problems of managing publicly owned industry' (*Public Enterprise*, p. 26). 'The importance of good management as the key to efficiency in the nationalized industries can scarcely be exaggerated' (*Public Enterprise*, p. 24). 'As companies grow larger and their affairs more complex, management becomes increasingly important, increasingly hierarchical, increasingly specialist and increasingly professional' (*Industry and Society*, p. 16). 'It is a specialized job the effective performance of which is essential to success' (*Public Enterprise*, p. 26). This signified the abandonment of whole chunks of traditional Socialist theory. For instance there was to be no more nonsense about workers' control of industry. 'Management is a job for specialists,' warned *Public Enterprise* on page 39, and then on page 41 said bluntly: 'Joint consultation is advisory in purpose and spirit: final decisions rest with management.' The bogeyman conception of big business was also renounced. 'The Labour Party recognizes that, under increasingly professional managements, large firms are as a whole serving the nation well' (*Industry and Society*, p. 48). On page 23 of *Industry and Society* 'conceptions of the national interest' are even listed among the four 'main incentives both for those on their way up and for those who have arrived in the Board Room'.

These two policy documents marked the opening of Hugh Gaitskell's struggle to make Labour Party thinking join contact with the real world. It is important to see how much they threw overboard of the wretched mythology that has bedevilled Socialism since the nineteenth century – the mythology of a society based on greed, with bloated capitalists, the law of the jungle, cut-throat competition, hard-faced business-men in ruthless pursuit of personal gain, the savage exploitation of the workers, not to mention the dream of workers' control of industry.

IV

Innocence of responsibility has affected the attitude of working-class people not only to economic affairs but to political tactics and a number of other things as well. Many people in the Labour Movement take it for granted that whatever that movement does, society will continue to be run and overall responsibility carried by someone else. They therefore aim not to direct society but to play a particular role within it. This is outstandingly true of the trade unions, but not only of them: it is true of everyone who wants the Labour Party to promote the interests of one class against another.

This is irresponsibility in the deepest sense. The Labour Party can only succeed in radically altering our society if it gains control of it by becoming the Government, and this means being responsible to all the people, as well as for the cost of all its proposals and for all the consequences of its actions. If it turns its back on this and opts for the role of permanent Opposition it will cease to be in any important sense an instrument of social change. This fact seems lost on the advocates of permanent opposition, such as R. H. S. Crossman in his Fabian pamphlet *Labour in the Affluent Society*: 'It is, I believe, for this creeping crisis of the 1960s and 1970s that the leadership of the Labour Party should hold itself in reserve, refusing in any way to come to terms with the Affluent Society. . . .' This attitude is one of practical

Conservatism, for not only does it acquiesce in the *status quo*, it positively advocates a quarter of a century of Conservative Government. It is greatly encouraged by the fact that the Labour Party has been in almost permanent opposition since its birth. In more than sixty years of existence it has had power for only six – an extraordinary record of failure for a party claiming to represent the mass of the people. For decades its members could do little but protest – march in processions, make demonstrations, carry banners, sign petitions, send telegrams and letters, hold mass-meetings. And the fact that there was little else they could do made many of them come to think of politics as consisting in these activities – and that in turn blinded them to what it is really about: power, responsibility, running things, changing things. They became opposition-minded.

Furthermore an organization whose activities are oppositional attracts into itself people who like opposition. The Labour Party was born of grievance – it would never have come into existence but for the deeply held feeling that there were things radically wrong with society that could and should be changed. And much of the support it got on its upward struggle to power came from people who believed that it would abolish not only poverty, unemployment and war, but also, as we saw in previous chapters, every other social evil from crime to disease. And because it laid *total blame* on the existing form of society it became a natural point of attraction for the anti-social – for all who formulated their grievances in social terms – the lonely, the poor, the envious, the vindictive. There are plenty of such people in the Labour Party to this day. They are in it not to change society or help other people but to meet psycho-emotional demands of their own. Their Socialist attitudes are neurotic symptoms. When confronted with a political problem their natural reaction is to take not the course most likely to solve it but the course most satisfying to their own needs. They would get more out of going to a psychiatrist, but they do not know this and spend their lives looking to politics for what it cannot give. They think they are on the 'Left' of the party, but that is only because they are permanently dissatisfied. These 'aginners' are fond of founding sects of their own, but if one is at all active in left-wing politics one soon comes to know plenty of them as individuals. They are incessantly sending telegrams in protest, walking in processions, carrying banners. Many of their organizations keep a permanent banner and simply paint each new slogan on it as required. I once heard the chairman of a ward meeting say: 'At the demonstration last Sunday, Comrades, I couldn't find our section. Finally I came across our banner lying on the grass and our members sitting round it! I hope that next Sunday our banner will be clearly visible. The demonstration next Sunday will be about the hydrogen bomb. We shall start from Marble Arch as usual.'

The simple but absolutely fundamental thing that such Socialists fail to understand is that politics is about policy – what schools to build, and where and when; how to organize the country's economic life, its medical system, its welfare services, its defences; how to run its colonies, and when and in what circumstances to make them independent; how to manage its relationships with other countries. Politics is *doing*, not saying or writing or thinking. Politics is not, except in trivial respects, an activity with words – it is not speeches and articles and processions and protests: it is houses and factories and office-blocks and art galleries and ships and roads and hospitals and schools and hydrogen bombs and concert halls. Defence policy is what goes on in the factories and laboratories and airfields and ship-yards, not what goes on in the speeches of Canon Collins or the columns of the *New Statesman*. In years of intensive political activity I have rarely been able to get an opposition-minded Socialist even to see what this means. Opposition-minded Socialists see the whole point of political activity as lying not in responsibility and achieve-ment but in struggle. They enjoy the challenge and the fighting, with the emotional release these bring, and what actually gets done is to them of secondary importance. They get more pleasure out of exciting meetings and brilliant articles than out of schools built and sick healed. This, of course, is a neurotic attitude carried over into public affairs. It is the politics of self. The ego is at the centre of everything, and what matters are personal feelings of triumph, anger, indig-nation and the rest – self-expression, not objective accomplishment. Such people are in politics not 'for the work's sake' but for kicks.

Among Socialists of this kind I can discern at least nine common motivations: (*1*) envy and resentment of people more fortunate than themselves, (*2*) hatred of authority, (*3*) revenge, (*4*) anxiety, (*5*) guilt, (*6*) what has been called 'aestheticism', (*7*) immaturity, (*8*) priggish-ness, and (*9*) the need for a religion-substitute.

(*1*) It is easy to identify Socialists who are motivated by envy and resentment. When they see that something socially desirable is available to too few people their natural instinct is not to make it available to more people but to destroy it.[1] This they term 'an attack on privilege'. Politics for them is a state of warfare against all who arouse in them feelings of social inferiority – whether with respect to education, style of life, income, possessions, power or class, or even sometimes personal appearance, dress or accent. This attitude is the life-blood of the class-war. Class-war has many of the characteristics of ordinary war. You must keep to your own side: you must not consort with the enemy or enter his haunts. (When Aneurin Bevan was kicked down the stairs of Whites several years ago the deputy leader of the Scottish mineworkers said to me bitterly: 'What we'd like to know is what the hell was he doing in Whites in the first place?') You must be clearly distinguishable from the enemy: hence you must not wear the same uniform or speak in the same way – a number of Socialists, such as Michael Foot, refuse ever to wear evening clothes and have developed synthetically proletarianised accents. The worst crime of all is to be a traitor. Socialists still think with active hatred of Ramsay Macdonald (whereas they have almost forgotten Stanley Baldwin, who did much more harm.) Socialists of this kind get most of the pleasures from politics that can be got from war: the sense of purpose, the easy cameraderie, the wonderful feeling of 'belonging', the joy of hating other people, the thrill of fighting, the continuing pleasure of reliving old battles. For this they pay by accepting the myths of class. They, too, judge people by their position or power or wealth or education or titles – only adversely instead of favourably. For reasons of class-consciousness there are innumerable things they cannot do, places they cannot visit, people they cannot befriend. In short they are snobs – inverted snobs are snobs, and like all other snobs they are social invalids. And the fact that they choose to fight mainly those who stir their resentment means that they feel inferior to their oponents, a fact which is a source of incurable distress. In the last big speech of his life, at Blackpool in 1959, Aneurin Bevan burst

1. For instance good secondary education. In 1958 'The Leadership put forward modest proposals for reform which utterly failed to excite the party in the country or the conference hall. The policy document was attacked as not being sufficiently socialist. Opposed to the leadership was nearly half the conference, who were not in the least interested in education but who wanted to abolish public schools. The assumption underlying the whole debate was that the state system is inferior, must remain so for a long time to come and that the public schools would always be privileged. *The party did not seriously consider making the educational standards of the privileged available to all.*' (Tyrrell Burgess: *If We Cared About Education:* Socialist Commentary, May 1961.) (My italics.)

out (with reference to 'the Tories'): 'I despise them! They are neither intelligent nor moral! Why on earth we should have an inferiority complex about them I do not know!'

(2) The haters of authority are in an odd situation, because the authority that impinges most on them in political matters is the leadership of their own party, which thus becomes their chief enemy. However, this seems odd only to others: to themselves it seems entirely natural. Anthony Howard, now political correspondent of the *New Statesman*, wrote in the *Sunday Pictorial* on 22 November 1959 (under the name 'Charles Wilberforce'): 'No one has ever denied that Gaitskell has courage. He shows it again next Saturday by choosing to speak at the beginning of the Labour Party's election inquest. . . . Gaitskell puts himself right up in the firing line at the beginning. Which is where a leader should be.' Mr Howard takes it for granted that a leader's function is to be shot at *by his own followers*. It does not occur to him that in saying this he has said anything peculiar. Whoever the leaders of the Labour Party were, and whatever their policies, they would be abused by Socialists of this sort. For example on 25 June 1960 the *New Statesman* wrote: 'Ever since Mr Gaitskell took over from Earl Attlee, the leadership has appeared to be manipulated by a small and much-disliked group of anti-Socialist zealots who do not only oppose, but even scorn, most of the traditional causes which still inspire the rank and file.' Yet when Attlee was in fact leader he and his colleagues came in for precisely the same sort of lambasting. I remember the *New Statesman's* fulminations in those days, quite clearly, week in week out, and no doubt if I pored over back numbers I could find some really juicy quotations. Yet even picking up a volume at random and opening it I see this on the page: 'Since Christmas Mr Attlee, Mr Morrison, and Mr Shinwell, by a series of tactical manœuvres, have been trying to evade the necessity of re-formulating the Socialist attitude to the Foreign and Defence policies of a Tory Government.' (*New Statesman*, 15 March 1952.) And then, flicking over the pages, I come to: 'Some Right-wing leaders of the Labour Party live haunted lives; their utterances are inspired by nothing except a terrifying vision of Soviet hordes pouring over Europe like molten lava over a fertile plain. On that assumption they are prepared for Britain to be an American satellite; if necessary, they will jettison the Welfare State, the creation of which is the only justification for their political existence.' (*New Statesman*, 5 April 1952; from a signed review written by the Editor, Kingsley

Martin, of Aneurin Bevan's book *In Place of Fear*.) This hatred of the party's leadership is the one persistent characteristic of the dissident 'Left'. The actual issues change – German re-armament, Clause IV, unilateralism, etc. – but they are always fought in these highly emotional personal terms. The leaders also change, but whoever they are they are always regarded as anti-Socialist betrayers who are also personally contemptible. The Socialists who feel like this are well-organized and very active. They even have their own weekly paper, *Tribune*. Because their chief aim is to destroy the leadership of their own party they tend to be popular with Conservatives and Communists, who naturally give them every encouragement. Lord Beaverbrook makes extensive use of them in his newspapers.[1]

There are also historical reasons why so many Socialists always distrust the leaders of the Labour Party no matter who they may be. These date partly from the *débâcle* of 1924, when 'the Labour Government thus ended in inglorious fiasco, as the result of a series of muddles, the making of which is still wholly beyond understanding. Their followers were already restive before these events, and naturally they added to the vehemence of criticism. . . . From the episode of Labour in office, in 1924, certainly dates the emergence of a new type of 'left-wing' Socialism, hostile to Communism on the one hand and to moderate Labour on the other. . . .'[2] But the real trauma happened in 1931, when the Labour Party's leaders deserted it altogether, had the Labour Government removed from office and a conservative Government formed under Ramsay Macdonald still as Prime Minister. The Labour Party has never quite recovered from this unimaginable betrayal, and the 'Left' of the party has been haunted ever since by the fear of being betrayed again – by the suspicion that the leaders, whoever they may be, do not really believe in Socialist policies but are crypto-Conservatives who, once they get into office, will adopt conservative policies. The Candidate for Buckingham at the time of the 1959 Annual Conference spoke the truth when he said: 'There can be no mistake about it – and let it be said quite frankly – that a great many people at this Conference suspect that most of the leaders of the

1. Michael Foot, long Editor of *Tribune*, was formerly editor of the *Evening Standard*. Robert Edwards, another ex-Editor of *Tribune*, was briefly Editor of the *Daily Express*. Tom Driberg was the original William Hickey, and has written a biography of Lord Beaverbrook. A. J. P. Taylor's admiration for Lord Beaverbrook is reciprocated, and he is a frequent contributor to his newspapers.

2. G. D. H. Cole: *A Short History of the British Working-Class Movement*, p. 411.

Party want to *dilute* Socialism as it has been understood to stand in the past fifty years.'

One of the most striking differences between Socialists and Conservatives is in their attitude towards leaders. I once asked a friend with a job in the Conservative Central Office if working there had affected his political opinions, and he replied that everything was much as he had expected except in one respect: he had been astonished to discover the full extent of the *Führerprinzip* and its all-pervading practical influence. I myself have seen Conservative leaders addressed with ostentatious deference by junior ministers, called 'Sir' by backbench M.P.s, and treated with servility by constituency activists. The difference between this and calling your leaders 'Hugh' and 'Clem' is not just a difference of language: it reflects a division in the psychology of political attitudes that goes deep below the level of consciousness to origins that have nothing to do with politics at all – it stems from attitudes to authority conditioned by our earliest relationships, and perhaps beyond that by hereditary factors. In addition to whatever these may be in my own case I dislike reverence for leaders for the organic relationship it bears to the hierarchic principle, belief in privilege and ultimately to authoritarianism and the pernicious faith that the validity of an utterance is determined by its source; above all for the practical consequences of these assumptions. Conversely I like irreverence both in itself and for its organic relationship to egalitarianism and rationality, and the practical consequences of these. But I wish all Socialists could be irreverent and critical without impugning the personal integrity of their leaders – whom they themselves elect, after all.

(3) People who want to revenge themselves on society find their natural home in the Communist Party rather than the Labour Party. I think the chief reason why there are disproportionately high numbers of Jews, ex-immigrants, Negroes and *declassés* among the Communists in Britain is simply this: that it is natural for people to feel antagonistic towards a society which in any way discriminates against them. There is an overspill of people with feelings of this sort into the Labour Party, people who feel that society has given them a raw deal and want to get their own back. They devote themselves almost entirely to 'attacking existing society', and no doubt some of them do some good. But their purposes are destructive, and hence their criticism tends to be the same; also the unremitting hostility that characterizes their behaviour and utterances tends to alienate reasonable people.

(*4*) Anxiety is another trait which normally drives people into parties other than the Labour Party – either into the Conservative Party, where they can fiercely resist any attempt to upset the *status quo*, or into the Communist Party with its belief in the inevitability of cataclysm. But again some people dominated by this trait are in the Labour Party. They tend to insist on the imminence of catastrophe, usually in the form of war or slump. In 1951 they genuinely believed that if the Conservatives won the General Election there would be world war, and in 1955 that there would be mass-unemployment. Some, like Thomas Balogh, have been prophesying an American slump every year since I can remember. At every annual conference they get up and say that our prosperity cannot possibly last, the bubble is bound to burst. For such people the Campaign for Nuclear Disarmament is ideal.

(*5*) The guilty, alas, find their perfect home in the Labour Party. In the days of mass poverty, guilt did more to make middle-class Socialists than any other emotion. It is common to find Socialists automatically laying blame on groups to which they themselves belong: in any conflict between Britain and another country Britain is always in the wrong; in any conflict between blacks and whites the blacks are always in the right. Even when someone else's behaviour is utterly indefensible the blame is still somehow ours. Even the evils of Communism are 'our fault'. Here is a typical expression of this view:

'That was how matters stood in Eastern Europe as late as the end of 1946. There seemed every prospect that the social revolution would be an altogether more humane and civilized affair than in the desperate conditions of Soviet Russia, bringing Social revolution to 17th century and primitive peoples and battling for its life against Allied intervention, and that democracy and political freedom would soon spread to countries where they had never been known before, in a new and more hopeful social context.

'But by 1948 Anglo-American intervention had changed all that. Under the impact of the growing hostility and menace from the West the more intransigent elements in the Communist and Socialist parties got the upper hand and were provided with all too plausible reasons for relying on the Secret Police and getting tough with political opponents. The threatened régimes drew together and mounted guard against the enemy without the gates and his real or suspected allies or agents within.'[1]

This has been the standard Socialist apologia for Communist terror ever since 1917. To the general advantage of laying guilt on ourselves it adds the more specialized advantage of avoiding hostility to Communism. It was maintained through collectivization, through the purges, through the terror, through the Nazi-Soviet pact, through the Russo-Finnish war – the whole unending bloodbath was due to nothing but our own unfriendliness. The attitude continues. Even Bertrand Russell adopted it in an argument I had with him in December 1958. Every time its inapplicability to the facts reaches another climax, pained bewilderment sets in all over again – the classic case of this in recent years being Hungary. 'To all western Socialists at least, the Russian action is indefensible and unforgivable. It is also very nearly incomprehensible. Despite the emergence of some counter-revolutionary elements, there was never any real danger that the Hungarian revolt would end in the restoration of the Horthyite Fascists, or that the 'western Imperialists' would move to create a military base in Hungary.' So said the *New Statesman* on 10 November 1956, for all the world as if the excuses Communists had always given for butchering opponents had been the actual reasons. At all costs the belief must be maintained that Communism is fundamentally a good thing; so when crimes are committed in circumstances such that they cannot possibly be our own fault then this is represented as a lapse from normal Communist standards – a failure of nerve or self-confidence. For instance when the Russians announced their killing of Imre Nagy (the Prime Minister of Hungary during the revolt who took refuge in the Yugoslav Embassy in Budapest – the Russians, it will be remembered, gave him and three colleagues a safe-conduct pass to come out and then arrested them when they emerged and murdered them) Basil Davison wrote in the *Daily Herald*) 18 June 1958): 'They[2] will note that these executions took place in the 41st year of the Russian Revolution. The Soviet Union had become the second strongest power in the world. At last it seemed to be throwing off the constraints and growing pains of enforced isolation. **They will note these executions as a sudden failure of nerve and self-confidence.** They will note that they took place at a time when Hungary was under

1. Konni Zilliacus: *I Choose Peace*, p. 399.

2. This refers to 'our children'. The heavy type later in the quotation is in the original.

no conceivable threat from outside and when the Soviet leaders were talking more and more of the need for co-existence.'

The Socialist conscience, when not kept under control, can assist in fundamental reversals of the truth and can be deadly dangerous. The opposite Conservative vice of complacency, of assuming that you or your country or your colour are always right and others wrong, does even greater damage, and must not be rebounded into. There is a need for conscience in politics, but conscience is neither a fact-finder nor a judge of truth, and in any case its workings should no more be exempted from criticism than anything else.

(6) By 'aestheticism' I mean the pursuit in politics of the kind of pleasure yielded by the formal qualities of good art or the solution of problems. This was attacked before the war by Orwell in *The Road to Wigan Pier* (Chapter XI): 'The underlying motive of many Socialists, I believe, is simply a hypertrophied sense of order.' This vice is found only among intellectuals, but among them it is quite common. One can easily understand the appeal to the intellectual of the ordered society – or rather the contemplation of an ordered society. It is aesthetically satisfying, and furthermore planning gives the intellectual a sense of power. 'But here I must protest. I do not believe that human lives may be made the means for satisfying an artist's desire for self-expression. We must demand, rather, that every man should be given, if he wishes, the right to model his life himself, as far as this does not interfere too much with others. Much as I may sympathize with the aesthetic impulse, I suggest that the artist might seek expression in another material. Politics, I demand, must uphold equalitarian and individualistic principles; dreams of beauty have to submit to the necessity of helping men in distress, and men who suffer injustice; and to the necessity of constructing institutions to serve such purposes.'[1] Furthermore the whole aesthetic approach rests on the pre-scientific assumption that society is perfectible, and like every political approach based on this superstition it is authoritarian.

(7) This brings me to the role of immaturity in Left-wing politics. Freud long ago taught us that growing involves building a workable compromise between the self and the environment. 'Since the individual can neither extirpate his instincts nor wholly reject the demands of society, his character expresses the way in which he

1. Karl Popper: *The Open Society and Its Enemies*, Vol. I, p. 165.

organizes and appeases the conflict between the two.'[1] The notion that conflict is avoidable, that it is possible for us to have all our own way, is a childish wish that we grow out of into the mature realization that living involves keeping a dynamic balance among conflicting forces. There is a direct analogy here between personal and political maturity. Every society will always contain not merely differences of opinion about social policy but direct clashes of interest, and broadly speaking these can only be settled by either the use of force or compromise. The use of force, which admittedly may result in someone getting all his own way, is the primitive method: compromise, which results in no one getting all his own way, is the mature or civilized method. Compromise as a permanent feature of the way in which political differences are settled is absolutely essential to democratic government, to free institutions, to any form of society which is not to rest on the use of violence – and hence essential to civilization itself. But to some Socialists this realisation is alien. Like children and adolescents, they believe that society can and should be shaped wholly to their demands. Responsibility would cure them of this illusion, but being immature they have no taste for it. To them compromise is wrong *in itself*, a 'sell-out', cheating them of the ends they think attainable and desirable. Socialists who compromise are not Socialists at all: they are traitors in league with the other side. Along with this hostility to actual democratic politics, and this belief in the attainability of absolute aims, goes the belief in panaceas which will bring about the latter without any need for the former. 'If only x were done everything would come right.' For most of Socialism's history 'x' has been public ownership of the means of production. For many people now it is unilateral nuclear disarmament. For quite a number it is both: the former to solve all domestic problems, the latter to solve all international problems. There is no logical connection between a belief that the Labour Party's domestic aims should be formulated exclusively in terms of public ownership and a belief in the efficacy of unilateral nuclear disarmament, but there is this *psychological* connection, and that is why the two beliefs are commonly held by the same people.

(*8*) Not all such people are prigs, but some are – the conviction that one has inside knowledge of Absolute Truth tends to make one so. But priggishness is usually found among Socialists for other reasons. Over the years the organizers of local Labour Parties have tended to

1. Philip Rieff: *Freud: The Mind of the Moralist*, p. 28.

be energetic working-class people of above-average intelligence who, unlike most of the people among whom they lived and worked, took an interest in affairs beyond their daily lives, kept up with the news, read books. With a liking for self-education that commonly amounted to a passion they were sensitive to the indifference and ignorance of the people round them and it was not unnatural for them to become exasperated with their indolence, their narrowness and self-absorption. 'Of course they don't understand . . .' – how many times have I heard local activists begin a sentence with those words? I have a lot of sympathy for such people. They are normally victims of our class-structure who have not been educated up to their abilities, and they realize, though the realization is not always fully conscious, that they are capable of an altogether richer, more intelligent, more responsible life than the one they have and than most of the people round them seem able to imagine. Until the last few years our society has been such that the only way a working-class boy of outstanding gifts and no education could fulfil himself without sycophancy was through the working-class movement – either the trade unions, like Ernest Bevin, or the Labour Party, like Herbert Morrison and Aneurin Bevan – and this has been so at all levels of the movement. Nevertheless the urge that many of these key party workers have to demonstrate superior understanding remains a vice. Of course it is not only working-class Socialists who can be priggish: on the contrary, the vice is found at its worst among middle-class intellectuals. These also get a kick out of despising the people among whom they live, and tend to be less unsure of their own cleverness. But all kinds of Socialists are prone to consider themselves morally superior *by virtue of being Socialists*: Mrs Barbara Castle, when chairman of the Labour Party, explained that we lost the General Election of 1959 because 'our ethical reach was beyond the mental grasp of the average person'. Even Socialist women can be priggish *vis-à-vis* other women – Mrs Renée Short said to the Labour Party Conference at Blackpool in 1959: 'Women in this country – I am sorry to have to say – are by and large, *except those in the Labour Party*, politically illiterate.'

(*9*) To large numbers of the Socialists motivated by these drives that have no necessary connection with politics Socialism is a religion-substitute. They even commonly talk of Socialism in religious terms: 'our Socialist faith', 'the gospel of Socialism', 'preach', 'crusade', 'convert', 'sacrosanct', 'desecrate', 'zeal', are words heard over and over again in Socialist speeches. Aneurin Bevan's most quoted phrase

– 'the language of priorities is the religion of Socialism'[1] – takes for granted, as it were, that Socialism *is* a religion. Socialist gatherings have a lot of the characteristics of religious gatherings: things are often discussed in the same sort of terms; there is often the same sort of fellowship and fervour – and the same sort of self-righteousness. People not only sing 'The Red Flag' like a hymn, they stand to sing it, and take their hats off. My objections to this kind of thing are many, but one of them is the same as my objection to petitions, processions and protests: emotional outburst is often salutary, but if it is allowed to become a habitual part of one's approach to politics it is destructive of good judgement. When the fervent singing starts and faces are shining with uplift, then is the time to subject assumptions to ruthless analysis.

The pre-scientific outlook – in everything, not only in politics – has a great hold on people's minds, and there are many reasons for this. Habits of thought which have characterized human beings since the beginning cannot be eliminated in a few generations. Some of them appeal to basic instincts, which is no doubt why they have been so long-lived and all-pervading and why they come naturally to children. For instance they assuage fear of the unknown. If you accept some theoretical system that explains everything you can never be in serious ignorance or perplexity. Whatever happens you can explain it – and what is more, whatever happens you have a guide to action. Another aspect of the unknown that you cease to fear is the future – which loses most of its terrors when it is 'known', and loses all of them when you want what you know it must bring. Thus belief in the inevitability of Socialism, or of a classless society, or even merely of progress, fulfils the same deep need as belief in heaven or a life after death. These are some of the reasons why people so often talk of 'clinging to their faith' in times of adversity: it meets their compulsive desire for security, for 'something to hold on to', as they themselves often put it. It gives life a pattern and a purpose, it buoys them up, it expands the area of certainty and confidence in their lives and diminishes the area of darkness and doubt, and above all it assures them a happy issue out of all their afflictions. The only real problem becomes that of relating the fixed faith to the changing facts.

1. This exhibits the same characteristic mixture of brilliance and muddle as the quotations on page 29. How can a language be a religion? Yet it was this phrase that introduced the fruitful concept of 'priorities' into the common currency of Socialist thought in England.

Those of the faithful who show ingenuity at this will make great reputations for themselves and often acquire positions of power. As the delegate from Bury and Radcliffe at the 1959 Conference said: 'Mr Gaitskell criticized philosophies and doctrinaire policies – but where would Morgan Phillips, Dick Crossman, Nye Bevan and many more be without these doctrinaire policies? I feel that doctrinaire philosophy has served these men more than anything, because of their understanding of it. And I feel that there is a basic failing in our movement on doctrinaire policies.' These feelings of course are much stronger in Communist parties and the Catholic Church, but many Socialists likewise cling to a theological conception of Socialism because it is a stable reference point in the flux of political events, the huge, ever-changing complexities of the modern world in which many of them would feel lost and overwhelmed if they had to find their own bearings and make their own way. It gives them a sense of security and relieves them of responsibility. Most people are frightened of responsibility – I believe this is why most people fear rationality. I am reminded of Bernard Shaw's maxim for revolutionists:[1] 'Liberty means responsibility. That is why most men dread it.' Psychologists agree in explaining the ease with which not only individuals but whole populations can embrace totalitarian faiths partly in these terms – the best-known book by a psychoanalyst about politics is called *The Fear of Freedom*.[2] Quite apart from politics, all children and most adults like being told what to do, or (what amounts to the same thing) having a routine mapped out for them, because they get frightened if they have to accept unlimited responsibility for themselves. And a faith is like a routine: once you have accepted it you simply follow it, and the burden of decision is lifted from your shoulders.

Socialists to whom Socialism is a religion are liable to indulge in the same vices as are traditionally associated with religion. They are liable to regard all people who are not of the faith as infidels with whom the only permissible relationship is holy war; to regard all who accept the name of the faith but disagree with them personally as schismatics and heretics; to reject any questioning of the traditional faith as blasphemous; and to put all this intolerance of thought and feeling into practice. Like the Church throughout its history, they hate critical rationality when applied to what they regard as their province, and even more when applied to themselves. Unfortunately

1. Appended to *Man and Superman*.
2. By Erich Fromm.

E*

most of them seem to have such a strong need for religion that they can give up their faith only in exchange for another. Nor do they appreciate the poverty of this condition, but rather sneer at the notion of living without superstition and dogma as unworthily materialistic or opportunist. Between religious Socialists and rational Socialists there is a gulf which seems at times unbridgeable. The former are usually impervious to argument, responding only when their prejudices are stimulated. The passion and intensity with which they approach politics grow from roots so deep in their personality that no consideration of politics alone can get down to them.

What I have said in this section will give a misleading impression unless I add a number of riders.

First, the *proportion* of Socialists to whom it refers is low. The great majority of people vote in accordance with what they conceive to be their material interests. This is simply a fact, statistically demonstrable. Emotional factors are never wholly absent – for instance in all classes a higher proportion of women vote Conservative than men, presumably because they have a stronger conscious desire for stability, and hence fear of change, and because they do not have the same trade-union loyalties – but in most people the influence of emotion is marginal. This fact, or rather the ignoring of it, invalidates a lot of the 'scientific' study that has been done on the psychology of political attitudes. For instance Eysenck's work, though interesting, tends to ignore it, and can itself to that extent be ignored.[1] On the other hand the people whose political attitudes are shaped by factors independent of their own material interests tend to think or feel about politics – in other words they are people to whom politics is in some way personally important. It is to this minority, but only to this minority, that Eysenck's work applies. But most of the people who take an active interest in politics come under this heading; so although they are a tiny minority of the population at large they form a huge proportion of M.P.s and candidates, political journalists, local activists and so on.

My second point follows on from this. It will be clear that I am not accusing opposition-minded Socialists of being alone in being motivated by psycho-emotional needs, since this applies to everyone active

1. Eysenck's main work in this field is *The Psychology of Politics*. After my own brief survey of the more unpleasant Socialist attitudes it might be interesting to quote Eysenck's summary of typical Conservative attitudes: 'As we shall

in politics. I do not even accuse them of being alone in exhibiting neurotic patterns of behaviour in politics – rigidity seems as common on the 'Right' of the Labour Party as hysteria is on the 'Left' – while the psycho-emotional basis of Conservatism can throw up worse aberrations than any I have written about (and as for totalitarian beliefs in a free country, these are an exclusively neurotic manifestation). What I accuse opposition-minded Socialists of is being, alone among Socialists, motivated by *destructive* urges. By no means all the Socialists who are politically active are impelled by these unadmirable emotions. There are many benevolent and constructive people among them – gifted organizers, practising Christians, genuine philanthropists, natural egalitarians, people who enjoy helping others or solving social problems, or initiating worthwhile change.

Thirdly, as I said at the very beginning of this book,[1] the motives of people in politics may be psychologically or biographically interesting but they are not politically important. The proof of the pudding is in the eating. What matters is what people do or advocate, and the way they go about this, and the consequences of their going about it; not why they go about it. This is why, in the case of each destructive emotion I have dealt with, I have written of its undesirable *consequences*. The Labour Party does not contain more cranks than the Conservative Party, nor are its cranks nastier, but the trouble is they do more damage. *The Guardian* said precisely this in its leading article on 9 October 1961: 'The floggers and hangers, the Suez group, and the Salisbury supporters are more unlovely than the Marxists, neutralists, and unilateralists in the Labour Party. Numerically, too, they are probably at least as large a proportion of the party. But they count for less, both in the pressure they can bring on party leaders and in their effect on the public.'

---

see later, a person who is anti-Semitic will also tend to be religious, in favour of flogging and the death penalty, hold strict views on the upbringing of children, be patriotic, and ethnocentric. In other words, attitudes themselves are correlated and give rise to what we might call super-attitudes or ideologies. A particular ideology which is defined by the various beliefs outlined above would be the Conservative ideology; as will be shown later, all the views mentioned above tend to be held more frequently by Conservatives than by Liberals and Socialists . . .' (page 113).

1. Chapter 1, section I, p. 22.

V

Opposition-mindedness is the curse of left-wing politics, but it is a curse that cannot easily be removed. The fact that a man is active on the Left is an indication that he is seriously dissatisfied with existing society and wants it radically changed, so it is scarcely surprising if he to some extent dissociates himself from it and does not want to accept responsibility for it. Radical governments have a curious relationship to the societies they run: they are responsible for them yet do not approve of them. However quickly they implement changes they must still run the country while the changes are taking effect. And the limited nature of material and human resources means that they cannot tackle everything at once; so they cannot avoid drawing up a list of priorities, neglecting some problems in order to cope with others, so that there will be social evils of which they are aware but which they are quite deliberately not removing – a decision which can cause bewilderment to the politically unrealistic, and makes the government vulnerable to attack from supporters as well as opponents.

Idealists, seeing that the attainment of power is followed, as it must always be, by the compromise of some of their ideals, conclude that power has corrupted their leaders, who now no longer really want what they have always said they wanted. For this reason many regard power as an evil to be avoided – quite a few Socialists in their heart of hearts want the Labour Government never to be in power. Many of them say so. Only recently at a Labour rally, when a speaker said there was nothing wrong with the Labour Party's wanting power, the woman behind me, an enthusiastic Labour Party member, shouted: 'Oh yes there is!' Many such people spoke at the Annual Conference held at Blackpool in 1959 after Labour's third General Election defeat in succession – for instance the Candidate for Ormskirk: 'Let us show at this Conference that we are basically a moral party who believe in truth and believe in Socialism. If we do that it does not matter whether we become the Government in 1964 – or 1974 – or 1984.' The answer came from Denis Healey in the most powerful five-minute speech I have heard at a Labour Party Conference.

'. . . There are far too many people who have spoken from this rostrum in these last two days who seem to think it is all right to do without votes. Some have even said so: it is better to lose elections, they say, than to win them, so long as we know we are fighting on the Socialist policy. And they seem to face with equanimity the idea of staying in Opposition – an Opposition that gets smaller and smaller at every election.

'If they want to luxuriate complacently in moral righteousness in Opposition they can do it – but who is going to pay the price for their complacency? You can take the view that it is better to give up half a loaf if you cannot get the whole loaf – but the point is that it is not we who are giving up the half loaf. It is the people whom we are trying to help, in the country and in the world – they are the people who suffer if we lose elections. In Britain it is the un-employed and old-age pensioners; and outside Britain there are thousands and millions of people in Asia and Africa who des-perately need a Labour Government in this country to help them. If you take the view that it is all right to stay in Opposition as long as your Socialist heart is pure, *you'll* be all right Jack. You'll have your TV set, your motor-car and your summer holidays on the Continent – and still keep your Socialist soul intact. The people who pay the price for your sense of moral satisfaction are the Africans – hundreds of thousands, millions, of them – being slowly forced into racial slavery; the Indians and the Indonesians dying of starvation.

'If you are prepared for them to pay the price of your sense of moral superiority, all right. But don't come to this Conference and say that because of that you are better Socialists than those who want to get a Labour Government in Britain. We are not just a debating society. We are not just a Socialist Sunday School. We are a great movement that wants to help real people living on this earth at the present time. We shall never be able to help them unless we get power. . . .'

The Labour Party exists in order to change society, and to do that it must become the government. This means taking on responsibility for society *as it is* and starting from there. Wherever you want to go you have to start from where you are. A Labour Government could not, for example, put into instant operation a programme for educa-tion that required three times as many teachers as there are. The best education system you can get is not the best you are able to think of but the best you are able to turn the one you have got into. For you do not begin with what you would like: you begin with what you have got. This limits what you can do. But the limitation is entirely unavoidable. If instead you try to start with a blueprint, an imagined society or system instead of the one you have, you cannot possibly actualize it. This is the major reason for all the lying that characterizes totalitarian régimes. (See again the quotation from *Dr Zhivago* on page 50.)

To 'help real people living on this earth at the present time' is a task for which a love of life, a love of people and of the world, is almost indispensable. At least it is important to be able to distinguish in broad outline what is good in human affairs from what is bad. If British Socialists developed this faculty a little more they would be less opposition-minded, more eager to take over the reins of society and more in sympathy with ordinary people. For we in Britain are lucky: we live in one of the few liberal democracies. These are the only societies ever to have given literacy, high living standards and political freedom to most of their members, and for this reason they are the most admirable societies that have ever existed.But make that statement to a Socialist or a Socialist audience and the chain of reaction will be shock, incredulity and dissent. I know – I have done it. But then challenge them to name a single other society that is or ever has been preferable, and there will be an interminable silence, which I should advise speakers to allow to deepen. Most Socialists are stunned at being made to face this. They are so used to criticizing our society, attacking its faults, deriding its absurdities, that they have become alien to the realization that it is the best form of society there has ever been. Yet this is, to put it mildly, a pretty important thing to get in proper perspective. Of course it would be ridiculous to make this a reason for conservatism – such an attitude would put an end to all development of everything: 'This anaesthetic (machine, institution, way of doing things, etc.) is the best yet, so let's resist all further development and keep it unchanged for ever.' Such an attitude is so obviously absurd that any Socialist who refused to acknowledge the unprecedented merits of the liberal democracies out of fear of lending support to it would be afraid of a shadow. It is perfectly consistent both to assert that Britain, along with America, Scandinavia and a few other countries, represents the best form of society yet achieved by man, and at the same time to assert that her government of some of her colonies is tyrannical, her aid to backward countries inadequate,

her class structure odious, her education system in need of reconstruction from top to bottom, almost everything – industry, the arts,
medicine, transport, social welfare – in need of a vigorous infusion of
public enterprise, and the whole population in need of waking up.

There are so many major things wrong with our society in Britain
that it is trebly grotesque to see Socialists disliking it for its affluence:
grotesque because all opposition to the abolition of poverty is
grotesque; doubly grotesque because the traditional purpose of
Socialism – the very reason it came into existence – was to abolish the
poverty in which most people lived; and trebly grotesque because
there is so much else that really does cry out for opposition. When
Aneurin Bevan said with such passion and emphasis at the 1959
Annual Conference: 'This so-called affluent society is an ugly society
still. It is a *vulgar* society. It is a *meretricious* society' . . . and then
later in his speech '. . . it is a vulgar society of which no decent person
could be proud', he was revealing a total lack of historical sense, and
betraying much of what he had stood for throughout his life. If the
same rise in living standards had taken place under a Labour Government he would have vaunted it with golden tongue. Yet his sentiments
are the clichés of contemporary Socialism. Socialists have stopped
thinking of most people as poor and come to think of them as
vulgar. Perhaps this reflects the need, which I referred to a few pages
back, to feel superior to others. It certainly reflects an unforgiving
resentment of the fact that the electorate declines to return Labour to
power. But it is a myth to suppose, as many Socialists do suppose,
that this is because they have been seduced by material affluence: far
fewer people voted Labour in any election before the Second World
War, when most people were poor, than have voted Labour at every
election since. As Aneurin Bevan pointed out in the speech I just
quoted: 'Even the unemployed voted against us. Even in the areas
where there was as much as 20 per cent and 30 per cent of unemployment we lost seats.' But whatever the reasons may be it has become
strikingly common for Socialists to speak *patronisingly* of ordinary
people. A few hours before this speech of Aneurin Bevan's, another
M.P., John Baird, said: 'Do we go to the electorate, with their hire-
purchase television sets and their prosperity based on overtime, or
do we try to educate the electorate to come to us and to Socialism?'
It is seldom working-class Socialists who talk like this. It is
usually Socialists who are themselves better off than the people
whose material aspirations they despise. John Baird has probably

paid for his television set, and his prosperity is not based on overtime. Aneurin Bevan enjoyed an income of several thousand pounds a year, world-wide travel, a flat in London and a farm in the country; and he was a convivial man who loved good food and expensive drink. I do not begrudge him any of these things – if anyone deserved them he did, and if it comes to that I would enjoy them myself – but it ill becomes someone in that position to despise the humbler material pleasures of ordinary people. If a man works overtime to give his wife a holiday abroad, or if they buy a television set on hire purchase, this is not a mark of inferior morality, nor do they need educating to go to John Baird.

I have written earlier of Marxism as one element I strongly dislike in the Socialist tradition: another is puritanism. The non-conformist churches, and Methodism in particular, have vastly enriched British Socialism, but they have also acted as carriers of puritanism and infested the Labour Party with it. Socialists include a disproportionately high number of people who equate the world and the flesh with the devil – sabbatarians, vegetarians, teetotallers – people who tint with grey everything they touch. They have every right to order their own lives as they wish, but they have no right to order the lives of others, and their influence on legislation should therefore be resisted. Their lamentation over the rise of living standards, though it cannot be stopped, does the Labour Party great harm. And their opposition to social reform acts as a dead weight of conservatism in a progressive party. I agree wholeheartedly with Anthony Crosland when he says,[1] under the heading *Liberty and Gaiety in Private Life: the Need for a Reaction against the Fabian Tradition:*

'Much could be done to make Britain a more colourful and civilized country to live in. We need not only higher exports and old-age pensions, but more open-air cafés, brighter and gayer streets at night, later closing-hours for public houses, more local repertory theatres, better and more hospitable hoteliers and restaurateurs, brighter and cleaner eating-houses, more riverside cafés, more pleasure-gardens on the Battersea model, more murals and pictures in public places, better designs for furniture and pottery and women's clothes, statues in the centre of new housing-estates, better-designed street-lamps and telephone kiosks, and so on *ad infinitum*. The enemy in all this will often be in unexpected guise; it is not only dark Satanic things and people that now bar the road to the New Jerusalem, but also, if not

1. *The Future of Socialism*, p. 521.

mainly, hygienic, respectable, virtuous things and people, lacking only in grace and gaiety.'

A lot of the things Socialists call 'evils' and ascribe to 'Capitalism' are not products of Capitalism and not in my opinion evils. I am thinking particularly of popular entertainment. After the 1961 Annual Conference the young delegate from Coatbridge and Airdrie, Tom Clarke, began a report in *New Advance – The Journal of the Young Socialists* with the words: 'Blackpool was an appropriate place to hold our Conference. For here – with its bingo stalls and amusement centres – was the very expression of capitalism which we had come to challenge.' Attitudes like this are common among Socialists and usually embrace television (but not radio), the cinema (but not the theatre), pop music, Conservative newspapers and, above all, advertising. Such attitudes, however one may feel about them – and I abominate them – are factually in error. For advertising, to take the biggest of the bogies, is not a specific product of Capitalism: its purpose is to stimulate consumer demand, and the need to do this is felt in every society *once it reaches a certain level of economic development*. There used to be little or no advertising in Communist countries, but this was because the last thing their governments wanted to do was to stimulate the demand for consumer goods – as I pointed out on pp. 64–65 the basic economic function of Communism is to repress this demand in the interests of capital accumulation. But when the point is reached at which a particular industry can expand only, or expand faster, if a market is created, then the government at once begins to advertise. And once it begins to advertise it seeks the most effective forms of advertisement – and before long it is exploiting bathing beauties, strip cartoons and all the rest. On successive visits to a Communist country I have seen these developments take place with great speed: the Yugoslav mass-media seemed to me to be transformed between the summer of 1960 and the summer of 1961, and on the second of those two visits I found Yugoslav television like an inferior copy of British Commercial Television, and Yugoslav newspapers not only looking like the magazine sections of American newspapers, with their funnies, pin-up girls and the rest, but syndicating actual American features like Ripley's *Believe It Or Not*. Michael Shanks, author of *The Stagnant Society*, brought similar impressions back from a visit to Bulgaria in 1959[1]: 'I was impressed, as any Western visitor must be, by the surface similarities between Western

1. *The Stagnant Society*, pp. 13–14.

and Soviet society. The average better-off citizen of a socialist country is as keenly interested in keeping up with the Joneses and increasing his or her share of the currently fashionable gadgets as we are in the West. There, as here, we tend to measure out our lives in washing machines and TV sets. . . . Tastes in dance music are depressingly similar, and the bronzed bodies of holiday-makers on Black Sea beaches could as easily belong to the bourgeoisie of Western Europe as they do in fact belong to the *nouveau-riche* factory managers and intellectuals of East Germany, Czechoslovakia, and Russia. . . . To compete with the West in consumer goods the Soviet world must copy Western techniques – not only of production but also of salesmanship, design, and advertising.'

The fact is that this is the way the whole world is going. America is in the van, with a longer lead than most people who have not been there can even visualize (consumption per head in America is more than twice what it is in Britain) and all the other countries of the world are scrambling along behind, hoping to catch up. The Marxist prophecy about Capitalist societies developing into Communist societies is the opposite of what is happening: Communist societies are developing more and more to be like Capitalist societies. America shows to Russia the image of its own future. But the old labels such as 'Left' versus 'Right', 'Socialism' versus 'Capitalism' and the rest blind many Socialists to the actual historical development of the world. They still think in terms of economic antitheses, with the 'Left' and the 'Right' going in opposite directions and yet the 'Left' being somehow more advanced than the 'Right', whereas in fact there is one general course of economic development common to all existing societies, and the 'Right' is decades in advance of the 'Left'.

It is certainly open to Socialists to dislike the way the world is developing, but it is not open to them to attribute these developments to 'Capitalism'. J. B. Priestley has coined the term 'Admass' for the culture based on a mass market for consumer goods, with advertising therefore playing a crucial role, and he loathes it, but he realizes that it is a world phenomenon and not a product of Capitalism. Speaking for myself, I quite like it in many ways. And to those Socialists who do not I would point out that most people do – most people, whether in Britain, Russia, Africa or anywhere else, *like* popular newspapers with pin-up girls and funnies, *like* dance music, bright lights, vulgar entertainments such as 'bingo stalls and amusement centres', *like* television sets, refrigerators, washing machines, cars and so on – and if they have not got them, want them. And if they want them, why should they not have them? I don't think I have ever been in a bingo stall, but it has never entered my head to resent their existence, or object to the people who enjoy them enjoying them. To regard them as a social evil is ludicrous. This puritan strain in Socialism, of hostility to popular enjoyment, is immoral in itself, because it is anti-libertarian; it is also politically costly, because it propagates the image of Socialists as killjoys. If most people perfer boogie-woogie to Beethoven that is their business. The Socialist's job is to see that they are given the choice, not to see that they have only what Socialists think is good for them.

CHAPTER EIGHT

The Conservatism of the Left

MOST left-wing institutions in Britain are noted for their conservatism. Even the major ones – the Trade Unions, the Co-operative Movement the Labour Party itself – have a positive and deserved reputation for being backward-looking.

I

The whole structure of the trade unions in Britain is archaic. They have developed out of the craft unions of the nineteenth century, with the result that they are largely organizations of people in the same trade and not organizations of people in the same industry. Most large factories contain members of several different unions – Electrical Trades Union, Amalgamated Engineering Union, Transport and General Workers' Union and so on – so that 'in a typical motor-car factory there may be anything up to three dozen different trade unions represented'.[1] No one union is concerned with the running of the factory as such: each is concerned only with the sectional interests of certain workers within it. This leaves the overall running firmly in the hands of a management whose employees do not confront it as an organized body. The unions administer themselves on a *geographical* basis, and they bargain with employers on a national level. Thus differentials within each factory are not decided by the workers in that factory, nor do they relate to the actual differences between the jobs being done there: they are determined by the relative bargaining strengths and skills of myriad union leaders representing different groups of workers at a national level, negotiating blanket agreements that operate all over the country regardless of local conditions, and sometimes not very well related to the conditions of other workers in the same factories, who of course are represented by other unions with other leaders. Meanwhile within the factories themselves each little

1. Michael Shanks: *The Stagnant Society*, p. 82.

148

group of craftsmen on the shop floor has its own spokesman, the shop steward, who protects their day-to-day interests and voices their complaints, but speaks for only his group, and in matters not dealt with at national level, and has no major bargaining power. 'A shop steward of a craft union is likely, in any matter involving changes in industrial methods, to be a reactionary force. He can hardly avoid being so on occasion, since his sole task, after all, is to seek the comfort and advantage of a particular group of men bound together by a fairly narrow interest. He is not supposed to look beyond this. The union official looking at the plant as a whole [would be] more likely to accept the fact that a certain amount of change and discomfort at one spot may be unavoidable in the interests of the efficiency of the works as a whole, and therefore of its capacity to pay high wages.'[1] One of the inevitable results of this system is an incessant conflict of interests between different unions engaged in the same industry. Some of the outstanding industrial disputes of recent years in Britain have been not between union and employer but between union and union.

The whole system from top to bottom is inappropriate to modern industry and to the interests of the workers. Contrast it with the organization of American unions in those key manufacturing industries that set the wage pattern for the United States. These are organizations of people in the same industry, which administer themselves on a factory basis, and negotiate with employers separately. The workers in each factory confront management as a single organized body. Not only are they able to insist on determining their own internal affairs, such as differentials and promotions, they also demand a major voice in the overall running of the business. And the unions as a whole (as distinct from their branches in each factory) are able to get maximum wage-rates by what they call 'key bargaining', which means picking on the most advantageous firm to get concessions out of, and then forcing the other employers in the same industry to follow suit. 'In negotiating with the leading company in a particular industry, the union is dealing with the concern that is generally in the soundest economic position – i.e. most able to accede to the bargaining demands of the union. In multi-employer negotiations, on the other hand, the ability of the group to meet union demands is likely to be limited by the ability of the most marginal producer in the group to meet such demands.' That is how a number

1. Andrew Shonfield: *British Economic Policy Since the War* (Revised Edition 1959), p. 22.

of American union officials describe the strength of their position.[1] And the justification for it: 'To accept lower wages or less adequate benefits because a company is not as profitable or efficient as its competitors is, in effect, to subsidize managerial inefficiency out of the welfare of the workers and their families.' And its effect on the rest of the working community: 'It is generally accepted . . . that any settlement made with a major corporation in the auto or steel industries in the United States will soon be reflected in varying degree throughout all organized industries and, to a lesser extent, even in unorganized companies and industries.'

As if we were still in the nineteenth century the British unions are oriented almost entirely towards protecting sectional interests. They do not regard the management of industry as part of their job: their attitude is oppositional and defensive. So opposition-minded are they that when the Labour Government nationalized most of the country's basic industries the unions refused its offer of representation on the boards. The they-us mentality – the notion that there are 'two sides of industry', with the corollary that you cannot be on both – goes to their very roots. This was plainly expressed at the Labour Party's 1957 Annual Conference by the delegate from South Coventry, a member of the Transport and General Workers' Union, in opposition to the plan to invest public money in private industry: 'We feel if the Labour Party took us over lock, stock and barrel, at least we would get a fair deal, because we would be dealing with our own people. For example, with regard to the share buying, when we had the big disputes in Coventry and in Briggs our people, like Bill Carron and Frank Cousins, were down there fighting in their interests. The position would be completely reversed if we pursued this policy and we were a 40% shareholder as against 58% or 59%. They would have to support the Capitalists against us.' This general attitude on the part of trade unions debilitates them in many ways. Even in their own internal organization they are class-conscious and anti-intellectual (the speaker quoted above had earlier commended a resolution on the ground that 'even stupid people like me can understand it') and this means in practice that they dislike middle-class people and university graduates. In modern educational conditions this in turn means that fewer and fewer people of first-class talent are becoming union officials. In any case the unions refuse to pay their officials com-

1. In an article quoted by Andrew Shonfield in *British Economic Policy Since the War* (Revised Edition 1959), p. 20.

petitively with the company executives with whom they are supposed to deal on equal terms. The consequence of all this is that union officials are almost always of lower calibre than their opposite numbers in management, and this only strengthens their attitudes of defensiveness and suspicion, their secret sense of the superiority of 'them'.

These class-war attitudes had a certain validity when the unions' chief aim was to wring out of employers a larger share of the profits of industry in the form of wages. But they are still thinking in these terms after taxation and the equalization of personal incomes have brought us to the point where no significant increase in workers' incomes can come from further redistribution.[1] The only way now is to increase the size of the national income itself – and this requires a revolutionary change of outlook on the part of the unions which has not yet been forthcoming. It no longer makes sense for them to leave all the decisions affecting economic growth to management: modern conditions demand that they participate in the direction of industry themselves. As Andrew Shonfield says (op. cit.): 'The United Automobile Workers or the United Steel Workers of America . . . start their negotiations with the explicit demand on the employers that they must do whatever is necessary – by way of investment or improvements in organization – to increase output per man by a substantial annual amount in the two or three years ahead during which the wage contract is to run. They now take the adjustments for *future* productivity just as much for granted as the automatic adjustments to current changes on the cost of living sliding scale. But of course, in making these technological demands on their employers, they have to be ready to accept radical alterations in plant and methods, and the dismissal of workers, if these become redundant as a result of improved methods of output. They try to screw as much money as they can out of the employers for the people who lose their jobs; but they do not insist on a process of dilution of labour which will keep them in work at their old jobs. They insist on the opposite. Here is something which it hurts the average militant trade unionist in Britain even to contemplate. . . . It is, for example, scarcely conceivable that an American union should refuse, as a matter of principle, to include in its wage negotiations a discussion of methods of increasing productivity,

1. The last part of this sentence is simply a statement of fact and is not meant to imply that I am opposed to further redistribution: on the contrary I have drastic views about this (see pp. 189–190).

insisting that the wage demand was a separate issue – as our own Associated Society of Locomotive Engineers and Firemen did in the spring of 1957. It takes a craft union with its spiritual roots firmly embedded in the nineteenth century to stand pat on a position like that – and not even ask itself whether the formula, as a guide to working-class action, does not make all wage increases perfectly pointless, since they would be swallowed forthwith by increases in prices.'[1] Altogether when one surveys trade union activities in Britain what, again to quote Shonfield, 'catches the eye is the ferocious determination to stay put, expressed in the compacts that are made by certain groups of working men, for instance in the shipbuilding industry, that no member of the group will earn more than an agreed maximum sum in any week. In the conditions of today in the shipbuilding industry this cannot conceivably be aimed at protecting anybody from being worked out of a job. It is just an automatic gesture, derived from the past, which holds up progress. Right through the economy there are the endless demarcation lines between one job and another, dividing industry into rigid compartments, in each of which a determined effort goes on to maximize costs. And behind all this is the widespread feeling that none of it matters a damn, because whatever is done things are not going to change very much anyhow.'[2]

These militant conservatives hate technological change. Instead of fighting to see that everyone has a job they fight to see that everyone keeps his *present* job – for example they resist every attempt to help industry abandon coal for more efficient forms of fuel on the ground that it creates unemployment in the mining industry.[3] Innovation is their enemy, as are personal independence and social mobility. They fear automation. They are the full-employment equivalent of Luddites.

This whole complex of trade union attitudes makes me angry. What enrages me most about it is not the social conservatism, though that makes me angry enough, but the acceptance of the role of underdog – more than acceptance, the passionate clinging to an inferior, irresponsible position such that overall policy-making and decision-taking are always the role of others; the refusal to look at the whole

1. Andrew Shonfield: *British Economic Policy Since the War* (Revised Edition 1959), pp. 20 and 25.
2. Shonfield: op. cit., p. 18.
3. Jobs like coal-mining are such an abuse of human life anyway that I should have thought the fewer the people who had to do them the better. On purely humanitarian grounds the working-class movement should be trying to *save* its members from having to go down coal mines, not trying to keep them there.

of any situation, on the ground that the whole situation is not one's concern; the bitter resistance to assuming responsibility and executive power. It is servile. It accepts and perpetuates the nineteenth-century stratification of our society. It accepts the immoral values on which that stratification rests. It is content with the role of object, of people whose lives are at the disposal of others. I am even reminded of Rousseau's 'Slaves, in their chains, lose everything, even to the desire to be free – they *like* their servitude . . .' a phrase coined, in *The Social Contract*, eighty-six years before the Communist Manifesto. Marx and Engels would have done well to think of it instead of writing that facile sentence: 'The proletarians have nothing to lose but their chains.'

II

After a quarter of a century in which the Co-operative Movement's share of retail trading in Britain failed to go up but stayed at around 11 %, it is now going down. The reason is quite simply that, like other left-wing organizations, the Co-op is stuck in the past. The age of mass abundance on which we have entered is bringing about a revolutionary change in the outlook of consumers, but so far the Co-op has failed even to keep abreast of this change, let alone lead it.

Consumers are demanding ever-higher quality in the goods they buy. And with increasing prosperity, marginal differences in price matter less to them. This means that the dividend repaid to customers, which used to be the Co-op's chief attraction to its members, is now of less concern to them, and is admitted to be so by the Co-op itself. What attracts customers nowadays is a high quality of goods and services. And they like their shops to be attractive – clean, bright and friendly, efficiently run, modern-looking and informal. They like what they buy to be pleasant to look at – in other words they are increasingly susceptible to design and packing. And they like to have the feeling of choice, even if this feeling is largely an illusion sustained by advertising. In all these respects the Co-op's standards are low, except in one or two localities. Their goods are mostly of a lower quality than can easily be got elsewhere; their shops are dowdy and uninviting; their packaging and advertising are alike dull and old-fashioned. In short, they are still geared to the society they used to serve before the war.

Like the trade unions, the Co-op has a conception of its role which is cramped, unadventurous, and completely out of touch with modern needs. In many other countries, especially Scandinavia, co-operative housing exists on a huge scale and of the highest modern standard. But not here. Consumer research, a natural territory for the Co-operative Movement to pioneer, was left to the initiative of others. The Co-operative Movement could have transformed the whole nature of commercial television in Britain by starting its own company, but the idea did not occur to it until too late. In short, the Co-operative Movement seldom seems to think of doing anything other than what it has always done. And even in its traditional fields of manufacturing and retailing it usually leaves the breaking of monopolies and artificial price-levels to enterprising private companies.

Again like the trade unions, the Co-operative Movement perpetuates its own inadequacy by deliberately closing its doors to people of first-class education and talent. It recruits few people with even a grammar-school education, let alone a university education; it pays them derisory salaries; and then instead of letting them get on with the job of management it elects amateur boards to harry them in all their doings. So just as the unions ensure that their leaders are lesser men than the people they have to negotiate with, so the Co-op ensures that its top management is in the hands of lesser men that its competitors'. As a result these competitors leave it standing. There is scarcely a single aspect of its operations – research, manufacture, retailing or marketing, even internal organization and staff relations – in which it is not manifestly inferior to such combines as Unilever, or to the other multiple stores. As for the public, a bigger change has been effected in our social life by Marks and Spencer in any five years since the war than by the Co-op in the whole post-war period.

All this, and more, has been said to the Co-op many times. But now comes my last indictment: even when the situation is spelled out to it in detail by its own nominees it continues to oppose, and bitterly, any radical change. In 1956 the Co-operative Movement, worried by its declining share of the market, the under-utilization of its factories and so on, set up a commission of enquiry of the highest calibre, with Hugh Gaitskell as chairman and Anthony Crosland as secretary. (Mr Crosland devoted himself solely to this task for two years.) The commission's main proposals were radical, and were rejected by the Co-op, which is adopting some of the lesser ones – just enough to keep it from falling too far behind its competitors. For the rest it proposes to continue in its old ways.

III

The Labour Party is a federation of several autonomous institutions, including the trade unions. Other institutions, including the Co-operative Movement, are affiliated to it. Its structure is something of a mess. The leader is elected by the Members of Parliament, i.e. the Parliamentary Labour Party; but the National Executive Committee, which in the words of the Constitution is 'the Administrative Authority of the Party', is elected by the Annual Party Conference, in which the Parliamentary Party has no votes but which is dominated by the trade unions. It is also Conference that decides party policy, but only so long as it passes that policy with a two-thirds majority. It is a joint meeting of the National Executive Committee and the Parliamentary Committee which decides what items of the policy are to go into the Party's election programmes, and what the programmes are to say about all matters that Conference has not pronounced on with a two-thirds majority.

Quite apart from anything else, then, there are three power centres in the party – the Parliamentary Committee, the National Executive Committee and the General Council of the T.U.C. And they are elected by, and responsible to, different assemblies – the Parliamentary Party, the Annual Conference and the trade unions respectively. Inevitably the process by which policies are arrived at is cumbersome and subject to almost innumerable formal procedures. This and the sheer complication of it all places it outside the understanding of everyone except the 'experts'. More germane to this chapter, every policy which is to get adopted must be acceptable to a number of differently-based groups of interests – and as we have seen already, not all those groups are even liberal in outlook, let alone radical. So the very structure of the party makes for horse-trading and compromise, at best moderation, at worst conservatism. This is bound to exist in any party, even a homogeneous party of congenial individuals, but it is tragic to have a party structure that so hugely magnifies the tendency.

There are politically desirable and politically undesirable brands of compromise. The former, as I have shown in earlier chapters is the only alternative to violence in the solution of problems. The latter loses sight of the problems – in other words compromise becomes morbid when situations are no longer seen as wholes. I will give an example of what I mean. A defence policy must (*1*) be such as to meet the country's defence needs, (*2*) fit the country's resources of money, manpower, etc., and (*3*) be such as the electorate will not vote against. Unless it is all three it will not result in any defence – not for long. Yet in recent years we have seen the Labour Party frame successive defence policies which are none of these things. Policies have been made or abandoned for no better reason than to unite the party. Proposals have been dropped not because they were mistaken or impracticable but because dropping them would put an end to internal opposition from this or that quarter. Others have been advanced not because they were right and practicable but because So-and-So's co-operation could be bought with them. Some people – Richard Crossman was the arch-offender – seemed concerned no longer with whether policies were right and arguments valid but only with the small-change of their effects on the disagreements among Socialists. Sometimes the country's actual defence needs were not discussed at all – it was as if the significance of alternative defence policies lay solely in their respective effects inside the Labour Party. In the end the whole search openly became one for a policy that would unite the Labour Party and not for a policy that would defend the country, and all proposals came to be judged in that light. It was contemptible and humiliating – and a perfect example of what I mean by morbid compromise. The point and purpose of defence policy were wholly lost sight of behind lesser considerations. Also lost sight of was the fact that the Labour Party might unite on a policy which the electorate would repudiate. And the meaninglessness was lost sight of of the very notion of an Opposition defence 'policy' four years before a General Election. I know from my own door-to-door canvassing and campaigning that the treatment of defence issues in the above way earned the Labour Party a lot of scorn. It gave the impression, correctly, that the Labour Party cared more about its own unity than about the defence of the country and was quite capable of sacrificing the latter to the former. Every time Dick Crossman came up with another wangle for uniting dissident groups and, as he thought, reviving the Labour Party he drove another nail into the coffin of its electoral chances.

However, all this I use only as an example of how the Labour Party's structure encourages conservatism and morbid compromise. It provides every incentive to evade issues instead of grapple with them. It encourages the fixer, the politician whose chief interest is not in solving problems but in reconciling the different pressure groups to which they give rise. For entirely different reasons it is absurd to have party policy fashioned in the first place by an Annual Conference which is dominated by the block votes of the trade unions. The unions cast a vote on behalf of each individual trade-union member who has not positively contracted out of paying the small contribution to the Labour Party which is a normal part of his membership fee. As a result, hundreds of thousands of Conservatives have votes cast for them at Labour Party conferences. Worse still, several members of the executive committees of the various unions, who are the people who actually *decide* how all these votes are to be cast, are members of the Communist Party – for example twelve out of the forty members of the A.E.U. Executive at the Scarborough Conference of 1960 (which used its 696,523 votes to turn what would otherwise have been an endorsement of the official policy of multi-lateral disarmament into a defeat). I do not see how anyone can defend a Constitution which provides that the most democratically elected people in the party – the M.P.s, who have been first selected as candidates by local parties on which Trades Councils, Co-ops, etc., are also represented, and then personally voted for by many millions of the electorate – do not even have individual votes at the Conference which decides party policy, while vast blocks of hundreds of thousands of votes are cast by committees on which sit people who are barred from even being members of the party.

There are so many things wrong with the Constitution of the Labour Party that some of them seem to have escaped notice altogether. For instance I have never heard anyone criticize Clause III (3) (b) which says that 'Each Individual Member must, if eligible, be a member of a Trade Union affiliated to the Trades Union Congress or recognized by the General Council of the Trades Union Congress as a *bona fide* Trade Union.' Yet whatever the historical reasons for this there is no justification for it now. It is morally unacceptable that someone who wants to join the Labour Party should be barred from doing so unless he also joins a trade union which perhaps, for reasons unconnected with politics, he does not wish to join. And it leads to absurdities, like Anthony Greenwood's being a member of the Transport and General Workers' Union. I am not criticizing Anthony Greenwood: irrelevant membership of trade unions is common among Labour M.P.s, precisely because it is forced on them. I once tried to join the T.G.W.U. myself. When I first became a parliamentary candidate I was a freelance writer with almost no work, living by the skin of my teeth and devoting most of my time to writing a book. I was not a member of a trade union. This worried my local party, who were afraid it might lead to trouble – for instance if as a result of some internal dispute opponents tried to get my candidature quashed on this technicality. I replied that I was not eligible for membership of any union, but they said, correctly, that anyone can get into some union or other, if he really tries. (This is how 'eligible' is interpreted.) So I tried to join the National Union of Journalists, but could not because I was not 'regularly employed' as a journalist. I then tried the T.G.W.U., on the ground that I was a general worker, but was told they did not admit 'professional people'. Then it occurred to me that my Oxford degrees automatically made me a qualified teacher, so although I was not a teacher and had no intention of ever becoming one I applied to join the National Union of Teachers, who were only too glad to accept my subscription. The element of farce in all this was not lost on me and I grew ashamed of the whole proceeding. However, I remained a member of the N.U.T. until the General Election of 1959 was over – in fact I did not resign until I was in the middle of fighting a by-election campaign in 1960, and then I did so quite deliberately. So long as Clause III (3) (b) and Clause IX (7) (a) remain in the Constitution the word 'eligible' should be given a natural interpretation. But they should not remain in the Constitution.

Clause III (3) (a), which comes immediately before the words quoted above, says: 'Each Individual Member must accept and conform to the Constitution, Programme, Principles and Policy of the Party.' This is appropriate only to a totalitarian party. A democratic party can exist only on the basis of the freedom of individuals and minorities to campaign against majority decisions. If every individual who broke this clause were expelled there would be almost no one left in the party, so it can serve only as an excuse for victimization. And when it is invoked against individuals, as it recently was against Bertrand Russell, Barbara Wootton, Canon Collins and Lord Chorley, it brings the party into public contempt.

Without needing to take further examples I think I have proved my assertion that the Constitution of the party is a mess. Ideally it should be scrapped. If this is not possible in practice then it should be radically revised. As it is, it positively imposes divisions on the party – casts votes for Conservatives, gives influence to Communists, divides the leadership from the policy-making body, and enjoins phoney membership of other institutions.

As if the structure of the party were not alone a strong enough force for divisions and conservatism there is a statement of political aims written into the constitution. This is a foolish thing regardless of the aims stated, and is bound to be a conservative factor. As I said to the Annual Conference at Scarborough in 1960: 'We could today put down the most up-to-date statement of Socialist aims that anyone could conceive, and yet, as the years went by and the seventies arrived, we should be stuck with an expression of the attitudes and aspirations of 1960. I can give you an obvious example. Every one of us believes – it is one of our most burning beliefs – that the colonial peoples of the world must have their independence at the earliest possible moment. But 75% of Africa is already free – and the other 25% will almost certainly become free very soon. Therefore while it would make wonderful sense to embody colonial freedom as one of our aims *now*, it might make no sense at all in ten or fifteen years time, because there may be no colonies to become free. The truth is that if you put a statement of aims in your Constitution then it recedes farther and farther into the past. And there are inevitably many members of this party with deep loyalties to that statement of aims, who therefore are loyal to something which is relevant to the past and not to the future.' Of course there is need for a progressive party to be continually putting out up-to-date policies, pressing forward with new ideas, and not only coming to terms with fresh situations but also revising attitudes to old problems. But none of this should be put in the Constitution, because it is simply a fact that from the moment a political policy is put on paper it begins to date. And it is not practicable to keep changing the Constitution. It would of course be possible to have a statement of aims so vague that it would not be affected by social changes or intellectual developments. But what would be the point of that?

As it is we have a statement of aims that was written and adopted during the First World War. The adoption, in fact, was in February 1918, in the first intoxicating months of the Russian Revolution, and the statement is straight Marxism: 'To secure for the workers by hand or by brain the full fruits of their industry and the most equitable distribution thereof that may be possible, upon the basis of the common ownership of the means of production, distribution and exchange, and the best obtainable system of popular administration and control of each industry or service.' Also 'generally to promote the Political, Social and Economic Emancipation of the People, and more particularly of those who depend directly upon their own exertions by hand or by brain for the means of life.'

The errors packed into the small compass of these two quotations, which incidentally include every word in the Constitution relating to Labour's policy aims, are obvious: the illusion that everything about a society depends on its economic organization, and hence the conception of political aims in narrowly economic terms; the ignorant assumption that it is even possible to secure to the workers 'the full fruits of their industry', as if communal saving, capital investment and unsuccessful experiment could be dispensed with, and as if nothing should be given to backward countries; the dream of 'popular administration and control of each industry or service', from which the Labour Party awoke at Brighton in 1957;[1] the Marxist theory of the state implied by proposing 'the political emancipation of the people' in what is already a parliamentary democracy; and the commitment throughout to the myths of class. Anyone who had not lived in England in recent years might be excused for taking it for granted that any party, let alone a progressive one, would unite as one man to jettison this farrago of fallacies. The leader of the Labour Party thought this after the defeat of Labour in the General Election of 1959. 'Can we really be satisfied today with a statement of fundamentals which makes no mention at all of colonial freedom, race relations, disarmament, full employment or planning? . . . I am sure that the Webbs and Arthur Henderson, who largely drafted this Constitution, would have been amazed and horrified had they thought that their words were to be treated as sacrosanct forty years later in utterly changed conditions.'[2] He did not propose to dispense altogether with a Constitutional statement of aims, he proposed only to bring the old one up to date. And he assumed that he would carry the broad Centre of the party with him – that only the traditionalist wing (the neo-Bevanites, *Tribune*, and what is now known as Victory for Socialism) would resist. In this he was wrong. The Centre, instead of rallying round him, rallied round the traditionalists, leaving him isolated and defeated on this issue.

A passionate attachment to the past is not unconscious in the people who oppose Gaitskell. On the contrary, they have been declar-

1. See page 124.
2. Hugh Gaitskell's speech to the Party Conference at Blackpool, 1959.

ing it openly since at least 1957, when his campaign to modernize the party began with the document *Industry and Society*. The central argument of that document was that each industry had its own problems and therefore before we could solve them we must find out what they were. It was no good, said the document, inventing one blanket solution and then imposing it on every industry regardless of the facts. It might prove to be in the country's best interests to nationalize some whole industries but to leave others in a state of internal competition among several firms. Or in some industries it might be best to nationalize a group of firms, or perhaps just one firm, or to buy shares in firms. It might be best to control the supply of capital or raw materials to some, to dictate their export policies to others. Any one of a dozen different policies might be the best, depending on circumstances. The only way to find out in each case was to examine the facts of the industry in question. Therefore the next Labour Government should make it its business to institute thorough-going enquiries and then, on the basis of findings, to do whatever seemed in the best interests of each industry and of the community as a whole.

This approach is the only sane one for a progressive party – and I mean the adjective 'sane' quite literally: it is the only approach that is compatible with rationality. Thus *Industry and Society*, for all its vaguenesses, omissions and repetitions, was a historic document, because it marked the Labour Party's official break with pre-scientific supersitition. For the first time in the history of the Labour Movement a policy-statement proclaimed that political action must proceed from observation of the facts and not by argument from first principles. But the traditionalists were and are flatly opposed to this, because they *believe* in arriving at policy by argument from first principles. I, for example, happen to have no views about what changes, if any, should be made in the metal canning industry, because I do not know anything about the metal canning industry. Traditional Socialists, on the other hand, can tell you that it should be nationalized. They do not know anything about the metal canning industry either, but they would not claim that their view was based on a know-ledge of the facts of the industry; their only demand of the facts is to fit their theories, and the sole purpose of any fact-finding committee would be to produce a report supporting the case for nationalization. Their view that the metal canning industry should be nationalized would be subsumed by their view that all industries should be

F

nationalized. This in turn would not – could not possibly – be based on a knowledge of the facts of all industries. It would have been arrived at by argument from first principles – like Aristotle's proof that men have more teeth than women, or Marx's theory of the dialectical development of history.

When *Industry and Society* was put before Conference (Brighton 1957) the traditionalists attacked at once. In the very first speech after it was moved the leader of the National Union of Railwaymen, Jim Campbell, said: 'I am proud of the fact that I am an old-fashioned Socialist. I do not care whether I am described as "one of the old guard" or not.' He was immediately followed by Maurice Edelman, M.P., who said: 'I have no objection, like Jim Campbell and I believe practically everyone here, to being called an old-fashioned nationalizer.' And so the debate went on. The delegate from Govan declared proudly: 'Let us all be Rip Van Winkles, old-fashioned Socialists, old-fashioned nationalizers. In the past it produced tremendous enthusiasm. The Party was built on the old-fashioned nationalization idea. We have to go back to what we were....' And those words – 'We have to go back' – echoed on into the afternoon. 'Let us get back to 1918,' said the M.P. for Kilmarnock, Mr W. Ross. He was followed by the delegate from Crosby saying: 'I ask you to go back and get George Lansbury's book *These Things Shall Be*, and Fred Henderson's book *The Case for Socialism* – both men of blessed memory.' This latter attitude became at its most extreme a kind of ancestor-worship. Mr Ellis Smith, M.P., representing the Patternmaker's Union, said: 'During the past forty years it has been my privilege to enjoy the close friendship of most of the best of our movement, both nationally and locally, and I am convinced of this: that . . . all the best would be bitterly disappointed with the anti-Socialist proposals contained in part of this document. I say to the miners' delegates that if the Bob Smillies, the Tom Richardses and the Peter Lees were here today I knew them sufficiently well to say that they would support the N.U.R. amendment. I say to the Transport and General Workers' Union, having enjoyed the close friendship of great men like Harry Gosling and Ernest Bevin, that if they were here this morning they would be making a powerful indictment against some of the proposals in this document.'

While sitting in the hall listening to these incredible speeches I began to wonder if the delegates who were denouncing the betrayal of early Socialism felt the same way about early methods of transport or early medicine. Did Maurice Edelman, I wondered, travel everywhere on horseback and floating logs, proud of the fact that he was an old-fashioned voyager? Did Mr Smith, before taking the advice of his doctor, ask himself if St Luke, who was as great a man in his way as Harry Gosling, would have agreed with it? Before undergoing an operation did Mr Ross urge his surgeon to go back to the works of Lister? What, I wondered, made people *proud* of recommending nineteenth-century attitudes in the second half of the twentieth-century, and to a party that was supposed to be progressive? How can people who insist that they are advocating changes in the very basis of society be in such terror of changing the basis of their own outlook?

In the July-September 1960 issue of *The Political Quarterly* Peggy Crane wrote: 'Throughout the entire movement fear of ideas and vested interests play as large a part as in any other organization or section of society that socialists so berate. A younger generation, unsteeped in the traditions of the Labour Party, must indeed often wonder how a movement so resistant to change and to organizing itself can really be capable of guiding the political life of this country.' That is putting it mildly. We have now reached the paradoxical situation where the Conservative Party, because of its opportunism, has more readily come to terms with some aspects of the contemporary situation than the Labour Party, and is more up-to-date in some important respects. For instance it is the Conservative Party that has applied modern advertising techniques to political campaigning. It is a Conservative Government that is taking Britain into the European Common Market against a deal of Socialist and Trade Union opposition. In these matters Left and Right have, as it were, changed places. This has happened much more completely inside the Labour Party. The more traditionalist Socialists are, the more they consider themselves on the 'Left'. Those who are altogether lost in the past – who keep starting sentences with 'I think we ought to go back . . .' – consider themselves the Leftest of all, the most progressive people in the country and, it goes without saying, the only true Socialists.

These keepers of the flame have always organized themselves within the Party, at least since 1924. To consider only the post-war years, there was first the Keep Left Group, then the Bevanites, then the *Tribune* Brains Trusts and now Victory For Socialism, all of which organizations have consisted of the same people – the name changes but there has for years been the same party within the party, controlling one of the only two Socialist weekly papers, *Tribune*, and being until recently supported by the other, *The New Statesman*. They have worked actively in the constituencies to get control of committees, frame the resolutions for Annual Conferences, vote for congenial National Executive Candidates and pick parliamentary candidates. The active traditionalists have always been only a small minority of the party, but because of their organization and vigour they have had an influence out of all proportion to their numbers. In any party it tends to be the extremists who are the most active members, for obvious reasons. The extreme traditionalists have included numberless people whose whole inner life has been given over to politics. Meanwhile, the mass of members remain somewhat inert, unorganized and inarticulate. Even those Socialists who actively oppose the traditionalists have mostly been better adjusted individuals for whom politics was one interest among many, and therefore they have not competed on equal terms – not with the same attack and single-mindedness, giving their all of time and money and emotional resources. There is an ideological basis for this difference. Most of the traditionalists are to some degree Marxist in outlook and tend to accept the Marxist belief that politics is co-extensive with life. Their more progressive opponents do not hold this primitive belief, and tend as individuals to value a number of interests and pursuits which they regard as having little or nothing to do with politics. Furthermore traditionalists on the whole tend to enjoy personal acrimony, as is plain from their speeches and journalism. One of their most striking characteristics is a common inability to discuss a question on its merits. I do not think I can recall a single controversy between traditionalists and others in which the traditionalists generally accepted that the others were people of no less intelligence, integrity and goodwill than themselves who genuinely believed in what they were advocating. The chief ingredient of *Tribune* is personal vilification of other Socialists. *The New Statesman*'s profile of Anthony Crosland was one of the most spiteful pieces of journalism I have ever seen. The defamation and misrepresentation of Hugh Gaitskell that have gone on in recent years have been nauseating – and have reached fantastic lengths. Ever since his Clause Four speech at Blackpool in 1959 his opponents have said that he is against more public ownership, but in fact his speech repudiated such a position at length, in a passage ending: 'I cannot agree that we have reached the frontiers of public ownership as a whole.' Ever since his 'fight and fight and fight again' speech at Scarborough in 1960 his opponents have said that he is against Britain's giving up the manufacture of hydrogen bombs, whereas what he said was quite the reverse, culminating in the words: 'We are agreed that in the future Britain should not attempt to produce and provide her own effective nuclear weapons.'

Healthier Socialists have been sickened by all this, some to the point of retiring from politics. They neither can nor want to compete with those who enjoy it. And at all levels, from the national to those of local party committees, they have too frequently allowed themselves to be swamped. Their confidence has been further undermined by the fear of being thought 'Right-wing'. 'Left', as I said on page 97, is a hooray-word, and I have seen at more local party and committee meetings than I care to remember how representative Socialists would rather not speak up against organized traditionalism than be thought to be 'not Left', much less 'anti-Left'. One or two national figures in the party are entirely dominated by the need to be 'on the Left' in every case, regardless of the merits of that case. In his last years Aneurin Bevan was deeply disturbed by the fact that he was no longer 'on the Left'.

All this has meant that the public's image of Socialists has been largely formed by the traditionalists. More people think of the typical Socialist as being someone like Michael Foot than as being someone like Hugh Gaitskell. And of course this does the party serious damage. It is what more than anything else has created the public's picture of an old-fashioned party still fighting the battles of long ago without relevance to contemporary life.

Included in the ideas that many Socialists have preserved unchanged are their conception of their opponents and their conception of society. One of the costliest illusions to be found in the Labour Party is that the Conservative Party has learnt nothing and forgotten nothing since the nineteen-thirties. In fact the Conservative Party has changed almost out of recognition. Its attitude to economic affairs has been transformed by Keynes, so that it is now associated by the electorate with full employment and mass prosperity. Some of its colonial policies have been as progressive as Labour's. In these and many other respects the actualities of Conservative rule are quite different from what you would suppose from listening to many Socialist speeches. This is largely the result of the cataclysm of 1945. The Conservative Party was shattered and bewildered by the magnitude of its defeat, and when the shock began to wear off enough Conservatives realized that the party would have to be completely reoriented if it was to win elections in post-war Britain. The radical extent of the reconstruction that then took place went unobserved by most Socialists, even when it resulted in the Conservatives' return to power. In all the endless discussion about why we have lost seats in each of the last four elections I have heard all kinds of blame laid on the Labour Party and on the electorate but seldom credit given to the Conservatives. The discussion is almost always in terms of why we lost, not why they won; yet a little consideration given to the latter question might improve many Socialists' understanding of both the Conservative Party and the electorate.

More serious is the refusal of many Socialists to acknowledge that the society they confront has changed. When at Blackpool in 1959 Hugh Gaitskell gave this refusal as the basic reason for Labour's successive defeats – 'I do not believe that the social and economic changes of which I have spoken were bound to react against us. They did so simply because we did not take them sufficiently into account' – many members of the party's Annual Conference did not understand what he was talking about. His analysis of social changes had been mild enough – far more conservative than I would have wished. Yet I could tell from the reactions of some of the delegates round me, and from subsequent conversations, that many of the party's key workers were hearing these arguments for the first time. And they were too much for many of them to stomach. The very first one to follow Gaitskell finished his speech with the words: 'Now we have Mr Gaitskell who talks about a mixed economy. What the heck is a mixed economy? We have a Capitalist economy – and where is this tripe getting us about a mixed economy which is non-existent? Engels many years ago wrote: "Nothing is; everything is becoming." What kind of tripe is a mixed economy? Where he is going to be at the end I do not know. I hope I am not there when he is.' And as at Brighton in 1957, delegate after delegate came to the rostrum to assert that nothing had changed. One of them had so lost touch with the world that he did not know that Stalin had been dead for several years: 'I do not agree with the bomb. Perhaps it is a good thing in a way that Joe Stalin and his boys have got it, because if they didn't have it we don't know what the Americans might have done.'

However, increasing acceptance of the truth is discernible in the party. Ray Gunter's speech at the next Annual Conference, at Scarborough in 1960, used some of the same arguments as Gaitskell had used at Blackpool but got a noticeably better reception for them. Even so the Bourbons of the Labour Movement still spoke in force – Emanuel Shinwell talked of 'the silly nonsense about adapting ourselves to a changed situation', and said: 'Rely on our principles. Do not depart from them. They are sacrosanct.'

It is tragic to see the Labour Party so far outstripped by historical change. In fact the pace of change in society is so much faster than the pace of change in the Labour Party that instead of leading the movement for reform the Labour Party is all the time trying to catch up with it. For the last ten years it has been society that is modernizing the Labour Party, not the Labour Party that is modernizing society.

IV

In anyone familiar with efficient and successful modern organizations it makes the spirits droop to go into Transport House. One's first impression is that things are drab, dirty and out of date; one's second that the work is ill-planned and wrongly directed – directed, if at all, in accordance with the past (you might find for example that the work of one member of the research staff is entirely taken up with Scottish affairs while no one is working full-time on the Common Market). I have come in contact with Transport House in several capacities over several years – as a parliamentary candidate, a writer, a television reporter – and I have learned to take for granted a lower standard of professional competence there than anywhere else I know. No one in the organization seems to know what anyone else is doing, they take days to arrange things by letters written in gobbledygook ('We hope to have your reply to hand at any early date . . .') that I can do on the telephone in half an hour; they constantly get things wrong or forget them altogether. Certainly any profit-making organization that operated in this way would soon be out of business. And in the field, among the local parties, the drabness and lack of professional competence are worse – the squalor of some local party headquarters has to be seen to be believed. In the internal organizations of the trade unions and the Co-ops, standards are scarcely better.

Why is all this? One reason is that the Labour Movement is the nearest thing left to an old-fashioned 'Capitalist' employer. It is fundamentally unwilling to employ the right amount or quality of labour, or to pay the full market price for what it does employ. It is unwilling to carry the cost of providing proper training for specialist work, or even of providing decent surroundings and working conditions. The result is that it does not get good people (except for a few, whom it seldom manages to keep for long – usually young men in their first job). For however enthusiastic and idealistic a Socialist may be it is not right to expect him to sacrifice the living standards of his wife and children to the Labour Party. Why should he? The Labour Party should pay the rate for the job. To say it cannot afford to do so is to grasp the wrong end of the stick – it would get more out of the same money by employing a dozen outstandingly gifted people at high salaries instead of two dozen ordinarily gifted people at low salaries. In the refusal to do so lurks an element of class feeling. It is felt to be right and proper for working-class organizations to lumber along at the pace that comes naturally to inexperienced, uneducated working-class people and is in keeping with their natural conservatism, while the drive and initiative of enterprising professionals is resented and liable to be categorized as 'slick'. Also such professionals are felt to be not working-class people, and it is better to have jobs done in a familiar way and at a comfortable pace by unqualified but like-minded people than to put oneself in the hands of untrustworthy, high-powered members of another class who talk a bewildering language and move at a bewildering pace.

As a result the Labour Movement is pervaded by amateurishness and a positive hostility to professionalism. The standard of administration at all levels is infuriating for people from other walks of life who are used to high standards. (The running of one particular by-election campaign of which I happen to have close knowledge was quite literally the most botched and bungled piece of organisation I have ever come across.) The movement prides itself on its indifference to public relations and its hostility to journalists, and derides the Conservative Party for employing a professional agency to run its poster and advertizing campaigns. Socialists associate successful organization with big business, successful propaganda with Fleet Street, and successful publicity with the advertising industry, and despise them all. They are satisfied with unsuccessful organization, unsuccessful propaganda and bad publicity. This ostrich-like attitude can be changed only by a vigorous and sustained initiative, and the most appropriate source for such an initiative would normally be the leadership of the party. But it is unlikely to come from there in the near future, for reasons which will emerge in the next section.

V

Any candid list of the sources of the Left's conservatism must include the leadership of the Labour Party. Not that Gaitskell's leadership has been conservative in the sense I have just been writing about. He has not been hidebound by Socialist traditions; on the contrary he has done his utmost to free the party from the dead weight of some of those traditions. What is lacking in him is vivacity of radical feeling. He has to be *pushed* into adopting radical attitudes – for instance he had to be pushed into supporting Anthony Wedgwood Benn's refusal to have a peerage clamped on him (and that issue is symbolic of some of the basic questions in British life). For a long time he was lukewarm about the Labour Party's superannuation scheme. It took him years to come round to the defence policy on which he finally staked his leadership at Scarborough in 1960. In a radical leader, as in a radical party, what is needed above all else is what Aneurin Bevan called 'passion in action in the pursuit of qualified judgments', and this Gaitskell shows only intermittently. When confronted with a difficult situation he instinctively sees it in terms of the snags rather than in terms of the challenge. It is no coincidence that he was so successful as a civil servant during the war, for his natural temperament is that of the civil servant rather than the politician.

Many Socialists are so bound up in outlook with society as it is that they are not 'free' enough when it comes to making radical proposals, and hence despite themselves are too conservative. Such a character is a defect in a radical politician, though a case can be made out for saying that it is in the Labour Party's interests to have a number of such people as a useful counterweight to the impulsives and the Utopians. However, for the leader of the Party to be of this stamp is a handicap. It increases the political caution proper to a party leader to the point where it becomes a failing. Under Gaitskell the Labour Party scarcely ever seems to take the initiative or make the running, let alone inaugurate nation-wide campaigns on radical issues. As a

F*

result, instead of being, as he should be, the national leader and symbol of all the radical forces in British life, he often seems little more than just another Establishment figure.

When his heart is in a cause he is unflinching. His bearing in defeat in the General Election of 1959 was dignified and moving, and no one who saw him face the Scarborough Conference of 1960 will ever forget his courage. So when he declines to promote a Labour Party campaign for such social reforms as abolishing the death penalty, on the ground that there are no votes in it, this is not lack of courage but lack of conviction. Like any other politician he does not willingly take risks over things he does not feel deeply about, and my complaint is that he does not feel deeply about them. If it is true, and I believe it is, that there are 'no votes in' abolition of the death penalty or radical revision of the law on divorce, abortion, homosexuality, drink, gambling and censorship, then the conclusion to draw, even on the most cynical vote-catching level, is not that the Labour Party should refrain from advocating these things but that it could conduct an all-out campaign for them without losing electoral support.

Gaitskell has great qualities. His combination of integrity, intellect, courage and industry is without equal in British political life. Unfortunately other qualities are also needed to lead the Labour Party successfully in opposition – size of personality, a shrewd command of political tactics, and above all spontaneous, natural radicalism. If Aneurin Bevan had lived I do not think there can be much doubt that he would have displaced Gaitskell within a year of the 1959 General Election; and despite all my reservations about Bevan I would have welcomed that. After being for many years the feared and fearless leader of the traditionalists he was in later life groping his way towards a rational view of politics. The fact that he was himself still in this painful process of shaking off the incubus of outmoded Socialist assumptions would have been all to the good, because with his imagination, his magic tongue and the deep traditional devotion he commanded within the party he would slowly, I am sure, have carried all but the lunatic fringe with him into the modern world. In addition he was a *big* man, potentially a world figure, such as none of our national leaders now is. However, it was not to be. And in his absence Gaitskell alone among the leaders of the Labour Party seems to realize with uncompromising clarity that the party's life-or-death need is to reconstruct its outlook and approach so as to take account of the revolutionary social and intellectual changes that have taken place since Socialist assumptions were first formed. Wanting to adjust Socialist attitudes to the society we live in is, of course, in itself a conservative aim, and as far as I am concerned it is acceptable only as an intermediate goal; but those attitudes now lag so far behind social developments that they cannot be modernized without a major upheaval in the party. Hence the paradox that Gaitskell is conservative outside the party and revolutionary within it. If I were an M.P. and had a vote for the leadership I would vote for him, because the task he has undertaken of the modernization of the party is the *sine qua non* of its survival, but I hope he will work himself out because he is the ablest man in the party and because the task he has undertaken of the modernization of the party is the *sine qua non* of its survival, but, at the same time, I should join forces with those – and they include some of his loyalest supporters – who are continually urging him to advocate more radical policies.

Let me be constructive in my criticisms. I would like representative leaders of the party and not his personal friends to be his closest political associates. (This now appears to be so: may it remain so.) I should like him to give a freer rein to radical impulse, both within himself (his bitter fight with the traditionalists has driven him into more rigid attitudes than he would otherwise have adopted) and in the party. And I would like him to do everything he can to extend the rationality of the party's approach in ways he has not even touched on. Some of these are not seriously controversial and would therefore involve him in no conflict. For example the whole Labour Movement has been infected by the assumption that our Socialism tells us how to deal with all political problems and therefore that it is unnecessary to inform ourselves further. One result is that we have never made any serious attempt to draw on the vast resources of practical experience and knowledge that are available to us. Although in 1957 the policy document *Public Enterprise* said: 'Too little attention used to be given to the problems of managing publicly-owned industry' I still, in 1962, know people who have sat for years on the boards of nationalized industries – people who have voted Labour all their lives and would be willing to give any honourable help they could to the party – who have never once been approached for their opinion or advice. The Labour Party goes on producing policies for industry, for public ownership and the rest, but all the discussion surrounding their formulation seems to go on *inside* the active Labour Movement, among people most of whom have no direct personal experience of the problems at issue, while sympathetic people outside with years of day-to-day experience of those problems are ignored.

Similarly with management generally, and with business. There must be tens of thousands of Socialist business-men in Britain, with every kind of background and experience, and many of these would be only too pleased to give their views on problems of which they have special knowledge; but there has been no attempt by the party to tap this source systematically as part of its normal workings. Then again with scientists and technologists: I have it from some of the most eminent in their fields that the Labour Party shows so little interest in their views that even when some of them have taken the initiative themselves and tried to establish talking-contact with the party they have been brushed off.

To have such huge reservoirs of practical knowledge and experience at one's disposal and yet ignore them is almost paranoid. It is due to two outmoded attitudes. First, the pre-scientific assumption that knowledge is obtained by argument from first principles, from which it follows that policy can be formulated without recourse to practical observation and experience. Second, the class-hostility a Labour Movement naturally develops towards business-men, managers and professional people. They are not 'our people', they have made their lives 'on the other side', and they are viewed at the very least with suspicion. But I should have thought that at this time of day there would be little opposition to a vigorous initiative from the leadership of the party to change all this – to establish wide-ranging contacts, both formal and informal, with the object of bringing this already-existing wealth of sympathy and expertise into the party's deliberations. As well as greatly improving our policies it would widen the base of the party and encourage thousands of extremely useful people to be active members. And it would do much to destroy the pre-scientific assumptions and the class limitations that still afflict the Labour Movement.

There are other areas where rationality needs to be encouraged. For instance ever since it left office the Labour Party has been the victim of serious inhibitions about criticizing the nationalized industries, fearing that such criticism would be turned against itself or its record or the case for public ownership. As a result it has put itself in the position of always seeming to defend publicly owned industries (and attack privately owned ones) regardless of the merits of the case, and thus of being bound by prejudice, refusing to learn from experience. When I said in Chapter Three that 'it is chiefly by the critical examination of theories that knowledge advances' I was giving an instance of a more general rule. It is chiefly by criticism that *anything* advances. Criticism is the key to progress. This is one of the innumerable connections between rationality and radicalism. When a progressive party becomes afraid to criticize it becomes conservative, for it is then defending, or at least condoning, the *status quo*. By taking all criticisms of nationalization as aimed at itself the Labour Party has played neatly into the Conservatives' hands. The Conservatives have been in power, and responsible for the nationalized industries, for over ten years now, yet we have the extraordinary situation whereby every criticism of those industries is regarded by the Government *and by the Opposition* as a blow at the Opposition. No wonder the public have come to look at it the same way! The Labour Party has given the Conservative Party more propaganda ammunition by not criticizing the nationalized industries than it would ever have done by criticizing them. Here, as so often, the dictates of political tactics and of rationality are the same. From the moment it went into Opposition the Labour Party should have shown itself as determined as ever to see that the nationalized industries were improved, and should have been unremittingly critical, pointing out weaknesses and suggesting changes, relentlessly holding the Conservative Government responsible for uncorrected faults.

These are all areas in which the Labour Party could become more effective, more vigorous and more radical without exacerbating its internal differences. It would be greatly to Gaitskell's personal advantage to give such an initiative, because his attempt to destroy the influence on the party of nineteenth-century ideas would be far more likely to succeed if it were clear to everyone that he opposed the traditionalists, as I do, *on the ground that they are a major obstacle to change, to radical reform, to progress*. So far he has given the impression of opposing them because he is cautious rather than because he is bold, imaginative, and impatient for the progress they impede.

VI

Unfortunately the Labour Party's conservatism is not confined to the effects of its ramshackle structure, its attachment to the dogmas of another age and the superfluous caution of its leader. There is also an emotional and personal attachment to the past on the part of many of its members. In some this takes the form of bitterness: in others, paradoxically, nostalgia. The bitter ones (I have heard many Socialists describe themselves as 'bitter') have what can amount almost to an obsession with the hardships of the inter-war years – the old wrongs, the old poverty, the old unemployment. Like the Irish, or the white Southerners in America, they seem unable to free themselves emotionally from the injustices of long ago. The nostalgic ones long for exactly those same times, because it was so thrilling to be a Socialist then. Socialists in those days had a full-blooded cause. There was no uncertainty about what they were against: they could see the bandy-legged children in every street, and Europe was full of villains to fight. Nor was there any uncertainty about what they were for: it was done, and more, between 1945 and 1951.[1] The Labour Party in those pre-war days was a militant movement with a clear purpose, and to belong to it was exciting, comforting, rewarding. In these days of affluence and impotence, uncertain aims and uncertain enemies, when the political atmosphere is cold and tense instead of flushed and heady, it is good to look back to the days of the rich emotional rewards.

Both these attitudes – the bitterness and the nostalgia – are understandable in individuals. But both are indisputably backward-looking No one who is strongly influenced by either can legitimately consider himself progressive. It is hard to tell people embittered by the injustices they have suffered to snap out of it, to live in the present and concern themselves with now and the future – it makes one feel smug and guilty. But the fact is that one can learn from the past without being imprisoned by it. In the inter-war slump the hardest-hit country of all was the United States, and American workers suffered far greater hardships than did British workers, yet the American labour movement does not keep harping on the past. For people in Britain to do so is understandable but not, I think, justifiable. In any case I do not think the ostensible reasons are the real reasons. People who have survived the concentration camps of Hitler and Stalin show that human beings can endure things that make unemployment seem like a holiday, things that inhabit an altogether different universe of suffering, and still go back to living normal, happy lives. Human beings are unimaginably resilient. When they live in the past it is because the present is unsatisfactory, and the reason is almost always to be found in the present. If people think life has cheated them because they did not get to a university, or because their fiancé was killed in the First

1. See page 13.

World War, or because father spent all his money on drink and did not leave anything when he died, or for any other reason, the chief thing this reveals is a *present* sense of dissatisfaction with life; similarly if someone keeps dwelling on how exciting the war was, or how well he played the piano before he had to give it up, or how successful he was in Canada. Nostalgic Socialists reveal themselves as people for whom politics is self-expression, not achievement. It may have *felt* good to be a Socialist in the inter-war years, but they were years of disastrous failure for the Labour Party – a stretch of helpless opposition punctuated by two debilitating doses of responsibility without power. When people live in the past they forget or ignore those aspects of it that are irrelevant to their purpose: the past they live in is imaginary but supplies their needs. For some people, I am afraid, the Labour Party is the source of supply.

The extreme livers-in-the-past are still in a world of wicked international Capitalism and not-so-bad Communism. Suez had a terrific impact on them but they have almost forgotten Hungary. At home they think everything can and should be nationalized. And they are still committed to the notion of class-war. But as for the world we are actually living in – the world of inflation and the welfare state, high living standards, full employment, automation; the world of nuclear energy, space travel, Communist terror, the clash of white and nonwhite peoples all over the globe, the liberation of colonies, the development of backward areas – this world is only on the fringe of their consciousness, less real to them politically than their memory-world of the thirties.

This helps to explain the striking similarities in outlook, so often remarked upon, between the Labour Party's 'extreme Left' and the Conservative Party's 'extreme Right'. It is that both are living in the past. The outstanding instance of this is their delusion about Britain's place in the world. When unilateralists trot out their basic argument about the need for Britain to 'give a moral lead to the world' they are making the same mistake as the Suez Conservatives, the mistake of assuming that Britain can by her own solitary decisions and actions shape the world's destiny. Other major attitudes common to these two groups are class-hatred and isolationism – in particular anti-Americanism, and now a growing opposition to Britain's joining the Common Market – together with a basic authoritarianism which makes them impatient of the actual democratic process and sympathetic to various forms of totalitarianism (Fascism in one case, Communism in the other). It is fortunate that neither group has any practical possibility of getting to control the government of the country. Their only major potential is for the infliction of serious damage on their own parties.

This damage takes many forms: continual party splits over particular issues; the tendency to catch the headlines with violent statements and regressive ideas, and hence to play a disproportionate and harmful part in forming the public image of the party; the alienation of reasonable people, the constant application of conservative pressure to which concessions have sometimes to be made; and the continual dragging of red herrings into public life. This last is particularly important. By compelling discussion on outmoded terms the traditionalists in both parties are all the time distracting attention from contemporary issues. This has been particularly marked in the Labour Party in recent years, which has suffered appalling injuries both internally and in the country by having not one but two internecine battles over cloud-cuckoo questions. Only the first was even a question which the Labour Party could decide, namely whether to retain in its Constitution a Marxist statement of aims written nearly half a century ago. The second – whether Britain should abandon her defensive alliances and become neutralist in world affairs – was something entirely out of its hands, since it was in opposition, yet it proceeded to bleed itself almost to death over it. There is something insane about a great party destroying itself in an attempt to specify a policy which it is powerless to implement. It represents in its most malignant form the opposition-minded assumption that political activity consists not in getting things done but in having opinions and carrying on discussions and arguments.

The mere fact of opposing the traditionalists gets one involved in controversy over the issues of yesterday. It should not be necessary in the 1960s to devote one's time to showing that the economic system does not determine all aspects of society, that education is more important than nationalization, that political freedom matters more than ownership of the means of production. It is like setting out the arguments against the belief that the earth is flat. And for the opposition to conduct a suicidal debate on defence policy is like medieval schoolmen arguing how many angels can stand on the point of a pin. Meanwhile – while these anachronistic or academic disputes are going on – the real problems of the day are relegated to second place: the Conservative Government either deals with them as it thinks fit or ignores them. And even those major spheres like education, which in many countries, including London, are controlled by Labour councils, take second place to theological disputes.

I am weary of all this. I think we should concern ourselves only with the real world. Let us get our attitudes right, and policy where it makes sense for us to have a policy, and leave theology to theologians. An Opposition has three main concerns: maximum implementation of its policies in those areas of government it still controls through local councils; effective opposition to the Government at all levels; and preparation for, and precipitation of, its own return to office. We shall do none of these things if we go on pouring our energies into irrelevancies. We should take issue with traditionalists only when it is of strictly practical importance to do so – never for its own sake but only when the damage done to the party by debates on outmoded issues is the lesser of two evils. For the rest we should devote ourselves to the world of the sixties and seventies, not the world of the thirties, and bring our force to bear against the Conservatives in office, not the conservatives in opposition. And if these latter then wish to leave a party which is not concerned with the things they are concerned with, so much the better. People who cling to the warmth and security of unchanging ideas have no place in a living radical movement.

Speaking for myself, I do not propose to spend much more time arguing with traditionalists about the outmoded issues that concern them or the outmoded categories in which they think, or language they speak. Time is too short and reality too urgent. But while still speaking personally, and before turning to a new chapter and more important matters, it is worth pointing out *in personal terms* just how archaic the traditionalists are from the point of view of someone of my age. During the 1960s some of the boys who were at my school at the same time as me will be having grandchildren, and already there is a whole generation of grown-up people younger than myself who regard me as standing on the threshold of middle age. Yet I was nine when the Second World War began, and with it the full employment that has lasted to this day. I was barely fifteen when Hitler and Mussolini were killed, and their régimes gone down in total ruin; fifteen when atom bombs were dropped on Hiroshima and Nagasaki; fifteen when a Labour Government was elected in Britain with a parliamentary majority of 148 seats over all other parties combined. I was eighteen and nineteen when I served on the Iron Curtain in the Intelligence Corps and learned the realities of Communism at first hand. The circumstances in which I and my generation grew up were the *direct opposite* of those in which pre-war Socialists grew up. They were obsessed by unemployment, and thought that it was 'inevitable under Capitalism': I take full-employment almost for granted – we have had it ever since I was in short trousers. They looked on Fascism as the greatest danger to world peace, and on Communism as a variant of what they themselves believed in: I look on Communism as the greatest danger to world peace and the opposite of what I believe in. They accept Conservative Government as the norm, and opposition as Labour's natural role; I came to maturity in an England governed by Labour, and spontaneously think of its natural role as governing the country. They think of atom bombs as the newest, latest, most revolutionary thing: for me atom-bombs are a childhood memory and have the same sort of relation to today's thermo-nuclear weapons as the Wright Brothers' flying machine does to a space rocket. It is little wonder that their whole way of looking at the world seems to me of little more than historical interest.

CHAPTER NINE

The Backwardness of Britain

THE conservatism of the Left in Britain is merely one aspect of the conservatism of Britain as a whole. 'A dogged resistance to change now blankets every segment of our national life. A middle-aged conservatism, parochial and complacent, has settled over the country; and it is hard to find a single sphere in which Britain is pre-eminently in the forefront.'[1] Observations of this sort about Britain are beginning to constitute a literature. And it is by no means only people active in politics who see Britain in this light. Before Crosland's article appeared the Principal of the Manchester College of Science and Technology, Dr B. V. Bowden, wrote in *Universities Quarterly* (issue of November 1959–January 1960): 'We seem to be suffering from a national neurosis which makes us accept our relative penury without being conscious of it; we seem to believe that if we are doing better than we were then no more should be expected of us, and we never seem to compare our institutions with their counterparts abroad. We have just ceased to make steam locomotives, but we shall be using them for years to come; the Dutch put their last steamer in a museum last year. Our telephone service is expanding more slowly than that of any other country from which data is available; almost every country in Europe has built more new hospitals than we have since the war; our cities still retain scars from bomb damage and our national productivity is rising appallingly slowly. An average English workman produces less than half as much as an American. Is it possible that the American educational system has helped to improve the productivity of American industry? Next October we hope to complete a hundred miles of modern road from nowhere to nowhere in particular, and we seem to be quite unaware of the fact that almost all other countries did much more years ago, that many American States open ten times as much new highway every year, and that we are spending less on new roads (per capita) than any other important European country.

1. The opening of an article by C. A. R. Crosland in *Encounter*, October 1960. Reprinted in his book *The Conservative Enemy*, p. 127.

We shall spend about £80,000,000 on new roads next year; this is far more than we have ever spent before, and the authorities seem to be very proud of themselves, but Western Germany will probably spend six times as much as we do. Why can they afford to be so much more enterprising than we are? We are told to admire the new London Airport, and many of us have come to believe that it is something to be proud of. Few Englishmen realize that in fact it does not handle as many aircraft as the Airport at Little Rock, Arkansas, that trans-atlantic passengers still use old wooden huts which would suit the bus station in a small provincial town and that London ranks about eightieth among domestic and international airports of the world.'

In the arts, too, this view of Britain has become familiar, par-ticularly in plays one associates with the Royal Court Theatre, Theatre Workshop and 'Angry Young Men'. Archie Rice, the central character of John Osborne's *The Entertainer*, says to the audience at the end of the play: 'Don't clap too hard, we're all in a very old building. Yes, very old. Old. What about *that*? (Pointing to Britannia.) What about *her*, eh – Madam with the helmet on? I reckon she's sagging a bit, if you ask me.' And earlier in the play one of the characters has tried to persuade another to emigrate to Canada: 'Look around you. Can you think of any good reason for staying in this cosy little corner of Europe? Don't kid yourself anyone's going to let you do anything, or try anything here, Jeannie. Because they're not.' And the central character of Colin MacInnes's novel *Absolute Beginners* – who thinks to himself: 'My God, my Lord, how horrible this country is, how dreary, how lifeless, how blind and busy over trifles!' – goes on to say something that nearly all these writers would echo: 'It's because I'm a patriot, that I can't bear our country.'

I

When I came down from Oxford at the age of twenty-three the only other countries I knew were countries which had lower living standards than Britain and had suffered more in the war. I had been to school in France for a time, lived for a year on the frontier of Austria and Yugoslavia, and done vacation work in Belgium, so I did know other ways of life and was accustomed to seeing Britain from the outside. But in almost all political and economic respects Britain compared favourably with those countries. I had not seen a more 'modern' country than Britain, a country in which people were more free, or more equal, or more prosperous. So I was still accustomed to thinking of Britain as being in the forefront internationally. My radicalism in practical politics was based not on actual comparisons but on ideal comparisons: I was saying in effect that this, that or the other aspect of British life was inferior to what I could envisage, not that it was inferior to what was actually happening elsewhere.

However, the first job I got on leaving Oxford was in Sweden, and I lived in Sweden for a year. Sweden has had a Socialist government since 1932, is the the most advanced welfare state in the world, has a far higher standard of living than Britain, is even freer politically and much more egalitarian, and has not been involved in a war since 1814. Living there transformed my view of Britain and had a great impact on my political outlook. For what had hitherto been for me only progressive *ideas* became actual experience: I was now living and working in a more 'advanced' society than Britain, and on every side I could see things in operation which would represent great forward steps for Britain – as I could also see mistakes for Britain to avoid. Travelling to and from Britain with Swedes, and running summer courses for them, I got used to their way of seeing my own country and noticed, as they did, all the respects in which it fell below the standards they were used to. My comparisons became real and ceased to be notional. But that was not the end of the change. For, two years after going to Sweden, I went to the United States, also for a year. And I discovered, as I said in the book I wrote about it on my return to England,[1] that 'it is not, as some people still imagine a more reactionary society than ours: it is a more radical, more progressive one, more accepting of change, more creative'. Of course America is completely different from Sweden in fundamental ways – seventeen times as big, with twenty-five times the population, a federation of states all dedicated to 'free enterprise' as a way of life. And it taught me completely different lessons. But for precisely that reason I came to see many aspects of British life not from one superior vantage point but from two, which were themselves at a distance from each other. I had had direct experience not merely of ways in which we might be better but of *different* ways in which we might be better. I have not felt the same about Britain since.

By the mid-fifties I had come, as a result of personal experience, to

1. *Go West, Young Man*, p. 17.

see Britain in pretty much the way expressed in the quotations at the beginning of this chapter: a stagnant backwater whose conventional ideas and conception of itself were grotesquely at variance with reality. And what struck me most forcibly about its social organization was the fraudulence of it. This is something that had been hitting outside observers in the eye for decades. Before the war an article about Britain in the American magazine *Esquire* (April 1937) contained the following passage: 'One-third of all Cabinet Ministers in the last hundred years have come from either Eton or Harrow. Those two schools have supplied twelve of the nineteen Prime Ministers during the same period. Today His Majesty's Ministers, numbering in all fifty-eight, can boast twenty-five Eton and Harrow men; of the fifty-five ranking officials of the foreign service, from Chargé d'affaires to Ambassador, Eton alone claims twenty-eight as well as ten of the thirty-four Governors and Governors-General. . . . The conclusions are therefore obvious. Either the type of education provided by the 'great' schools is so overwhelmingly superior that its beneficiaries are uniquely equipped to handle the vaster problems of the nation, or – if not – and I believe very few would care to support that thesis – then the virtual monopoly of the positions of power by the sometime-students of the 'great' schools, has, at least to the untutored eye of an American inquirer, a number of the earmarks of a highly successful racket.'

Most people imagine that this sort of thing has substantially changed since the war, but it has not. Post-war Conservative Governments have been worse than their predecessors, not better. At the time of writing more than a third of the Cabinet Ministers are from Eton alone; in the previous Cabinet it was exactly a third, and in the one before that, out of nineteen members, eighteen were from public schools and six from Eton. All this is partly what was in Jimmy Porter's mind in *Look Back in Anger* when he said of his brother-in-law, a young ex-public-school-and-Sandhurst Conservative M.P.: 'He'll end up in the Cabinet one day, make no mistake. But somewhere at the back of that mind is the vague knowledge that he and his pals have been plundering and fooling everybody for generations. . . . But it wouldn't do for him to be troubled by any stabs of conscience, however vague. Besides, he's a patriot and an Englishman, and he doesn't like the idea that he may have been selling out his countrymen all these years, so what does he do? The only thing he *can* do – seek sanctuary in his own stupidity. The only way to keep things as much like they always have been as possible, is to make any alternative too much for your poor, tiny brain to grasp. It takes some doing nowadays. It really does.'

The racket extends all the way down: it is our class-structure, as dishonest and debilitating at the bottom as it is at the top. Most people in England are not acutely aware of it because they have never known anything else and they take it for granted, as a slave born among slaves takes his slavery for granted. I find this exasperating, but the truth is I took most of it for granted myself until I had the experience of living in classless societies. Now I find it intolerable. Not only is it Britain's worst fault: it is the chief cause of her other faults.

Most British people have extraordinarily little idea of what the world is like. The physical fact that we live on an island has a lot to do with this – it encourages isolationism not only in politics but in every aspect of social life and outlook. (I know it is platitudinous to talk of the British being 'insular' but it is none the less true for that.) This sheer ignorance of other people is a powerful force for conservatism, because it means we do not learn from them. We tend rather to bumble along in our old ways, enclosed within our tight little horizons, until circumstances compel us to change. The same ignorance also enables us to persist in illusions about our relative merits. Most English people really do suppose that English people are better than other people, and English ways of doing things better than other ways. More bizarre still, they take it to be a generally accepted fact. So they can effortlessly talk, or swallow talk from others, about 'Britain giving a lead', 'other countries looking to us' and all the rest of it, without being aware that they are talking about a private world of the British imagination and not the world we actually live in. The fact that people in other countries do not 'look up to Britain', do not in the least regard us as their superiors, and go about their own affairs with no special concern for us, is as uncomprehended as it is obvious. At a party the other day I heard someone ask an American politician what the current talk was in Washington about England, and the politician replied politely that most people in Washington had scarcely any occasion to talk about England at all. The Englishman thought he was being insulting. I tried to help by suggesting that America was influenced by us in the same sort of way as we were influenced by Australia, but this met with blank non-comprehension.

So we drag along, knowing and caring little about the world we live in, falling farther and farther behind most other advanced countries, and yet still supposing that others share our view of our own importance. It is a pathetic spectacle – and not a unique one in world history. It is the common fate of ex-Imperial Powers: Spain experienced it two hundred years ago; then Portugal; and now France as well as Britain. It multiplies the need for a radical party to challenge outmoded assumptions, tell home truths, prick bubbles, topple the idols of the past. It also multiplies the need for radical policies, because the more sham there is in a society the more the actual abuses and wrongs go unrighted. There is no compulsion for us to be so seedy and second-rate about so much: we could be a dynamic, creative society if only we would adjust our outlook and policies to the truth of our situation. We are like an individual who prefers to keep himself slightly ill all the time, spending more than his income and straining to cope with jobs beyond his capacities, living in a permanent atmosphere of shabby-gentility and recurrent crisis, rather than face the truth about himself and be healthy, happy, solvent and relaxed in what he would regard as 'a lower station'. A radical party ought to have the courage to tell the British people the truth. This would certainly not make it popular with everyone, but it would not necessarily lose elections either.

II

The stifling lack of opportunity and enterprise in Britain is due more to our class structure than to any other factor. Management and labour, staff and employees, officers and men, gentlemen and players, U and non-U, us and them – British society is slashed across with these distinctions. What is wrong with them is that although they are not moral distinctions they function as if they were. Human beings are evaluated in accordance with them, have their lives shaped by them. The following Table 2 of the 1959 Crowther Report is based on a survey of the school-leaving age of National Service recruits to the Army and R.A.F., and shows that the age at which a British child leaves school depends less on his personal ability than on the social class and income of his parents. There is only one chance in a hundred that the child of unskilled workers will get a higher education.

School Leaving Age	15 or less	16	17	18 or more
Father's Occupation	%	%	%	%
Professional/Managerial	25	24	17	34
Clerical or Non-manual	59	22	9	10
Skilled Workers	78	15	3	4
Semi-skilled Workers	85	11	2	2
Unskilled Workers	92	6	1	1
% on all Groups	72	15	5	8

Lower down the same page the report says: 'Among National Service men entering the Army, while nine-tenths of those in the top 10 per cent in ability stayed at school voluntarily for at least one year more than they had to, over four-tenths of them (42 per cent) left by sixteen and did not attempt the Sixth Form course to Advanced Level in the General Certificate of Education for which their ability would have made them strong candidates. It also shows that, among the next ability group [out of six groups] very nearly two-thirds left school as soon as they were allowed to. Of course there is a close association between the facts of under-utilized ability . . . and the facts of under-represented social groups shown in Table 2.'

So the notion that we now have equality even of opportunity in Britain is a myth. The great majority of people stay in the class into which they were born, *regardless of their merit*. Untalented members of the upper and upper-middle class stay in that class, thanks chiefly to our education system (and our tax system, which I shall deal with in a moment) while more talented members of the working and lower-middle class leave school and start work by the age of sixteen. The exceptions draw attention to themselves, some of them making quite a splash as Angry Young Men, and though few they are much more numerous than a generation ago, so an altogether exaggerated estimate of social mobility is built up in people's minds. In present circumstances lack of education is 'inherited' along with bad housing conditions, lack of money, and all the other inadequacies that surround the upbringing of most people, and the doors of opportunity are closed not only where money is required but also where the only requirement seems, on the face of it, to be personal fittedness. You need no property to become a clergyman, and most clergymen are poor, yet how many working-class boys become clergymen? The working-class constitutes, say, three-quarters of the population – yet what proportion of barristers are of working-class origin? What proportion of authors, of doctors, of artists, of architects? Success in the professions may depend chiefly on personal ability *once you are in them*, but you have little chance of getting into them unless you already belong to the most privileged quarter of the population.

When I went into industry I was interviewed by some of the biggest companies in Britain. At every interview I was asked what school I had been to and what university, what games I played, what regiment I had been in in the Army. I was often told approvingly that I was 'the sort of chap we want', because I spoke 'well' or dressed 'well'. (On the other hand an interviewer at the BBC once told me I would be handicapped for the rest of my life by the fact that I had been at Keble, Oxford's least fashionable college.) Little discussion was given to the job I was being interviewed for – sometimes none at all. When I was 'on the inside' I got used to people being evaluated in this way. Whenever it was a question of taking on a new person my colleagues were concerned not about whether he would do the job well but whether he would 'fit in'. If he looked like doing the job too well he would be turned down. The important thing was to be a good chap, saying the right things, slapping the right backs, thinking the right thoughts. In British industry a boy from a 'good' family, 'good' school and 'good' regiment does not start at a lower level than management trainee, however untalented he may be. A labourer rarely rises higher than foreman, however able he is. Quite apart from human considerations, which are the most important considerations, even in mere economic terms there is a double loss here. First, most of the nation's ability is running to waste, as shown by the Crowther Report, and second – because many if not most people in the ranks of management were recruited on the basis of class and not ability – our average level of business management is scarcely even third rate. 'Empirical studies show that a high proportion of British managements, in contrast to a minority of their compatriots and a majority of their competitors abroad, are slow to introduce new products, display unaggressive salesmanship, maintain inadequate after-sales service, belittle market research, fail to seek new markets, decline to attend trade fairs abroad, send catalogues to South America written in

English, are afraid of foreign competition, and generally show a
spirit neither of thoroughness nor of innovation.'[1]

Unfortunately most English people suppose that a class system
such as ours exists in every society, so instead of seeing it for the
vulgar swindle it is they take it as part of the natural order of things.
Even the intelligent and educated are quite commonly unable to envisage life without it. I once told an anecdote to a
clever young woman doctor who had never lived outside England,
which involved, among other things, my being taken to a party in
America given in his palatial house and vast estate by a millionaire I
had never met, and mistaking the gardener for my host. She remarked
that she could not even imagine what life would be like in a society
in which a gardener's presence at his employer's parties was as
natural as that of any other guests, let alone a society in which
one couldn't tell the difference. The point here, of course, is not
that the two men looked alike – they no more looked alike than I look
like my next-door neighbour. The point is that all the visible differences between them – of physique, grooming, dress, speech and
manner – were differences of individual personality, not class-
differences. This is the answer to people who assert that classlessness
would bring uniformity. The opposite is the truth. It is class distinctions that type people, thickly disguising not only differences between
members of the same class but similarities between members of
different classes, for they lump people together on some basis quite
other than their personality. The more you approach classlessness the
nearer you get to that ideal condition in which the differences between
people are the differences between them *as people*.

British acceptance of the class structure is positively incited by the
Government, the Conservative Party and most of the mass media, in
that they incite complacency. All the familiar concepts of the Affluent
Society, together with Conservative trumpetings about the 'Opportunity State' and slogans like 'You've never had it so good' encourage
the British people to think that everyone is well off and getting a full
chance in life, and everything in the garden is lovely. And of course
most people *are* better off than they have ever been before and *do*
have a better chance in life. But they compare the way things are with
the way they were, and are pleased, instead of comparing the way
they are here with the way they are elsewhere and being discon-
tented. They allow themselves to be fobbed off with an education

1. C. A. R. Crosland in *Encounter*, April 1961.

system that fails to educate most people, and they accept in consequence a fantastic inequality of opportunity; they are encouraged to ignore the plight of large minorities, such as the old, who live in great poverty, along with five or six million other casualties of the Welfare State. And they accept a tax system that perpetuates the economic basis of the class-structure by taxing earned wealth more heavily than unearned wealth – which indeed does not tax a lot of unearned wealth at all. I suppose one must expect the people who do well out of a racket to promote it vigorously, but it is a bitter thought that those who do most to foster belief in the myths of equality of opportunity and the Affluent Society would yell blue murder if called on to accept average amounts of opportunity and affluence – if they had to stop being educated and start work at the age of sixteen regardless of their abilities, and then at the height of their careers earn the £14 a week that is the average wage in Britain, and send their children to the Secondary Modern Schools that most children go to.

It is rare nowadays for people to defend class distinctions openly. This, together with the fact that when they are defended the arguments are fatuous, makes it unnecessary for me to spend more than a few lines on the subject. The standard defence, from Plato and Aristotle down to today, has been that equality would be all very well if people were the same, but they are not the same: there are wide and obvious differences of character, ability, energy, intelligence and so on; the able will always do better for themselves than the incompetent, and it is desirable that they should; therefore equality is not desirable, and whether it is desirable or not it is impossible. This argument is fatuous because it assumes or asserts that class differences are founded on differences of personal ability, whereas this has never been so in any society known to history. In all class-ridden societies, including present-day Britain, the self-made man has been regarded as an upstart by the people who were born into the station he has reached by his own ability, and looked down on by them, and his family is only fully accepted after a generation or two, when there can be no question of its members having established their social position for themselves. In other words personal merit is openly and positively ruled out as a fully-acceptable justification for privilege, and it is only when someone's privileged position is not in any way due to his personal merits that he can deploy the full aura of social superiority. The class structure of Britain today is quite flagrantly not based on personal merit –

if anyone were inclined to doubt that my quotations from the Crowther Report are alone enough to establish it. I say 'if anyone were inclined to doubt that' because the notion that the privileged are *personally* superior has such seductive appeal to the privileged that they almost always believe it, and is so invaluable in perpetuating their privilege that they vigorously encourage it with all the means that their privilege gives them, with the result that in most societies it is quite widely believed. But it is flatly contradicted on every side by manifest fact.

The Labour Party and all radical organizations should be conducting a frontal assault on the British class structure with maximum destruction as their avowed aim. Education, I think, is the key – if there is another Labour Government it should make education policy its chief domestic concern. Abolishing the situation revealed in the chart on page 185 should be given priority. It means spending 7% of the national income on education. At the moment we are spending $4\frac{1}{2}$%. We should build more schools, universities, and technical and teacher-training colleges; get more teachers by paying them more, using more part-time teachers and conducting recruiting campaigns for the profession; make classes smaller; abolish the eleven-plus examination and end the division, tripartite in theory and bipartite in practice, of our children; incorporate the private schools into the public system; and do more for handicapped children, both directly and by making greater provision for their teachers. This is only a beginning. The social background of educational inequality must also be attacked, not only in immediate ways like providing poor families with grants to keep their children at school beyond the minimum leaving age, but in indirect ways like a really determined effort to solve the housing problem.

The tax system should be radically altered. At the moment we have a looking-glass situation in which if one earns a lot of money, it is taxed more heavily than any other form of income, whereas if one gets the same sum without working for it, it is taxed either less or not at all. This fact alone contributes a lot of the fraud to our Fraudulent Society. In Britain today there are two ways in which a person can come into a large fortune: capital gains and inheritance. (You cannot work yourself rich.) Long-term capital gains are not taxed at all. If a person inherits a fortune the tax to be paid on it rises to a maximum of only 16/- in the pound, and reaches that level only on estates worth more than a million pounds. By contrast, the tax on earned income rises to a maximum of 17/9 in the pound and does so on all income over £15,000. So, to take an example, if a married man with two children earns £15,000 in a year he is liable to pay £7,662 2s. 6d. of it in tax. But if he inherits an estate of £15,000 he will pay only £1,200 of it in tax. I do not see how anyone can conceivably defend this. It is plainly unjust. The case for taxing inherited wealth more heavily, and much more heavily, than earned wealth is overwhelming. Furthermore the social results would be highly desirable. For inherited wealth is still the financial basis of our class structure, and its near-abolition would be a major step towards equality.

There are yet other important things that a Labour Government could do to end the class-racket. It could see to it that entry and pro-motion in all organizations under ministerial control – the nationalized industries, the civil service, the armed forces and so on – were based on individual fittedness, and drop all this nonsense about accent and school, and all the other class-characteristics. Such a policy pursued in a dozen of our major industries and all our public services would com-pel private industry to follow suit, however reluctantly and however belatedly. Then again a Labour Government could, and indeed is already committed to, abolish poverty in old age by means of a national superannuation scheme. In these and other ways the attack on the class-structure should be launched on a very wide front. It would require energy and courage from individual members of the Govern-ment, but if conducted with vigour and imagination the transforma-tion effected in British society by this alone would be greater than what took place between 1945 and 1951 – and I have not yet men-tioned all the other important aspects of policy.

Nor is the liquidation of the class structure a job for government alone. Local Authorities can make important contributions especially in housing, education and social welfare, and those controlled by Socialists should do so. At whatever points they are obstructed by the Government they should make bold use of publicity to fix the blame where it belongs. The trade unions should expand their outlook to include the whole of our society and start large-scale activity in such things as building housing estates, colleges, hotels and hostels; banking and insurance, publishing and television, even subsidizing the arts and entertainment. Above all they should run their own factories and businesses. The same things go for the Co-operative Society (insurance and housing estates should prove especially rich fields for them). Then there is a great deal to be done

by bodies quite outside the Labour Movement, like Consumers'
Association Ltd and the Advisory Centre for Education. All these
activities, as well as dealing mortal blows at our class structure, would
bring much-needed diversity, dynamism and enterprise to our stagnant society. And, perhaps most important of all, they are worth
doing for their own sake.

There is a great need for more democracy in British working
life, and the trade unions should pioneer it in the way their counterparts have done in some industries in the United States. I am not
suggesting workers' control of industry. What I am suggesting is
much more workers' control *over their own level of operations*. For
example if it is a question of promoting one of the workers on a
particular stretch of production line to be foreman of it, why should
he not be chosen by the workers themselves instead of by management? Critics of this suggestion say that the men would choose either
indulgent or extremist foremen, or simply the fellow who happens to
be most popular, but in the American factories where this system
already operates that does not happen. On the contrary, it becomes
quite clear that the workers concerned, like everybody else, prefer to
work under people whom they respect and who they feel could do
their job as well as themselves, if not better. And knowing each other's
personal strengths and weaknesses better than management they
make better choices; as a result they are happier and the foreman is
not looked on as an agent of the boss. It is when management chooses
that the wrong man is more likely to be promoted – someone chosen
for his compliance, or some other not-fundamentally-desirable
quality. This is only an example, but it is a vivid one, I think, of how
responsibility and egalitarianism could be extended in every walk of
British work.

III

If one points out to an Englishman that Sweden is much more
'up-to-date' than Britain the reply is likely to be: 'Of course, the
Swedes haven't had a war.' If one points out that the United States is
more up-to-date the reply is likely to be: 'Of course; we were bled
white by the war, losing all our overseas investments and being bomb-
damaged into the bargain; whereas the Americans, thousands of
miles from the fighting, did jolly well out of it.' If one points out that

West Germany is more up-to-date the reply is likely to be: 'Of course; their economy was totally destroyed by the war and their cities razed to the ground; they had to start building everything from scratch again willy-nilly, so naturally it's all bright and new and modern; whereas we emerged from the war with our pre-war economy and cities relatively unscathed, so we've been stuck with them.' There is something in each of these answers, but the chief thing they show is that we are more ready to make mutually contradictory excuses for our deficiencies than to remove them.

Nevertheless the reasons that have been given so far for the backwardness of Britain – our class-structure, the fact that we are a declining imperial power, and our ignorance not only about the rest of the world but about ourselves in relation to it and as seen by it – are not an exhaustive list. There is also, for example, the crucial fact that we were first in the field at the Industrial Revolution. We built the first railways, before their full importance and potential were realized, so we built them on a narrow gauge: other countries, following us, learned from our mistakes as well as from our example and built their railways on a wider gauge. There was never subsequently a time at which we could afford simply to scrap our whole national system and build another, so we were stuck with an out-of-date one simply as a result of being the first to have one. This is typical of what has happened across a whole range of industries: not only our railways but our coal mines and our textile industry are old-fashioned partly because their basic structure was laid down before that of other countries and is therefore more outmoded now. Nor is this true only of industrial organizations – it is true of all the institutions that sprang out of the Industrial Revolution, including the Labour Movement. I showed in Chapter Eight how the trade unions in Britain were outmoded because their structure was adapted to conditions of the nineteenth century and not conditions of today; and how the Co-operative Society was oriented towards a public that no longer existed. In politics, as in social economy, the radical pioneering of today becomes the conservative vested interest of tomorrow.

But this is to explain, not to excuse. The fact that the past lies more heavily on us than it does on other countries means only that we need more irreverence for it. Society is for us, its economy is for us, its institutions are for us, and we must make them serve us, not subordinate ourselves to them. (Jesus insisted on this, even of the most hallowed institutions: 'The sabbath was made for man, and not man for the sabbath.') We must treat institutions in the light of our present and future needs, not in the light of their former usefulness. Similarly with the material equipment of our society: English visitors to America are commonly astonished at the readiness with which Americans will tear down, say, a perfectly usable skyscraper to make way for a better one. It is a major symptom of decadence in the English that they are now more interested in preserving than in creating. I believe very strongly in preserving beautiful things. But it is idiotic to campaign for the preservation of pseudo-oriental towers and pseudo-Doric arches merely because they are there: if we insist on preserving everything the country will eventually become a museum, and one that does not even have room to accommodate new exhibits. We are a lot of people on a small island, and we cannot meet our changing needs by filling more space and adding to what we have; we must also show a radical willingness to discard the old and replace it, to destroy and rebuild. People who want to preserve everything that is outmoded merely because it is old are people who wish to return to the past. Conservatives can be as bad in sacrificing the living to the dead as Communists are in sacrificing the living to the unborn. Society is for the living and their children.

IV

If we as a community devote more productive resources to things that are privately owned, like hotels and cars, the general feeling is that we are adding to our income. But if we devote the same resources to things that are publicly owned, like hospitals and roads, the feeling is that we are adding to our expenses. The former things are looked on as more assets to be enjoyed, the latter as more burdens to be borne. There is no economic justification for this distinction. Its basis is purely psychological. If our personal incomes increase we can gratify private desires in immediate ways, like going out and buying things; also the freedom conferred by having the money and being able to do what we like with it is itself enjoyable. We are deprived of both of these pleasures if we have to spend the money on taxes. Although it is still we who consume it, in the form of new hospitals, new roads or whatever, the gratifications are neither private nor immediate, and we no longer have individual freedom to decide what they shall be. So each one of us likes to keep as much of his income as he can and spend it in accordance with his personal wishes.

This attitude, which we all share to some extent, is a short-sighted, selfish one and has tragic consequences. The public expenditure we want less of is for the most important things in life – health, education, justice, the arts, research, insurance against poverty and old age, defence against crime, accident and fire, effective freedom of movement – while the private expenditure we want more of is for enjoyable but, increasingly, secondary things. We are playing a sort of confidence trick on ourselves. We are cheating ourselves of necessities in order to have more luxuries. We are doing without new hospitals in order to have more hotels and bowling alleys. We are building fewer roads so that we can have more cars. We are sending our children to fifth-rate schools so that we can have television sets and washing machines. And the grotesque thing is that we are proud of it, revelling more and more in a *sense* of prosperity that is itself increasing.

All this is largely the result of a dozen years of Conservative government. For if there is one thing that unites Conservatives everywhere it is a fundamentalist belief in low taxes, with a consequent and passionate hostility to social expenditure. The British Conservatives have starved the public services ever since they came into office. In addition they have displayed a doctrinaire hostility to the nationalized industries even when they themselves are in charge of them. At the same time they have encouraged the private speculator and the private-consumption industries – in return for which they are massively assisted by commercial interests. The whole tendency of advertising is to persuade the public that private consumption constitutes happiness. 'The engines of mass communication, in their highest state of development, assail the eyes and ears of the community on behalf of more beer but not of more schools. Even in the conventional wisdom it will scarcely be contended that this leads to an equal choice between the two.'[1]

The Labour Party should lead an onslaught on these commercial values. It should do so in such a way as to make it absolutely clear that it is campaigning *for* 'the good things of life' and not against them, and it should do everything in its power to educate the public in the simple political issue underlying the choice. It should make its appeal colourful and dramatic – emotional as well as rational. There

1. Galbraith: *The Affluent Society*, p. 202.

should be no taint of drabness or austerity about it. On no account should Socialists allow themselves to appear as if opposing prosperity: they should talk of maximising prosperity, and prosperity where it matters most – in the public services.

This brings me back to a point I approached earlier from a different direction, namely the need for more public enterprise. Not only are bold new departures required in the education system, the health service and the nationalized industries: the very face of Britain itself is in need of urgent public attention. At the moment the development of our cities and the use of our land are being chiefly determined by the speculator and the spiv. 'Powerful social and economic forces are rapidly changing the landscape. Much of it is being defaced, even devastated in places, but it is not yet irretrievably ruined. What happens in the next two decades will decide whether it is to be de-spoiled beyond recovery.'[1] There is urgent need for the re-establish-ment of the Ministry of Town and Country Planning, with wider responsibilities than before, to co-ordinate building, land-ownership and land-values, transport and the location of jobs, in a way that has never yet been done in this country. In an overcrowded island like ours these are matters to be decided by public discussion and demo-cratically elected bodies, not by irresponsible private citizens in search of quick returns.

V

Our beliefs in liberty, rational government, decent standards of life, and freedom from exploitation are only morally defensible so long as we do not restrict their application to ourselves. If we demand them for ourselves yet refuse them to others they are nothing but rationalizations of selfishness. And we in Britain have a special responsibility to others because we have a colonial empire in which millions of people, whether they like it or not, are ruled by us.

The Labour Party never had much of a colonial policy until after the war, largely because of its opposition-mindedness. It used the colonies chiefly as indignation-fodder, and most Socialist activity in connection with them consisted of protest against topical abuses. In

1. *The Face of Britain*, a special committee report published in *Socialist Commentary*, September 1961, and available separately.

other words they were looked on more as sticks to beat the Tories with than as countries full of human beings who needed our imaginative help. It is only since the war that Socialists have given much constructive thought to the real problems of social rescue, investment, education, medical organization, and economic and political development. It was lack of a policy that lost the post-war Labour Government most of its goodwill in the colonies. When it was elected in 1945 the reaction in the colonies was ecstatic: a revolutionary change at last, a new deal! And of course in some colonies there was a new deal – in India, Ceylon and Burma, for instance. But in too many places there was not. Kenya, Malaya and Cyprus were only the most glaring examples: there was also the Middle East, the beginnings of Central African Federation, and such remote spots as British Guiana, such whited sepulchres as the Bahama Islands. In too many colonies the Labour Government bumbled along in the black wake of the Conservatives simply because it did not know what to do. Naturally the colonials who had expected so much were disappointed, and naturally their disappointment turned to bitterness – and naturally they tend now to say 'One party's as bad as the other as far as we're concerned: they're both the same.'

The historic purpose of the Labour Party has been to improve the lot of the British workers, and British workers are rich and privileged compared with the people of the colonies. As a result many Socialists *in practice* have similar attitudes towards colonial people as those they traditionally complain of in capitalists towards workers. They care far more passionately about pay rises for the already privileged people they represent than they do about ameliorating the unimaginable squalor in which most coloured British subjects, for whom they are also responsible, live. They get a kick out of helping the underprivileged, but only provided the cost is too small to be felt. They do not mind how quickly the underprivileged rise, provided they themselves rise at least as fast and the gap is not closed. Before the 1959 General Election the Labour Party pledged itself to devote one per cent of the national income to developing the colonies: but since this was less than half the annual *increase* in our national income it suggested that the gap in living standards should go on widening and not start to close. One of the basic problems in the world today is that the poor countries are getting poorer while the rich are getting richer, and the Labour Party has still not faced the full implications of this for British colonial policy.

A simple truth, but one that needs stating, is that the need for radical policies is greater in the colonies than it is in Britain. And whether we like it or not the rate of colonial change is itself increasing. A friend of mine who travelled through East Africa in 1959 was generally told by White Settlers that they had twenty or twenty-five years in which to prepare for independence. When he told them he thought they had about five they laughed at him and said that he, being on his first visit, naturally did not know what he was talking about, while they, who had lived there all their lives . . . etc. In fact independence came in three years – faster than even the most ardent African nationalists or the most radical Europeans had dared to hope. It is silly for us to go on pretending that it is we who decide when colonies get their independence: the decision is forced on us by events which are not merely out of our control but which are continually taking us by surprise.

However, this seems to happen only when we avoid committing ourselves about dates. Such avoidance forces a direct conflict between us and the colonies. If instead we agree at the outset a specific time-table for accomplishing independence by stages over a maximum period of five years – which we did so successfully in Ghana – this transforms the local situation into one of co-operation in preparing for independence. The success of a newly independent country depends a good deal on how effectively that independence is prepared – the Congo shows what happens when it is not prepared at all. None of the British colonies are in the state the Congo was just before independence, but in most of them there is urgent need for crash programmes of development to be carried out immediately.

It has always seemed to me that the real crime of the colonial powers has been not exploitation but neglect. In March 1954 Krishna Menon, commenting on the Tanganyika Government's annual report to the Trusteeship Council of the UN, said: 'In the field of education a European child costs the Administration £223 a year, an African child costs the Administration £8 5s. 0d. a year, and an Asian child costs £31 a year. I am sure it is not contended that the European child is so uneducable that it requires thirty times as much effort to teach him.' At about the same time Julius Nyerere pointed out that under the existing programme would be '1986 or 1990' before every African child in Tanganyika was going to school. This is the kind of thing which has constituted the basic immorality of colonial rule, and which demands a radically new approach from the colonial powers. We should attack such problems with the same passion, determination and sustained hard work and investment as we would if they existed in Britain. If we ourselves cannot provide all the investment required we should make it part of our job to get it, whether from other governments, or the World Bank, or other UN agencies, or private sources, or new groupings like a reconstituted NATO. Any radical government worth its salt would be ashamed to do less for the people of the colonies than it does for the people of Britain.

CHAPTER TEN

The Oneness of the World

IN Chapter Four I gave some of the reasons why our moral obligations cannot be limited to this group or that. They bind us to everyone: morally the only collection of people to which we belong is the one that excludes nobody, namely the human race. Lesser groupings are either administrative conveniences or cultural limitations. This has been reiterated by great moralists for over two thousand years. 'I am not an Athenian or a Greek,' said Socrates,[1] 'but a citizen of the world.' 'A wise man belongs to all countries,' said Democritus,[2] 'for the whole world is the mother country of a noble spirit.' When Diogenes was asked what his country was he replied: 'Κοσμοπολίτης' ('I am a citizen of the world') and thus coined the word 'cosmopolitan'.[3] And so on through the centuries – in England in the seventeenth century we have Samuel Butler saying 'All countries are a wise man's home',[4] and in the eighteenth Thomas Paine: 'My country is the world, and my religion is to do good.'[5]

Until the Industrial Revolution, however, it was not possible for this principle to be put into more than very limited practice. For throughout history until very recently the people in each part of the world did not even know of the existence of most other parts of the world. Before the eighteenth century neither news nor men could travel faster than a horse. It is almost impossible for us now to comprehend these facts. People simply did not receive much news even from places of whose existence they knew, and such as they did would take weeks, months, perhaps even years to arrive. There is now more transmission of news in a single day, and more journeys are undertaken, than in any whole century before the advent of modern communications. We now have access to more information even about the countries we know least about, like Communist China, than people

1. According to Plutarch in *Of Banishment*.
2. Democritus: *Ethics*.
3. Diogenes Laertius: *Diogenes*.
4. *Hudibras*, Part 3, Canto 2.
5. *Rights of Man*, Part 2, Chapter 5.

had until the eighteenth century about the countries they knew most about. But the most important result of the unification of the world by modern communications is interdependence. It is not merely a matter of *knowing* what is going on elsewhere, it is a matter of being profoundly affected by it. This morning's events in Paris may cause this evening's riots in Algiers. The accidental death of a single man in the heart of Central Africa can plunge the whole world into a state of shock within twenty-four hours. An invasion in Korea or Egypt or Cuba will have all the governments in the world leaping to action stations simultaneously. And of course, macabre though it is, the communications that have done most to make all parts of the world interdependent are those that carry nuclear weapons.

If any country uses nuclear weapons again there will be no such thing as 'keeping out of it': everyone will be swept away, neutrals as well as belligerents. For this quite simple reason politics everywhere is everyone's concern. The invasion of South Korea brought the world to the brink of nuclear destruction. When Britain invaded Egypt the Russians threatened her with rockets. New civil or colonial wars might yet take us over the edge – in Persia for instance, or Germany, Laos, Korea, the Congo or Cuba. It is as much my business as anybody's whether, say, America gets involved in war with China, because if she does I shall go up in vapour. An Indian or an African could say the same. We are all in everything together. And mention of India and Africa reminds us that some of the most explosive forces in the world today are being generated in backward countries trying to emancipate themselves from poverty and colonial dependence. Indo-China's attempts to retain her independence after being liberated from Japanese occupation in 1945 involved her in war with the French, who tried to reimpose their former colonial rule by force, and this in turn involved first the Chinese and then the Americans, until the whole world stood on the threshold of a hydrogen-bomb war.

So the basic maxim of civilized ethics has now acquired a momentous significance. Although the world is a country in chaos it is only by insistently regarding it as one country, a single society to which we all belong, that we shall behave in such a way as to stop the chaos before it stops us. Human beings should think and feel and act as if they were all, without exception, members one of another, not only because it is right but because if they deny it they will be refuted by universal death. I do not say mankind is going to destroy itself, nor do I say it is going to survive – the whole point is that the choice has yet to be made, and is ours.

Some people believe that man is incorrigibly homicidal, and therefore that there is no choice. I do not believe this. I am sure we all have aggressive impulses so powerful that they have to be given expression, but there are countless forms in which we do this besides killing people: competitiveness at work, at play, in politics and social life, in the family and among our friends. The great majority of men and women live their whole lives without killing or trying to kill anyone, yet they exhibit aggression in all sorts of ways from argument to driving. In this age of high-speed travel, emergent colonies, dangerous medical research, space rockets and the rest, there is no lack of challenge, adventure and mortal risk for anyone who wants them.

It is an undoubted fact, as emphasized by Professor Eysenck in *The Psychology of Politics* (see especially pp. 251–5) that only our drives themselves, our aggressive or competitive drives, are innate, and that the activities in which they are given expression and the formation of the groups pursuing those activities are contingent. All history bears this out. Rulers down the ages have manipulated our aggressive instincts for their own ends. But one must not overlook the fact that this has taken *sustained* ingenuity, work, money and force, together with the massive exploitation of myth (usually in the guise of history) and religion. It seems that unless communities are driven and duped and drugged into warlike group-attitudes they cannot be relied on to maintain them. But given such remorseless conditioning they are liable to look on current enmities as 'natural' – it is 'natural' for Athenians and Spartans to kill each other, or Romans and Cartheginians, or Moslems and Christians, or Catholics and Protestants, or Englishmen and Scots, or Germans and Frenchmen, or Chinese and Japanese.

The innumerable nationalist heroes who have built up unified countries out of hitherto warring territories and tribes have almost always been looked on in their early days, before their practical successes, as fanatic dreamers attempting the impossible and flying in the face of nature; yet before long the very people who believed in the naturalness and immutability of the traditional hostilities come to believe equally in the naturalness of the new unification and the immutability of the new patriotism. Some sentimentalists go on maintaining that local allegiances are the strongest, but this is plainly untrue

– the sense of allegiance to the new, bigger unit becomes over-whelmingly stronger. Lancastrians would not be prepared to die on the battlefield to prevent the forcible incorporation of Lancashire in Yorkshire, but they would to prevent the incorporation of Britain in Germany or Russia. In the course of time it is totally forgotten what the former distinctions even were: in Britain today most people have never heard of the Mercians, though some are descended from them and others not – yet Mercia was once the proudest and most powerful of kingdoms, with its own language and its own history, at constant war with its neighbours. Being British is as arbitrary now as being a Mercian once was. Similarly it is quite clear that being a German is no more a 'natural' allegiance than being a Bavarian or a Prussian was before the unification of Germany – or being a Franconian before the unification of Bavaria; and so on back *ad infinitum*.

So far in history there seems to have been a steady move towards the building up of larger and larger units of allegiance. Now we have Russia covering a sixth of the earth's surface, and many other continent-sized countries whose people derive from a wealth of different backgrounds of race, language and religion – America, Canada, Brazil, India, China, Australia – and we seem to be witnessing the emergence of an 'African personality' before our very eyes. The farthest this process can go is to the development of a sense of belong-ing to the world. That is not inevitable, but the evidence of history makes it seem likely. Unless we manage to develop such an allegiance the world will probably come to an end.

To say that it is unrealistic to expect people to develop such feelings is to ignore fact, and in that sense is itself unrealistic. Many people *have* them, and for over two thousand years many people have had them. If Socrates could manage it in the fifth century B.C. I do not see that it is necessarily too sophisticated or advanced for us today. It is no more idealistic to expect Europeans to become citizens of the world than it was to expect Germans to become Europeans, or Bavarians to become Germans, or Franconians to become Bavarians, though in each case it appeared impossible to most people before it happened. Patriotism is a form of tribalism that has survived into a world in which tribal motivations in one society can bring death to all mankind. I have no great faith in the power of argument to alter most people's attitudes, but I have considerable faith in the power of brute fact to do so, and such basic drives as that of self-preservation.

What seems on the face of it the strongest argument against our being able to develop a world outlook is that hitherto there have always been in-groups and out-groups, however big the groups and despite the fact that their composition has been always changing; the human race cannot become a single in-group, the argument runs, because then there would be no out-group at all, and therefore no common enemy to bind people together. In the absence of an external group against whom to direct their aggression people would direct it at each other, so fragmentation and internecine strife will always continue. This argument overlooks many things. It overlooks not only the fact that many individuals already feel themselves as belonging to mankind rather than to this or that group, but the further fact that whole nations are already getting along very happily without conflict with their neighbours and yet without suffering internal disruption as a result. In Europe Sweden and Switzerland are obvious examples, and there are many others. It is not impossible for the world as a whole to do what these countries are already doing and have long done. The argument also overlooks the fact, pointed out earlier, that there are innumerable outlets for aggression besides war. I suppose there will always be crime, and therefore always the need for a certain amount of legal violence in its prevention and in the apprehension of criminals. The Army quite sensibly channels potential delinquents into the Military Police so that their love of fighting will be used to restore order instead of disrupting it. Most governments do the same sort of thing with their police forces, at least to some extent – even in docile England the police and the underworld overlap. My point here is that people with a thirst for physical violence can be used to uphold law and order instead of endangering it. I think all the things people are inclined to say cannot be done when one is talking in international terms are already being done in lesser causes.

The fact that aggression between groups does not arise out of the natural differences between them, but rather that whatever differences happen to exist are seized on as an excuse for aggression, is of the profoundest importance. So is the fact that governments have nearly always made it one of their chief concerns to cultivate and manipulate such aggression for their own ends. It should be clear by this time that I do not expect aggressive instincts to disappear and do not expect governments to stop manipulating them (though I do expect governments to stop cultivating them – for instance to stop the indoctrination of children with nationalist propaganda disguised as school history). I expect aggression to continue, and therefore I want manipulation of it also to continue so as to secure that so far as possible it finds its outlet in non-violent forms, and that what must take the form of violence is used to strengthen the rule of law and not destroy it.

What I am arguing for, of course, is the need for world government. This is not idealistic. Even Harold Macmillan has described world government as 'the only way out for mankind'.[1] Attlee, no soft sentimentalist either, is devoting the last years of his life to campaigning for it. I urge the impossibilists to think again. In the last chapter I showed how independence was coming to African colonies faster than even the most extreme idealists thought possible only two or three years ago. A mistake we consistently make in the modern world is to leave out of account the fact that the movement of change is accelerating. We go on thinking as if change will continue to take place at its present rate, whereas the rate, already bafflingly fast, is itself increasing. Changes that used to occupy fifty years now occupy five, and changes that now take five years will soon take only two. A couple of years ago we gasped with incredulity when told that a man would land on the moon by the end of this century, yet now the facts are such that he may already have done so by the time this book appears in print. Experience systematically misleads us over this vital question of how quickly developments will materialize, because they always materialize faster than they would at present rates of change.

I

Whether or not it is realistic to urge the need for world government the fact is we have not got it. To say that world government is the only long-term solution to our problems and leave it at that is to leave unanswered the most important question of all, namely what should we do in the short run? We live in the world as it is, not the world as we would like it to be. Until such time as we get world government the pursuit of national foreign policies is inescapable, and only the pursuit of the right ones will avert the end of the world.

So I wish to consider now what Britain's foreign policy should be, not in the long run – our long run aim should be the establishment of world government, 'the only way out for mankind' – but in the short run. And there are, it seems to me, three guiding principles we should

1. In the House of Commons, March 1955.

follow. The first and overriding one is quite simply self-preservation. In practice this means chiefly the avoidance of a Third and Final World War. The second is that we should do as much as possible to help and as little as possible to hinder the emancipation of people from poverty and tyranny. The third is that we should frustrate totalitarian attempts anywhere in the world to overthrow free institutions or to trick national liberation movements into exchanging one form of tyranny for another. These three aims deeply interpenetrate one another in obvious ways. Resistance to national liberation movements leads to war which may involve the nuclear powers. On the other hand blind encouragement of them, especially in Eastern Europe, could also lead to war involving the nuclear powers. Failure to resist Communist pressure, as in West Berlin, would result in the loss of freedom. Yet ever-zealous resistance to it could precipitate McCarthyism at home and, if persisted in, world war. Every policy must be looked at in the round and its side-effects ruthlessly calculated. I use the word 'ruthlessly' deliberately. We were right, for instance, to hold back while the Hungarian people were butchered in their own streets in a heroic attempt to shake off Russian colonial rule, for to have sent help would have been to launch a war between nuclear powers. Such decisions are hard and bitter. They seem inhuman to many and are intolerable to some. But they have to be taken. They impose terrible strains on the politicians who take them but, as I argued in Chapter Three, the need to take harrowing decisions is inescapable in politics. I hope I have said nothing in this book to suggest that being a responsible politician is easy.

So although I can deal only one at a time with the three principles I have set out I would like the reader never to lose sight of the fact that the operation of each is modified by the operation of the others. I shall deal with the first, self-preservation, in this section; with the emancipation of the oppressed in Section II; and with resistance to totalitarianism in Section III.

At the moment we have the famous 'balance of terror' between the two great Power blocs: each fears the other, but each fears to attack the other because of the certainty of instant retaliation. And the fear each feels at the prospect of the other's pulling ahead in technical development and gaining a clear preponderance of power urges both to more and more urgent preparations for nuclear war. This is a vicious circle, of course: the higher the pitch of preparedness in each the more terrified the other becomes, so that the tension and the destructive power mount side by side, each spurring the other on. If this goes on indefinitely, and if furthermore the possession of nuclear weapons spreads to more and more governments, I do not see how the human race can survive. In such circumstances it seems practically certain that hydrogen bombs will sooner or later be used. The arms race must be halted –and then put into reverse, with a gradual scaling down of armaments on both sides – and the spread of nuclear weapons to new governments stopped if Armageddon is to be avoided. How is this to be done?

It is crying for the moon to expect either side to agree to anything that would shift the balance in favour of the other, since it is fear of precisely this that is the whole dynamic of the arms race. Any proposals, to be serious, must be equally advantageous to both. Neither side will yield an inch unless it can be sure that the other is also yielding at least an inch. From this it follows that bilateral disarmament is the only hope for disarmament. As for ending the arms race in the first place and stopping the spread of nuclear weapons to new governments, this can be done only by an international agreement to have no more tests – for without tests the Great Powers cannot develop nuclear weapons much beyond their present stage, and if new governments cannot test nuclear devices they cannot develop their own hydrogen bombs. I should have thought it was clearly in the Great Powers' interest to see that no other governments acquired hydrogen bombs, and therefore to reach genuine agreement on tests. This may even have happened by the time this book appears. What is absolutely clear is that in this whole question of disarmament there is no substitute for negotiation. Neither side can get what it wants by unilateral action.

Since in practice neither side will agree to anything that gives the other an easy dominance a lot of the debate in the Labour Party about disarmament has been wasted breath. For instance to suggest that the West disarm unilaterally and leave Russia with a world monopoly of hydrogen bombs is as fantastic as to suggest that Russia disarm unilaterally and leave the West with a world monopoly of hydrogen bombs: in no conceivable circumstances would any of the governments concerned dream of doing any such thing. So to make proposals along these lines is not to confront the problem at all but simply to wish it away. But the problem does not disappear if it is ignored, it gets worse. However, to point this out – that whatever the rights and wrongs of the fact, it is a fact that neither side in the Cold War is going to throw itself on the other's mercy – is not to make a moral point: it is to make a practical point, and a point of supreme importance above all others.

Yet one can still ask, *ought not* either of the Great Powers to be prepared to disarm unilaterally? I myself have no doubt that America should not. Because ever since the end of the Second World War the Russians have not hesitated to impose Communist governments on other countries by violence when they were in a position to do so (the solitary exception is Finland). All the European countries liberated by America and Britain soon had free elections and democratic governments, even their half of defeated Germany, but the Russians broke the Yalta agreements on holding free elections in occupied countries and imposed Communist régimes by brute force on East Germany, Poland, Hungary, Rumania, Bulgaria, Albania, Estonia, Latvia, Lithuania and Czechoslovakia. Communists themselves now officially admit how indescribably savage those régimes were. All attempts at self-determination were crushed with the utmost brutality, the bloodiest incidents being in East Germany, Poland and Hungary. The Russians also encouraged civil war in Greece and Turkey and tried to establish their troops in Persia, but these ventures were not successful. Nor was their blockade of Berlin. In the Far East the Chinese Communist régime sent its troops into South Korea, Indo-China, India and Burma, and in the annexation of Tibet indulged in even more ferocity and slaughter than the Russians did in Hungary. Whatever the Western record since the war, that of the Communist states is heinous and shows determination to stop at no perfidy or bloodshed to promote Communist governments in other countries. For the West to disarm unilaterally and leave the Russians with all the hydrogen bombs in the world would be to invite the destruction of free institutions everywhere. For that reason it would be the most immoral act in history.

If the choice lay between Communism and nuclear war I should choose Communism – no question about that. But that is not the choice. People who present it as such are hysterical in outlook. At the moment we have neither world-Communism nor world-war, and we should aim to go on avoiding both. But exclusive concern to avoid *all risk* of Communism would probably lead us to launch a devastating surprise attack on Russia, just as exclusive concern to avoid *all risk* of war would lead us to unqualified submission to Russia. Both policies are neurotic, the former characteristic of the lunatic Right, the latter of the lunatic Left, and both results would be calamitous. There is no magic formula for the elimination of risk. This is something that the hysterical or simple-minded do not understand: there is no panacea such that if we do 'x' (e.g. disarm unilaterally) everything will be all right. There is only a choice of dangers. And since we do not wish to invite disaster, whether in the form of world war or submission to Communism, the only general line we can pursue is that of minimizing the *joint* risk. I am convinced that multilateral disarmament is a necessary part of any such policy.

I have given my basic reasons for believing on both moral and practical grounds that the West must keep hydrogen bombs just so long as – but not one moment longer than – the Russians do. Discussion in Britain, however, has centred on two other questions: should we allow American bases on British soil, and should we retain independent possession of hydrogen bombs? If it is granted that the Americans should not strip themselves of nuclear weapons while the Russians retain theirs, the first question becomes a technical one, for if it is the case that American weapons can hit Russian targets only if fired from overseas bases whereas Russian weapons can hit American targets from Russia then clearly the Americans must have overseas bases. The answer probably is that America still needs overseas bases for a little while longer but will stop needing them shortly. Meanwhile to say that the Americans must have overseas bases but these are so dangerous they should be in someone else's country is a profoundly immoral attitude.

The second question – whether we should have our own 'independent deterrent' – is academic, because we have not got it and are clearly never going to have it. Hydrogen bombs are useless without the means of delivering them to their targets, and the collapse of the Blue Streak project made it clear that henceforth we should be dependent on America for any such means. Nevertheless it may be important to enumerate the reasons why we should give up the attempt or pretence at independent nuclear-power status:

1. It does not add to the safety of the world. It is America that Russia is afraid of, not us, and whether we have hydrogen bombs or not makes little difference. (When we exploded our first hydrogen bomb and the British newspapers flew banner headlines such as WE'RE STILL *GREAT* BRITAIN, of the four New York newspapers only one put the story on its front page; two printed it inside, and one did not report it at all.) To imagine that our possession of the bomb is a

decisive factor in world affairs is to indulge in megalomaniac delusions about our status.

2. We cannot afford it. The cost of the nuclear arms race is not only (*1*) immense but also (*2*) rapidly increasing and (*3*) not delimitable. To enter the race is to commit ourselves to future levels of expenditure which we cannot even foresee, let alone meet. We are altogether out of our depth here.

3. Nuclear physicists of really high calibre are not numerous, and it is a waste of creative talent to devote most of their research to defence which has little practical value.

4. The fewer countries possess hydrogen bombs the better. Since we could give ours up without prejudice to our security we should do so. Perhaps the best use to make of this renunciation would be to try to make it part of an agreement with other secondary powers not to manufacture nuclear weapons. It is hopeless, as at present, to insist that we must have them for our own security while trying to deny them to others, e.g. Western Germany, on the grounds that in the hands of others they are a danger to world peace.

One basic question remains: having given up our nuclear pretensions, should we stay in the Western alliance or should we adopt a neutralist policy in world affairs? There has been one occasion since the war when we have cut loose from our alliances and 'gone it alone', and that was Suez. Immediately the Russian government – not impressed by our independent deterrent – threatened us with rockets if we did not withdraw our troops from Egypt. Two of the lessons underlined by the Suez episode are that Britain is helpless in the world without her American allies and that the moment we are on our own the Russians threaten us with extinction if we do not do what they want. For these reasons neutralism is for us a non-starter. As for talk of Britain 'leading a neutral bloc', this is the old megalomaniac delusion in a new guise. Why on earth should other countries want to follow Britain? The very notion of Nehru being 'led' by Harold Macmillan is laughable.

To sum up my views on disarmament: it is the *sine qua non* of human survival, but will come about only by negotiation between the two Great Powers, who in turn will agree only on proposals that do not give either a net advantage over the other. This means that bilateral disarmament is the only solution. Britain cannot play a star role in this, but can still make a useful contribution by giving up her own manufacture of nuclear weapons (which she should do in any case for her own good) though her security requires her to stay in the Western alliance.

The concept of unilateralism – that one can solve problems all alone, by direct action, without the co-operation of the other people involved in them – is common in politics. Psychologically it is related to the infantile fantasy of having all one's own way; also it offers an escape from responsibility and risk. It panders to the overestimation of one's own power which is also a commonplace in politics. (I have been stricken with sheer awe by America's repeated attempts, first with the Japanese Peace Treaty and then with SEATO, to make a post-war settlement in Asia without reference to India, Russia or China, which together comprise most of Asia and contain getting on for half the human race.) Negotiations involves concessions on both sides, so people who expect to get all their own way can seldom negotiate. They usually look on negotiation as appeasement. Such an attitude is mortally dangerous, since in the long run problems can be solved only by negotiation or by violence. The United Nations was created to provide permanent machinery for doing the former and averting the latter, but obviously it can work only if it is used. To keep out the most bellicose country in the world, China, on the ground that it is bellicose is an extraordinary inversion of values: if there were no bellicose countries we should not need the United Nations. The whole point of the organization is to provide a permanent conference table round which differences can be settled peacefully, and the more troublesome a state is the more important it is that it should be at the conference table. To shut it out is to ensure that it pursues its aim unilaterally and by violence, since you leave it no alternative. The British Government should do all it can to insist that the United Nations includes everyone, and that it is used wherever possible for the settlement of international disputes. It should also accept United Nations decisions, even when these conflict with what it would like. It is tragic that our Conservative Government has built up a black record for Britain of limiting the UN's membership by helping, until recently, to keep China out, even though Britain recognizes the Chinese Government; of defiance of the United Nations Charter, as at Suez; and, worst of all, of clandestine sabotage of its operations, as in the Congo.

II

Most of the nation states of Europe were formed in war, and it has been common for national liberation movements to stop at nothing to gain their ends – to form alliances with foreign tyrannies or to embrace tyranny themselves. Since this has been almost universal experience in Europe it should surprise none of us to find many of the newer countries of Asia and Africa going through a similar development. In their struggle for integration, independence and release from poverty the backward countries will grasp at any help that is offered. If it comes from the West they will take it, but if it does not they will turn to Communist countries for it. In this sense the development of the backward countries is prior in significance to the Cold War, because their Cold War attitudes are determined by what happens in their nationalist struggles, and not *vice versa*. Even in the Communist countries themselves it is probably true that nationalist loyalty is stronger than Communist loyalty. 'National communism is, in the strictest sense, a contradiction in terms, for a doctrine which claims the status of a scientific law cannot be true in one place and false in another. Yet in one country after another it has become clear that even the faithful themselves put national independence ahead of doctrinal uniformity. There are now at least five different varieties of communism in existence – the Russian, the Chinese, the Yugoslav, the Albanian, and the Polish – and if communism spreads still further others are certain to appear.'[1]

Conservatives seldom bother to distinguish between different forms of social revolution – in fact are commonly incapable of doing so. When Nasser defied Britain, Conservative newspapers and speakers branded him as 'a puppet of Moscow', whereas in truth he has always been defiant of Moscow and one of the toughest anti-Communists in the Middle East (the Communist Party is outlawed in Egypt and all well-known Communists are in prison). In the United States right-wing Republicans tend to regard everyone who is not conservative as Communist. Sir Roy Welensky calls his crusade against African nationalism a crusade against Communism, and the South African Government pursues its policies of race-hatred against all coloured

1. *The Guardian*, 11 December 1961.

people in the name of defence of the free world from the bolshevik menace. All powerful threats to the existing social order seem to evoke the same basic emotional reaction from Conservatives, who therefore tend to lump them all together as a single phenomenon. This is the chief cause of their grotesque and all-embracing failure to understand the world we live in. The mistake is suicidal, because for the reasons given in the previous paragraph our anti-Communism should make us pro-nationalist. Wherever we have co-operated with movements of national liberation, as in India, Pakistan, Ceylon, Burma, Nigeria, Tanganyika and even Ghana, we have non-Communist societies living at peace with the West – in fact all the above countries except Burma chose to remain in the British Commonwealth, to the bafflement of many foreign observers. But where the West has tried to destroy national liberation movements by force, as in Indonesia, Indo-China, Algeria, Cyprus or Egypt, we have (*1*) failed, (*2*) strengthened the very forces we wanted to destroy, (*3*) promoted the appeal of Communism in the world at large, and often in the particular territory itself, (*4*) made any rational settlement of the problem difficult or impossible, (*5*) killed a lot of people, (*6*) brought terrorism into existence, (*7*) done a great deal of material damage, and (*8*) created lasting hatred of ourselves.

Quite apart from moral considerations we should help national liberation movements simply on grounds of expediency. To meet movements for independence with force and chicanery is merely to exacerbate them. Instead we should be on their side. (In purely expedient terms it seems to me that an independent Algeria, for example, would have been better for France all along than the authoritarian government, the corruption of public morals, the national impoverishment, the strengthening of Chinese Communist influence, the appalling refugee problem, the endless catalogue of slaughter, torture, censorship, terrorism and right-wing *coups*, and the loss of the world's respect, that have been the price of denying that independence. If one adds moral considerations to the account, then what is already an overwhelming case of self-interest becomes a moral obligation. The rich nations have a *duty* to help that great mass of mankind that is still trying to struggle its way out of abject poverty. 'Of 800 million children born in the last ten years, 100 million have already died from hunger or disease. Two out of every three cannot expect to live beyond 35.'[1] In such a world it is not

1. Ritchie Calder in *The Daily Herald*, 27 November 1961.

enough for us to grant political freedom to the oppressed: we owe them massive personal, financial and technical assistance.

The backward countries need doctors, teachers, engineers, administrators – skilled people of all kinds. They need them not only to do their respective jobs but also to pass on their skills to the local inhabitants. They need opportunities to send their able people abroad to study. And they need huge amounts of capital for the construction of roads, railways, homes, hospitals, schools, colleges and public buildings of all sorts; to irrigate land, build dams, drain swamps, clear forests; to mechanize and, above all, 'chemicalize' agriculture; and simply to finance government, administration, education, health and all the other public services. But all these resources, both human and material, can come in the first instance only from the advanced countries. In other words what is required is a redistribution of the world's income, a gigantic redistribution of goods and services, and above all investment, from the richer to the poorer nations. If the term 'international Socialism' has any meaning it involves at least this – the unrestricted application of what Socialists have always advocated within our own local society. The refusal of the rich to help the poor, or to help them enough, leads, as we know, to desperation and violence on the part of the poor, and this in turn brings counter-revolutionary violence from the rich. In purely material terms it is not worth it. In some Western Societies – Britain is the outstanding example – even Conservative politicians have prided themselves on their sustained skill in staving off revolution with reform. At least the same degree of flexibility is needed in the world as a whole, even if one eschews all idealism.

A great deal of redistribution is already going on. Most of it is in the form of direct aid from one country to another. By far the biggest donor is the United States. But there is also a fair amount administered by the international agencies of the United Nations – the World Bank, the International Monetary Fund, the World Health Organization, the International Labour Organization, the Food and Agriculture Organization, UNICEF, UNESCO and the rest. In my view the latter system is vastly preferable to the former. Aid administered directly by the Great Powers is often used as an instrument in the Cold War, so that even when it is not it is suspect. It makes the recipient dependent on the giver, and this dependence can be exploited for political ends. On the other hand when aid is administered by United Nations agencies the advanced nations have to provide the resources just the same, but they get no direct *quid pro quo*, which is as it should be. If America and Russia directly compete with each other as donors this carries the conflict of Great Power politics into all the backward countries concerned and ties their development to the Cold War, whereas the United Nations can administer exactly the same aid in a way that keeps power politics and the Cold War out of it. The channelling of virtually all international aid through the United Nations, which I believe should be done, would give all countries of the world a say in how it was used, instead of leaving the decisions to the rich and powerful with their inevitably partial view of world affairs. And the immense strengthening of the United Nations as an international body for the service of mankind would bring world government substantially nearer.

There is limitless opportunity here for dedicated people, especially the idealistic young. Several of my personal friends have gone out to teach in African countries, or to work for United Nations agencies. They have commonly met with official indifference and sometimes with positive obstruction. Governments have been extraordinarily unimaginative in this whole matter. For example to call up hundreds of thousands of young men since the war and then waste them for most of two years on spit and polish, square-bashing and obsolete exercises, when they could have been doing construction work all over Asia and Africa and still be getting their basic military training, has been an almost total loss without any cause except stupidity. If you were to ask members of those whole generations of Englishmen that have fretted for years in camps whether they would not rather have gone out to some distant continent and helped with the building of railways and roads and airstrips I know what the answer would be in most cases. You do not need to be idealistic to prefer constructive activity to organized time-wasting when the latter is made deliberately unpleasant.

III

No Communist Party, so far as I know, has ever won a freely-conducted national election, and no people has voluntarily gone Communist. Every Communist régime that exists was set up by violence, in war or as a result of defeat in war. No such régime, contrary to the

Marxist prophecy, has been established as the result of a revolutionary rising of the industrial proletariat. This flatly contradicts the widespread assumption that Communism has mass appeal – its record shows quite plainly that it does not have mass appeal. This is illustrated even more startingly by the development of emergent nations. Only a dozen years ago Communists were confident, and most non-Communists mortally afraid, that Communism was about to sweep across the newly independent countries of Asia and Africa. It has to be rubbed in now that *all* schools of non-Communist thought, from right-wing Conservatives to Bevanites – and Communists more than any of them – expected at least *some* newly independent countries to go Communist. The Conservatives argued,— often in despair, that the position was so desperate that we must sink our democratic scruples and do everything we could to build up strong military governments all round the Communist world in order to 'contain' it. The Bevanites argued that the real danger of Communism lay not in a direct military threat but in a social and economic challenge through the uncommitted nations, so that unless the West spent a lot less on armaments and a lot more on aid these uncommitted nations would go Communist and the West would lose the Cold War by default. These two points of view, and others in between, were fought out verbally in fascinating debate while the world developed in such a way as to falsify what both sides were saying. For the astounding fact, which scarcely anyone would have credited even half-a-dozen years ago, is that *not one single newly independent country has gone Communist.*

Communism had been overestimated in almost every way. Not only was its appeal overestimated: its success had been absurdly exaggerated. I wrote something of this on pp. 51–54, and composed with India, and if one adds to this comparisons of Eastern with Western Germany, of Czechoslovakia under Communism with Czechoslovakia as a democracy, what strikes one is not even material success but the lack of it. From East Germany to China, Communist régimes are marked by famine and shortage. Mervyn Jones, whose own outlook is to a considerable extent based on Marxist assumptions, wrote in *The Observer* on 10 December 1961: 'Will Russia overtake the American standard of living by 1970, as Khrushchev has predicted? Returning from my travels in both countries, I find this the first question fired at me, and I ought not to dodge it. Fo be frank, I believe that the question could be put only by someone who has either never seen

America or never seen Russia. Russian backwardness, even by comparison with countries not normally regarded as advanced, is still glaring. If the Russians overtake Yugoslavia by 1970 they will have achieved something. Much too much credence is given to the claims Communists make for themselves. There is also too great a readiness to believe that Communist régimes have the support, or at least acquiescence, of their people – whereas the Hungarian revolt, in which 80% of the Hungarians killed were under the age of twenty-two, showed that even people who have grown up entirely under a Communist régime and been indoctrinated at school and elsewhere from early childhood can still not be brought to accept it. It is too easily believed by the undereducated that Communism is intellectually formidable, a philosophy pressing against the future, whereas it is intellectually indefensible, a relic of the past. And everything about Communism in practice, from the frequent revolts of anonymous workers along the periphery – in Poland, East Germany, Hungary – to the interminable struggle for personal power at the centre in the Kremlin itself, shows that it is inherently unstable and exists only on the basis of unceasing terror.

A lot of this is apprehended, though not always clearly, by leading politicians in backward countries. Some of them are not as hostile to Communism as I am, but virtually all have realized the unreality of its claims, and there is quite a common tendency among them to lump together the Western imperialist powers and the Communist powers as six of one and half-a-dozen of the other. I have interviewed some of them, and what usually emerges, at least when they are talking off the record, is an attitude excellently expressed by the ex-Marxist John Strachey in lectures given in Singapore in 1961 :[1]

'Certainly so far as the people of my own country are concerned, and I would say of the West generally, the appeal of Communism has been very largely lost. This is interesting and paradoxical. Because it is not that Communism has failed, in one sense. On the contrary, Communism has succeeded in industrializing a great country like Russia. Nobody denies that. It is the very character of that Communist achievement which has made Communism lose its appeal in the West. And I would say that this will happen, even if it hasn't happened already, elsewhere also, in the underdeveloped world. It will be the very character of its achievement which will

1. Published under the title *The Great Awakening*.

cause Communism to lose that Messianic appeal which undoubtedly it had twenty-five years ago.

'I take Russia as an instance, though you are more preoccupied, probably, with the other great Communist country, China. But I think it is fairer to take Russia, for there Communism has been much longer established; it has had more than forty years of power and you can see much more clearly the definitive results. And what you see is a very great nation, unquestionably; a nation of great economic achievement, a nation which has a rate of economic growth, a rate of growth of its G.N.P., of its 'Gross National Product', which is very fast. It is not, as a matter of fact, uniquely fast, if you compare it with other rapidly growing countries. It is by no means uniquely fast, but it is fast and well sustained; and then there are the impressive scientific and engineering achievements in space and the like. Undoubtedly Russia is a country making very great progress.

'But then, you know, Russia is a country which has great disadvantages too. Russia has a very primitive political system, a system in which the democratic mechanism is still absent. So the peoples of the West look at Russia and they say, "Yes – this is another big industrialized nation-state, very impressive, no doubt: but there is nothing unique about it." They look at Russia's external relations with the countries which are – what shall I call them? – her dependencies, her satellites, or quite frankly her colonies – the countries of Eastern Europe. My wife and I have travelled a good deal to those countries of Eastern Europe and I am bound to say that it may be argued that though Russia's treatment of her dependencies is no worse than the treatment of their dependencies, in the past, by many Western countries, yet it is difficult indeed to argue that it is any better. Here again we have the impression of just another nation-state, better in some respects but not so good in others, than other such states.

'What has all that got to do with those tremendous ideas, those tremendous ideals, for which Communism stood? For they were high, noble ideals for which we worked in agreement with the Communists in the 1930s. They were the ideals of the ending of the exploitation of man by man: ideals for which great suffering, great oppression even, might be justified. But now we see that after all that has happened in Russia, after "the forty terrible years" as the great Russian writer, Boris Pasternak put it, at the end of all that, the result is just one more nation-state. I tried to sum all that up in a recent article I wrote in the magazine *Encounter*. I put it like this: "The Communists' means have been terrible, their results commonplace!" '

These world-wide changes of attitude towards Communism have been sudden and unexpected, and most people still do not seem to realize consciously that they have taken place. But whereas a few years ago it was common for people to say that the West was obviously losing the Cold War, no one says it now. Until the nineteen-fifties the whole history of Communism could arguably be looked at in terms of continuous expansion. But just as it is undeniable that in 1950 almost everyone expected many newly-independent countries to go Communist, so it is equally undeniable that by the nineteen-sixties not a single one of them had, and furthermore it had become plain that almost none were going to. The nineteen-fifties therefore revealed themselves as a major turning point in history, the end of Communist expansion and the beginning of its internal disintegration. The age of Communism is past. But our thinking has not yet caught up with the fact, and the governments of the West are still behaving as if they were engaged with Russia in a struggle for the future of the new countries. They have merely progressed in their attitude from the Conservative mistake to the Bevanite mistake. (This is nevertheless an immense advance, to be quite fair, both because it makes possible – at least so far as the West is concerned – the ending of the arms race and because massive aid to the backward countries is urgent on other grounds.)

Why was everyone wrong? Looking back it seems to me that the major mistake everyone made was to discount the possibility and attractions of *independence*. The colonial countries always said that independence was what they wanted, yet on both sides of the Cold War everyone took it for granted that their need for aid from the Great Powers would soon make them dependent again, in a different way, on one side or the other. For example when the United States went back on its promise to help Nasser with money for the Aswan dam it seemed to almost everyone that this must lead either to the collapse of his régime (which was its purpose, presumably) or to forcing him into the arms of Russia for sheer self-preservation (which was the result foreseen by left-wing critics of Dulles's action). Yet not even the subsequent military invasion of Egypt by two of the Western

Powers brought either of these alternatives close. National independence was a hardier flower than anyone had dreamt. New countries really did prize it above all else, and really would not sacrifice it to other things. This has been the undoing of the Russians. For the chief objection of new countries to Communism, I am sure, is not its lack of political freedom or its use of terror as an instrument of government but the fact that it means subservience to the national interests of Russia – at least the Russians think it does, and any Communist country that wishes to assert its independence is committed to a permanent Cold War with Russia. Secondly, the West's ridiculous overestimate of Russia's economic strength caused a wild exaggeration of the amount of overseas aid Russia could provide. In fact the whole notion of economic competition between America and Russia in the backward countries has proved to be absurd because the Russians have never been in a position to provide more than the same sort of dribble of aid as, say, Britain, compared with the gigantic flood from America. These two facts taken together – Russia's ruthless policy of subordination and her inability to provide help on a big scale – make her seem like just another imperialist power, offering too little and asking too much. The new countries are not as hostile to her politically as they are to the West because they have never been in her clutches, whereas they have just shaken off subordination to the West after years of struggle, but they see no reason why, having just escaped from a submissive relationship to the West, they should contract one to Russia.

All this contributes to the growing feeling that I tried to illustrate just now, the feeling that the Communist bloc is part of an outmoded set-up, associated with precisely the sort of past that the newly independent countries want to get away from. As far as it concerns them the Cold War is an anachronism, dangerous to them in some ways if useful in others. It is like two rivals duelling for a woman who is out of love with both and has not the least intention of giving herself to either. Their conviction that the encounter might prove fatal to either or both is correct. What is false is their assumption that their fight and not the lady is going to settle her future.

The chief danger of nuclear war now comes from the mounting tensions being generated by the Communist bloc. These are three-fold: the accumulating frustration of its expansionist drives, the increasing disruption of its internal cohesion, and as a result of both of these the increasing hysteria of disputes at the top among the individiduals and groups advocating different policies. These dangers promote each other – for instance the traditional way to get internal cohesion is to have external enemies, so internal differences are likely to lead to yet more aggressive foreign policies. Confronted with this situation the West should stand firm, but at the same time avoid all provocation, and when confronted with a choice should strengthen the hand of the Communist conciliators as against the Communist warmongers – which for example America signally failed to do in its handling of the U2 incident. (I am no friend of Mr Khrushchev, but it is vitally in our interests to strengthen his hand rather than weaken it in his struggle with the Stalinists.) At the same time the West should vigorously pursue all the policies for lowering tension that were outlined in Section I of this chapter.

Meanwhile the great upsurging mass of underprivileged mankind is still there, as it were, outside the Cold War and largely indifferent to it except insofar as it might put an end to us all. There is need for scarcely any Cold War considerations in our policies towards them. In giving them aid we do not need to tie them down with political and economic strings or to badger them into treaty organizations whose obligations they cannot possibly fulfil. Merely to redress their wrongs is to deal the death-blow to already expiring Communist prospects. There is no excuse whatever for propping up corrupt and reactionary dictatorships – for that matter there never was: insofar as it affected the Cold War it allowed Communists to set themselves up as champions of freedom against us as the imperialist oppressors, and did us immeasurable political harm from which we are still suffering. I realize that it is impossible to give a country aid without to some extent strengthening its government, but at least the aid can be for specific constructive projects. In the past most aid has been for military purposes – we built up, financed and even trained the armies with which dictators kept their people in subjection so that they would be there as a defence against Communist expansion. And too much of the aid given for civilian projects went into the pockets of politicians. So instead of being used to lift populations out of misery and oppression, aid was more commonly used to keep them there. There are parts of the world where millions of dollars have been spent and there is virtually nothing to show for it. These abuses could be obviated by earmarking aid for special purposes and having it administered by an impartial body, presumptively the United Nations – but again this means keeping the whole operation outside the Cold

War. However, no matter what the nature of the régime in the recipient
country the result would be to develop its economy, provide employment and raise living standards, and this in itself is good. It is no way
to oppose a tyrannical government to blockade its subjects.

IV

I am flabbergasted when I hear Socialists say that our differences
with the Conservatives must be formulated in terms of domestic policy
because there are no fundamental differences over foreign affairs. I
can think of no greater cleavage between any two foreign policies open
to Britain than that between the one I believe in and the one the
Conservatives pursue. If after this Government's help to America for
ten years in keeping China out of the United Nations, its maintenance
of the Nuri-es-Said régime in Iraq, its invasion of Egypt – in open
breach of the UN Charter, but otherwise behind a smoke screen of
lies and double-dealing; its subsequent landing of troops in Jordan,
its treatment of the Bahreini prisoners, Hola, the Devlin Committee
Report, the chronic appeasement of Sir Roy Welensky, the years of
bloody repression in Cyprus, the special missions of friendship to both
Spain and Portugal, the support for Portuguese bestiality in Angola
and persistent failure to speak or vote in the UN against this and
other colonial terror (e.g. France's in Algeria), the open obstruction
of the UN in the Congo, the Immigrants' Bill, the readiness to squander
hundreds of millions on a chimerical independent deterrent while
frequently refusing loans to backward countries, even to British
colonies, for their economic and social development – if after all this,
to take only a selection from the brief record of the present Government, a Socialist does not feel himself in fundamental disagreement
with Conservatives over foreign policy he is in the wrong party.

Radical disagreement with Conservatives over specific issues such
as this is rooted in a profound difference of moral and political outlook. Nearly all active Conservatives really do believe in their hearts
that Britain and the British are inherently superior, and that whereas
everyone else is inferior some are more inferior than others. They
have a predilection for violence, and try to solve problems by the use
of it whenever they think they can get away with it. This is true over
the whole range of policy, from colonial government to the treatment
of criminals – indeed to the handling of interrupters at their own

Annual Party Conference. There is such a deep emotional attachment on their part to the use of violence that defence of it brings out the strongest of all their political responses. They savagely denounce people who oppose the use of violence abroad – as in Suez, say, or Cyprus – as 'unpatriotic', indeed 'anti-British'. They hold Army Officers in high esteem – far higher than doctors or teachers or artists. In 1961, a year of international crisis unprecedented since the end of World War Two, and major domestic economic upheaval, there were more resolutions at the Conservative Party's Annual Conference calling for an increase in hanging and flogging than on any other subject.

Modern Conservatism is a shotgun marriage between tribalism and democracy. The characteristic attitudes are all tribal – the primary division of human beings into our group and the rest, with an underlying hostility towards the rest, the belief that our group is the depository of civilization, the reverence for authority and leaders and the deep sense of hierarchy, the attribution of religious properties to social structure and in consequence a tendency to regard basic criticisms of it as sacriligious, the preference of violence to reason as an instrument for solving problems. The development of parliamentary democracy has forced Conservatives to contain these primitive passions within a framework of law, but the nature of the strain imposed on them reveals itself in their reactions the moment an individual steps outside the protection of that law, whether by committing a crime or merely by interrupting at one of their private meetings. The most satisfying of all outlets for tribal impulses are external: in the colonies, where most of the inhabitants are black and have few political rights, or in international affairs where there is none but the most tentative law; and in those cases the only important limit Conservatives set to racialism and violence is what they think they can get away with without causing eventual damage to themselves.

The basic attitudes and prejudices of Conservatives unfit them to cope with the modern world. Their failure to understand even the notion of equality, and their hatred and fear of its practical manifestations – this alone puts them outside any real comprehension of, or sympathy with, the major current of our time at home as well as abroad. With such people in charge of Britain's affairs we can expect only continued material loss and sullying of our good name. Unfortunately Socialist proposals on foreign affairs have too often been merely reactions to Conservative policies – partly because of the long

years of opposition, partly also because of opposition-mindedness –
with the result that they frequently inhabit the same nutshell world.
But a radical foreign policy should start from radical premises, not
Conservative ones. A foreign policy based on the classic radical
principles of freedom, equality and the brotherhood of man (or even
merely on enlightened self-interest) would not only immeasurably
surpass that of the Conservatives in scope and vision but would be
diametrically opposed to it on major issues and, most important of all,
might expect a little practical success.

Conclusion

THIS book has been about ways of looking at things. Chiefly, of course, it has been about ways of looking at politics, but since political attitudes do not exist in isolation this has involved mention of other important aspects of life and thought. The way we look at things is of absolutely fundamental importance because it determines not merely how we approach problems but what problems we approach. A Conservative in France or Britain might be overwhelmingly concerned with his country's status in the world, whereas a Socialist might be concerned with equality at home and abroad, and a Communist with Russia's interests in the Cold War. Thus three men of the same nationality and background might view the affairs of the world in such different terms, and concern themselves with such different things, that in practice they would have little to say to each other. These differences – so great that each is, as it were, living in a different world – derive from the fact that the assumptions on which the outlook of each is based are fundamentally different. It is with assumptions in this sense, with the foundations on which our political attitudes are built, that this book is concerned.

The Labour Party comprises groups of people whose outlooks in this sense are different. Among them there is permanent misunderstanding, conflict and distrust. Classifications are arbitrary, but it is useful to distinguish three kinds of active Socialist: the radicals, the traditionalists (whether conservatives or neo-Marxists) and the opposition-minded. The radicals are the mainstream of the British Socialist tradition, and the leadership of the party is in their hands. But in the nature of practical politics they are constantly having to make concessions to the other groups, who profoundly influence policy, are represented by prominent spokesmen, and largely shape the public image of the party. In any case it is particularly unfortunate that at the moment the leader of the party, though the best available, is only just radical, and a bad tactician. The conservatives are obsolete in the sense that the world has passed them by. After nearly a quarter

224

of a century of full-employment and the welfare state they are still thinking in terms of unemployment and destitution. They invest the Labour Party with an aura of 'cloth caps, mufflers and misery', and the general public laughs at them in the same way as it laughs at ostrich feathers and model-T Fords. The neo-Marxists are also obsolete, but in a different way. For whereas the point about the conservatives is that their attitudes used to be applicable but changes in our environment have made them no longer so, the point about Marxism is that it used to seem applicable but developments have shown that it never was. The difference between the two sorts of obsoleteness is the difference between the man who still believes it takes a year to go round the world and the man who still believes the world is flat. As for the opposition-minded, the only thing they have in common is the chip on their shoulders. Some detest all forms of leadership, including the Labour Party's; some feel themselves to have been victimized by society and want to revenge themselves on it, some are envious, some have an uncontrollable craving for anger, indignation and protest as indispensable emotional outlets, some are life-haters seizing on a substitute for puritanism, and none wants responsibility.

Because of all this the future of the Labour Party is in serious doubt. If the obsolete and oppositional retain their formative influence on policy and the public image the Labour Party will wither away just as other great parties in the past have withered away who lost contact with a changing world. But if it emerges as a full-blooded radical party it may again govern the country. In this fight for the party's survival the radicals are weakened by, among other things, the absence of a fully-worked-out 'philosophy', an up-to-date way of looking at things that can provide a common language in which their position can be made clear, as well as helping to suggest an accurate social analysis and being a spur to revolutionary change. They are often made to look like opportunists, or like driftwood. The only coherent 'left-wing' philosophy that most people know of is Marxism, and if you are not a Marxist their question is, How then are you different from the Conservatives? And they either believe that you are not really different from the Conservatives or, if they believe you are, that in spite of what you say you have common ground with the Marxists to precisely the extent of that difference.

My contention is that both the conservatism and the Marxism are essentially nineteenth-century ways of looking at things (they both happened to get a shot in the arm in the nineteen-thirties). Neither of them has come to terms with universal suffrage and all its revolutionary implications – democratic government, mass affluence, the disintegration of traditional class structures and so on. Neither of them takes account of the revolutionary advances in man's understanding of himself and his environment that are the Einsteinian revolution and the Freudian revolution and the revolution in philosophy. Both are hopeless instruments for understanding the world – distorting mirrors that will go on misleading until they are thrown on the conceptual scrap heap. And because they are obsolete the issue between them is obsolete. Therefore to suppose that what I am offering is in some sense a middle way is a total misunderstanding. I am not interested in a middle way between two forms of outmodedness. What is needed is also what I believe this book articulates: a dynamic philosophy free of the major conservative and Marxist fallacies, appropriate to the world as it actually is today, taking full account of the revolutionary intellectual as well as social developments of the twentieth century. It has been neither desirable nor possible to write it in nineteenth-century terms like Left versus Right, revolution versus reform, Socialism versus Capitalism, and all the rest. In so far as it is read in those terms it will be misunderstood.

Radicalism in politics is like the top of an iceberg, in that it is supported by a mass several times its own weight – it is supported by the tradition of all that is best in our civilization, above all by the belief in the unique moral value of each human being and in the pursuit of truth wherever it may lead. The basic Socialist values of freedom, equality and the brotherhood of man are merely a rewording – scarcely even that – of the classic liberal slogan 'Liberty! Equality! Fraternity!' – and so on, back to the New Testament: 'There is no question of relieving others at the cost of hardship to yourselves; it is a question of equality. At the moment your surplus meets their need, but one day your need may be met from their surplus. The aim is equality.' (II Corinthians VIII, 13–14); and beyond that to Socrates: 'Agree with me, if I seem to you to be speaking the truth; or if not, withstand me might and main, that I may not deceive you as well as myself in my enthusiasm, and like the bee, leave my sting in you before I die' (Phaedo, 40). Not all radicals are aware of the immensity and richness and force of this tradition, an endless source of encouragement and stimulus. (Not until our own time has it motivated governments, and the history of the world before that is taught on authoritarian assumptions, as if all that mattered were kings and emperors, popes, churches, armies, wars and governments, and everything is seen from their point of view.) The most important thing about it is that it is not a fixed philosophy. The questioning never stops. There is no final knowledge, no definitive solution, no infallible authority.

The need to be ever alive, ever thinking, ever seeking out new ideas and new approaches is more important in politics than in any other aspect of human life. It should be the mainspring of a radical party. But the purpose of such a party is to change things for the better, and as the changes it advocates come into effect it must advocate new changes, or else it becomes a conservative party. In other words the only thing it should cling to through time, the one constant to give it identity, is a tradition of criticism, the testing of beliefs against an ever-changing reality, the perpetual revision of outlook in the light of experience. Rational politics means the right adaptation of means to ends, and this is the only way of changing things in accordance with our wishes; for this to be successful each step must be short, but this does not mean that the pace of change must be slow. Sprinters take shorter steps than long-distance runners but they run much faster. Progressive politics seeks a bustling, unflagging, never-ending series of improvements, and the faster the better. 'It must achieve passion in action in the pursuit of qualified judgments.'

To become such a party the Labour Party will have to transcend its origins. It may have been born of the working-class movement in Britain but it cannot remain a baby for ever. The problems it came into existence to solve were those of poverty and exploitation in the industrial cities of Britain, but the chief problems it faces now are those accompanying the explosive emancipation of most of the human race, together with Communist imperialism and the threat of a man-made end to the world. It cannot meet these vast new global challenges with the attitudes, assumptions and forms of organization created in response to the old local problems of its early days. It must shake off its narrow nationalist and class past and rise to the stature of events. Its outlook must be as international as its responsibilities have now become, its policies as quick to change as the problems it confronts. I want the Labour Party to come out as a bold, radical party concerned with the present and the immediate future, not with the distant future and the past. I want it to spurn its various traditions of conservatism, Marxism and opposition-mindedness and develop along its central tradition of radicalism, adventurousness with ideas, eagerness for improvement, passionate realism. I want it to welcome responsibility.

I want it to enthuse individuals with a sense of the importance of what is going on in the world. People who are fundamentally out of sympathy with such an approach and consistently oppose the policies based on it should be free to pursue their political activities anywhere except in the Labour Party: the Labour Party should not only be a radical party, it should be unambiguously so, and clearly seen to be so. Only if it does all this will it ever again deserve to be the government of Britain.

Index